THE WORK PARADIGM

The Work Paradigm

A theoretical investigation of concepts of work

PAUL RANSOME
School of Social Studies
University of Nottingham
England

Avebury
Aldershot • Brookfield USA • Hong Kong • Singapore • Sydney

© Paul Ransome 1996

All rights reserved. No part of this publication may be reproduced, stored in a retrieval system, or transmitted in any form or by any means, electronic, mechanical, photocopying, recording or otherwise, without the prior permission of the publisher.

Published by
Avebury
Ashgate Publishing Limited
Gower House
Croft Road
Aldershot
Hants GU11 3HR
England

Ashgate Publishing Company
Old Post Road
Brookfield
Vermont 05036
USA

British Library Cataloguing in Publication Data

Ransome, Paul
    Work Paradigm: Theoretical Investigation of
     Concepts of Work
    I. Title
    306.36
ISBN 1 85972 183 4

Library of Congress Catalog Card Number: 95-83045

Printed and bound by Athenaeum Press, Ltd.,
Gateshead, Tyne & Wear.

Contents

Tables vii

Preface viii

Acknowledgements ix

1 Introductory discussion 1

2 Definitions and concepts of work 15
    Part One - The definition of the word 'work' 16
    Part Two - Basic themes in the concept *work* 27

3 The humanist definition of work 42
    Part One - The meaning and purpose of work 43
    Part Two - Fundamental principles and expectations of work .. 52

4 The work paradigm 74
    Part One - Ideas, ideologies and the work-ethic 75
    Part Two - Forces and relations of production 89

5 The work paradigm of Classical and Medieval society 99
    Part One - Classical and pre-Christian concepts of work 102
    Part Two - Early Christian and Medieval concepts of work ... 105

6 The work paradigm of sixteenth and seventeenth century European society 115
    Part One - The Protestant work-ethic 116

Part Two -	A critique of Weber's position	123
Part Three -	Discussion	128

7 The work paradigm of the late-twentieth century:
changes in the practice of work   140
    Part One -   Patterns of working   141
    Part Two -   Technological change   148
    Part Three - Discussion   163

8 A critique of the current concept of work   175
    Part One -   The arbitrariness of the contemporary
                    criteria of work   176
    Part Two -   The contemporary work-ethic:
                    the ideology of economic rationality   184
    Part Three - Towards a new concept of work   190

Bibliography   198

Tables

Table 2.1	Defining the word work	19
Table 2.2	Contemporary criteria of work	23
Table 2.3	Characteristics of the criteria of work 1	27
Table 2.4	Characteristics of the criteria of work 2	35
Table 3.1	Fundamental principles of action/work	54
Table 3.2	Key expectations of work	61
Table 3.3	Motivations and expectations of work	62
Table 3.4	The contemporary concept of work	63
Table 3.5	Assessing the potential arbitrariness of the criteria of work	68
Table 4.1	The work-ethic	83
Table 4.2	The work paradigm	95
Table 5.1	Principles of justification	102

Preface

This book grows out of a concern with the problem of job insecurity and unemployment. Adopting a largely theoretical approach, it is argued that each historical period is characterised by the development of a work paradigm which combines a particular manifestation of the productive forces with a particular concept of work. The success of the paradigm as a whole is determined by the degree to which these two elements are mutually supportive. In Gramsci's terms, a successful work paradigm provides the basis for an hegemonic social structure. In the late modern period the work paradigm of the advanced industrial societies has begun to collapse as job insecurity increasingly undermines people's expectations of the availability of formal paid employment. Given that technological advance will continue, and given that people cannot simply discard their needs for income, security, creativity and social contact, re-establishing equilibrium in the work paradigm can only be achieved if we accept the need for a revised conception of what 'work' is - we need to develop a new definition of work. Although a number of theorists have focused attention on the parameters of post-Fordist capitalism, precious little has as yet been written about the conceptual and definitional aspects of work itself. It is hoped that this book will provide a provisional theoretical framework within which this deficit could be rectified.

Acknowledgements

Inevitably, any book builds upon the ideas and research of its predecessors, and I would therefore like to acknowledge the work of all those authors referred to in the text. The initial research for the book was carried out in the Faculty of Social and Political Science, University of Cambridge, between 1989 and 1992, and I thank the Economic and Social Research Council for their financial support during this period. I would also like to acknowledge the expert guidance and encouragement of Gavin Mackenzie and Conrad Lodziak who commented diligently and enthusiastically on a number of earlier drafts. Finally, I would like to thank my parents, John and Evelyn Ransome, for providing much encouragement, Nick Stevenson for intellectual and moral support, and Helen Smith for reminding me of the dangers of the ivory tower. It is of course entirely my own responsibility to defend and rectify the errors and omissions of the following.

1 Introductory discussion

The aim of this book is to explore how members of the advanced industrialized societies have come to define and conceptualize what can be labelled 'the concept of work'. There is little doubt that in these societies, activities which we call 'work' occupy a central position in our overall perception of the meaning and purpose of daily life. At the same time however, it is also clear that the practical business of working - the physical activities themselves - have not remained constant over time, but are undergoing a more or less continual process of change. This being the case, it is likely that the conceptual and perceptual understandings which we have of work -the intellectual assumptions and expectations we make about the work we do and why we do it - will also change over time. In the current context for example, technological innovation has made it possible for a growing number of people to 'work from home' rather than 'from the office'. Taken together with other developments such as increases in part-time working, work-sharing and other forms of 'telecommuting', questions of whether we might be on the brink of a more or less radical change in how we perceive work, how it can be organized, and what meaning we should attribute to it, are gradually impressing themselves upon the public imagination. Inevitably, the question of 'the future of work' is a matter of growing concern for all of us.

In order to understand how current perceptions of work might be affected by recent and future developments in the practical organization of work, it is necessary to understand how these perceptions have evolved in relation to previous methods of organizing the practicalities of work. To what extent for example, did the first industrial revolution bring about important changes in the work-concept of pre-industrial society? Did pre-industrial society have what we now call a work-ethic, and if so, where did this come from? Is it the case that there are a number of fundamental expectations associated with work which remain constant despite changes in the practical organization of work?

Assuming that the economic stability and prosperity of a particular society is at least minimally dependent upon there being a satisfactory correspondence between how people work and what they consider to be the meanings and purposes of that work, this raises the crucial issue of what might happen if people's perceptions of work failed to keep pace with developments in the organization of work. At the very least, it would seem likely that economic stability would be seriously inhibited if such a correspondence did not exist or if it began to decay. In contemporary society for example, there is evidence of growing uncertainty over whether our prevailing perception of work as full-time and life-long can be sustained in the face of a more or less continuous reduction in the availability of employment brought about by technological innovation. Similarly, it is by no means certain that the new principles of flexibility and multi-skilling can be accommodated within the much more rigid and skill-specific definition of work of the recent past. To put it bluntly, there is growing evidence that members of the advanced industrial societies are facing something of a crisis in their efforts to come to terms with a revolution in the world of work.

This is not of course to say that these changes have gone unnoticed. Amongst academic researchers, considerable interest has developed in the fields of the sociology of work and labour economics concerning both the quantitative and qualitative effects of the 'technological revolution' upon the nature and organization of work. The impact of the microprocessor as the new driving force within productive techniques has been described in great detail, and the new paradigm of 'flexibility' has been set out. The development of the MINOS system for automated coalmining; the use of industrial robots and Japanese working practices in car manufacturing; computer aided design and manufacture (CAD/CAM); the use of electronic point-of-sale cash registers are clear examples of this impact throughout the economy. With further developments in fibre-optics, lasers and artificial intelligence it is inevitable that its future impact will be even more prodigious. Outside the academic field, writers and broadcasters have been quick to provide their readers and viewers with articles and programmes on how information technology will endow us with a new 'virtual' reality through access to the internet and world-wide web. Modernity it seems, is being pushed further and further forward by 'micro-power' surging along the conduits of the information superhighway.

Although these discussions and debates have certainly drawn our attention to many of the *practical* implications of the new technological paradigm, far less attention has been paid to possible changes in the *conceptual* and *perceptual* dimensions of work. Indeed, much of the current debate into 'the future of work' has tended to proceed on the assumption that underlying concepts and perceptions of work can be read-off in an unquestioning manner. Concepts of work simply follow along behind the practicalities of work and, if necessary, change their form without much ado. A number of interpretations of the relationship between belief systems and working practice have of course been put forward. The best known example is Max Weber's *Protestant Ethic Thesis*, where it is suggested that modern capitalism developed in the way that it did because of a close relationship between a Protestant religious ethic and a capitalistic business ethic. More recently, the emergence of 'competitive individualism' and 'entrepreneurialism' can be interpreted as an inevitable consequence of the growth of what Durkheim called the 'cult of the individual' where personal success and individual ambition have displaced more 'traditional' and 'communal' forms of economic motivation. For Durkheim, the social division of labour provides the indispensable mechanism through which the organic solidarity of modern societies is developed and maintained; without the division of labour, all other dimensions of social solidarity would collapse. While these interpretations have certainly contributed to our understanding of the relationship between the conceptual and practical aspects of economic practice during particular historical periods, and have shown that these two aspects interact with one another, it can be argued that recent changes in economic practices are sufficiently profound as to require a much greater concentration of effort into understanding the nature and dynamics of this relationship. In contemporary analysis in other words, insufficient attention has been paid both to the nature of underlying concepts of work, and to the relationship between these and the ways in which work is actually organized.

Against this background, the discussion in the following chapters seeks to develop a revised theoretical and conceptual perspective for understanding the relationship between changes in the practice and organization of work, and related changes in the concept and meaning of work. It will be argued that each juncture of social development carries with it a particular *work paradigm*. This paradigm is made up of a *conceptual aspect* - the cognitive meaning and purpose we attach to the category of activities we regard as work, and a *practical material aspect* through which work is actually organized. During periods of economic prosperity and growth, these two aspects exist in a largely harmonious relationship with one another; a state of balance exists within the work paradigm. Indeed, the emergence of a harmonious work paradigm is actually a pre-requisite for sustainable economic prosperity. Since social stability is dependent upon economic stability, we can suggest that the work paradigm not only gives a particular historical period its distinctive character, but also provides the foundation for social stability itself. Since however, the practical dimension of the work paradigm is subject to a more or less continuous process of change, due largely to developments in productive technique and business practice, and since there is a tendency for developments in technique to develop more quickly than developments in perceptions of work, harmony within the work paradigm is always under threat. Under these circumstances, the work paradigm passes through a period of disruption and possibly crisis until the conceptual and practical aspects are once more in equilibrium. This is of course an extremely complex process, since it cannot be assumed that practical developments and conceptual developments will occur in series, one following the other. Under some circumstances, the practical application of new techniques may be conditional upon real changes in attitudes towards working practices. Similarly, it may not always be possible to distinguish clearly between the conceptual and the practical aspects of the work paradigm if a series of changes follow rapidly one upon the other.

On the assumption that economic stability does depend upon the presence of a harmonious work paradigm, we can anticipate that if this harmony breaks down, and depending on the degree and extent of breakdown, disequilibrium in the work paradigm will have an extremely negative impact upon economic stability and progress. A partial breakdown would result in a change of direction in the labour process, while a complete breakdown would signal a complete transition of the social structure. Without wishing to anticipate the discussion in the following chapters, we can acknowledge at the outset that harmony within the work paradigm between the practical and conceptual aspects of work, is likely to be relative rather than absolute, that over time, it is dynamic rather than static, and that the strength and resilience of a particular work paradigm can be assessed by considering its ability to accommodate changes in productive technique. Historically, the most successful work paradigms are those which have survived a series of crises or periods of disequilibrium through continuous modification. The least successful are those which have collapsed in a relatively short period of time in the face of perhaps only a single significant change in productive technique.

In contemporary society, microelectronic technologies have already had a considerable impact on working practices. On the assumption that a causal relationship necessarily exists between the practical and conceptual aspects of the work paradigm, it is reasonable to expect that changes in the former will inevitably have an impact upon the latter. At present however, it can be argued that practical changes in the nature and organization of work are progressing so rapidly as to render current conceptions of the meaning and purpose of work obsolete in a number of important respects. Contemporary concepts of work in other words, have been left behind by developments in productive technique. Although as noted above, many individuals are now experiencing important changes in patterns of work such as increases in part-time working, work-sharing, and telecommuting, and although these changes will inevitably stimulate fresh conceptions of the meaning and role of work, and of how work can be organized, it is likely that this transition will be less than smooth. Equilibrium within our current work paradigm is, and is increasingly seen to be, in crisis. Growing unease about the stability, dependability and sustainability of our current work paradigm will become more and more acute as its conceptual and material aspects become ever more dislocated from each other.

A key feature of this dislocation, is the fact that new technologies have brought about major improvements in productive efficiency, which have in turn caused a significant and structurally embedded reduction in employers' demand for full-time and life-long employees. This became clear throughout Western Europe and North America during the mid-1980s, when unemployment particularly within the manufacturing sector rose to unprecedented post-war levels. At the time, considerable optimism was placed in the likelihood of a general growth in non-manual technical staff in manufacturing, and in manual and non-manual service sector employment. It was expected that once the general recession of the early 1980s had passed, a new balance would be established between the supply and demand for labour as service sector employment expanded to offset the effects of a contracting manufacturing sector. An expanding service sector would stimulate increasing demand for service-oriented products which would in turn further stimulate growth in this sector. Although it was acknowledged that this transition would require a high level of 'sacrifice' amongst traditional occupations and a considerable disruption of established working patterns, it was believed that the period of transition would soon be replaced by a new phase of stable employment and prosperity. By the end of the 1980s however, many Western economies had entered a second major recession again accompanied by further significant increases in unemployment. Most importantly, and confounding the earlier optimism, rising unemployment has had a strong impact on service-sector employment itself. This suggests that growing job *insecurity* has become a feature not only of manual, but also of non-manual service industry occupations. Writing in the mid-1990s, it seems that the revolutionising scope of the new technologies has been seriously underestimated; all occupations, in whichever sector of the economy, are equally vulnerable to reorganization and job loss through technological change.

The new reality then, is one in which the perception of work as full-time and life-long has become incompatible with actual reality. If, as is evidently the case, the post-war generations have grown up with, and have been led to expect, that stable employment can more or less be taken for granted, the new reality poses a considerable material and psychological threat. In material terms, for individuals in a society which has adopted formal paid employment as virtually the only means of gaining access to basic necessary resources, the threat of increasing unemployment and decreasing job security strikes at the root of our sense of material well-being. As employment becomes more and more scarce, competition for the diminishing number of jobs will inevitably increase. For the fortunate few, these jobs may offer high financial rewards, continuing increases in standard of living, and higher social status. For the majority however, the choice will be between accepting a range of poorly paid and largely unrewarding jobs organized on a part-time, temporary or casual basis, and increasing dependency either on the state or on various forms of 'informal' working or crime. In both cases, the priority will be to obtain an income; the means of doing so will be a secondary consideration.

In psychological terms, the effects of the new reality will be to undermine many of the desires and expectations associated not only with work, but with modern life more generally. To the extent that we articulate important aspects of our perceptions of self-worth, self-belief and social status through employment, loss of employment signifies a loss of our sense of security. Further still, and central to the concerns of this book, the disappointment of seeing our well-established assumptions and expectations about work betrayed, may increase our reluctance to accept the need for an alternative concept of work. The imminent collapse of our present concept of work in other words, is likely to create a deep sense of suspicion about how things might develop in the future.

On the positive side however, the technological revolution is extremely advantageous in a number of important respects. What after all, is the point in developing new techniques and patterns of working if not to increase efficiency and quality of products and of working life? Would it have been better to have acknowledged the potential of the micro-processor, but to have decided not to use it? Clearly, the opportunity to produce more products in a shorter working time; the more efficient use of raw materials and essential resources; the ability to reduce mundane and mechanistic work-tasks through automation, and the possibility of far greater personal autonomy in performing particular types of work would all seem to be 'a good thing'. The central motivation therefore, for understanding how a new equilibrium can be achieved within the contemporary work paradigm, is how to achieve these benefits without forcing a significant proportion of the population into transitory and peripheral forms of work on the margins of the formal economy. In the final chapters of this book, it will be argued that the solution to the present disequilibrium between the technologically possible and the socially unacceptable, is crucially bound up with the need to reassess the meaning and purpose of work in the technological world of the late-twentieth century. The need in other words, to take advantage of inevitable and far-reaching changes in present patterns and organizations of work, while at the same time reconciling these changes with the need for a mechanism for income distribution, requires us to reconsider our concept of work.

Developing a fresh understanding of the relationship between the conceptual and practical aspects of a work paradigm necessarily raises a number of important questions. Firstly, since 'work' is a very widely used and commonplace term, it is important to consider how the term 'work' itself is defined. If this term is used to describe a reasonably discrete realm or category of activities, it is necessary to consider what this realm is and what are its limitations. Secondly, it is necessary to consider the processes by which individuals attribute meaning and significance to their working activities. How and why do individuals make sense of activities described as 'work'; is it possible to differentiate and describe a set of principles which underlie all concepts of work - principles which could perhaps indicate the likely form and content of future changes in the contemporary work paradigm? Thirdly, on the assumption that there is a reasonably high degree of concurrence between individuals with regard to the attribution of meaning and purpose to work, what are the mechanisms by which these shared criteria become manifest in the context of wider cooperative relationships? To what extent are these shared perceptions accurate and expedient, and to what extent are they inaccurate and ideological? Finally, since personal and mutual perceptions of work evidently develop over time, it is necessary to consider what governs their continued evolution. This involves an understanding not only that there is a reciprocal relationship between the practical and conceptual of aspects of the work paradigm, but also of the direction of causation between the two. Do concepts of work originate in a more or less abstract way, perhaps out of allegiance to religious or other belief systems, or are they determined by the actual experience of working in particular ways? Is it the case that new ideas about work tend to follow-on from practical changes, or is it the case that practical changes are themselves initiated by changes in ideas about work?

Before outlining the order in which these questions will be addressed, it will be useful to indicate the broad theoretical perspective which has been adopted here. This account adopts a largely critical Marxian approach in analysing the relationship between the conceptual and material aspects of the work paradigm. Since the presence of a harmonious work paradigm is necessary for economic stability, and since economic stability is necessary for social stability, it is important to be clear as to how the relationship between conceptual or 'ideological' and practical or 'material' phenomena are being interpreted. Broadly speaking, interpretations of this relationship can be divided between pluralist or bourgeois-liberal interpretations on the one hand, and Marxian accounts on the other. From within a bourgeois-liberal perspective, the apparent stability of the economic and social structures is seen as a reflection of the fact that, in general, the majority of the population shares a set of coherent beliefs, norms and values. The legitimacy of the social structure in its present form, is therefore assumed to be demonstrated by the apparent lack of widespread social dissent. (A limited degree of social dissent can be regarded as 'functional', as it may ultimately tend to confirm the stability of the structure in the normal course of events). The mutual and unprejudiced exchange of ideas, and their combination into ideologies manifest through the practices of representative democracies, and 'transmitted' through 'superstructural' agencies including the education system, the Church, and the mass media, are seen as an accountable means through which the elected minority is lawfully pursuing the goals and priorities which the majority of the population seek to fulfil. The perceived flexibility and apparent responsiveness of the democratic processes are taken to guarantee that society will continue to develop in accordance with these goals and priorities. The practices and institutions of society provide the means by which these ends can be fulfilled, and are thus subordinate to them. In turn, economic practices and institutions are regarded as largely subordinate to the practices and institutions of the superstructure, and to the democratically determined goals, aspirations and purposes developed within them.

From a Marxian perspective, it is argued that appeals to a process of mutual awareness and legitimation of this kind amount to little more than a sophisticated means of pseudo-justification of the social structure on behalf of the disproportionately advantaged minority; a form of 'false consciousness' which must be dispelled through the re-education of the working class. The implication that the population as a whole adheres more or less automatically to an over-arching belief system which perpetuates the passive consent of the minority over the majority, is set aside. Rather, it is argued that in reality, the 'consent' of the population is primarily attained through a complex range of structural constraints, which 'physically' locate individuals both in respect of each other, and in respect of the resources necessary for survival. Any ideological means of persuasion or consent, are regarded as secondary to these primary material restraints, since the former have relatively little coercive 'power' when seen in the context of the latter. When dissent and social conflict emerge, they are taken to be symptomatic of the inherent contradictions which characterize capitalistic relations of production; relations which are based upon a fundamental opposition of interests between a disproportionately advantaged minority and an exploited and oppressed majority. Consequently, the institutional practices of the superstructure, including the legal and the parliamentary systems, the church and the mass media, and the ideas they put forward, are seen as deriving from and are 'determined' by the economic structure. Ultimately therefore, in order to change society it is necessary to change its practices, and particularly its economic practices, rather than its ideologies.

The position taken here with regard to concepts and ideologies of work, is that while both these interpretations offer valuable aids to analysis, the Marxian perspective offers a more pragmatic means of understanding developments in the work paradigm. A paradigm which, in its present form at least, is certainly characterized by inequality in terms of access to necessary resources. This perspective does however, sustain a number of important deficiencies of its own particularly with regard to the conceptual aspects of the work paradigm. In the first place, while it is reasonable to accept that the concept of work or 'labour' provides an essential foundation for developing a wider analysis of social structure, this perspective may tend to hold a relatively inflexible view of work. In the same way therefore, that the bourgeois-liberal concept of work has been left behind by technological progress, so too has the Marxian concept of work. In the second place, by emphasising the priority of material and structural aspects of the work paradigm over its conceptual or ideological aspects, Marxian interpretations have tended to *underestimate* the complexity and importance of the processes by which individuals attach meaning and significance to work. To some extent this tendency derives from the general suspicion with which 'ideas' tend to be treated within this perspective; a suspicion which is also applied to the intellectual and perceptual aspect of the work paradigm.

In the following account it will be argued that while it is certainly necessary to analyse the material aspects of work, a sufficiently rigorous understanding of developments in the work paradigm as a whole cannot be achieved without also considering the process by which individuals attribute meaning and significance to their working activities. Since it is likely that these processes make an important contribution both to an individual's sense of well-being and to the maintenance of productive co-operation, it is reasonable to expect that the conceptual component of the work paradigm deserves close attention, and should not be dismissed as some form of mass deception. It cannot be denied in other words, that individuals inherently achieve a conscious, intellectual understanding of their work which cannot be explained solely in terms of 'false consciousness'.

Finally, it will be useful to point out the particular meaning which is being attached to the word 'work'. This is a very widely used term which has inevitably attracted a broad range of definitions. As will be illustrated in chapter two, the criteria used in deciding which activities fit into the category 'work' have varied over time. Perhaps the most useful definition is that work constitutes a range of activities through which individuals and groups of individuals seek to gain access to resources necessary for their survival. Since in contemporary society these resources primarily take the form of monetary income, this definition of work can be refined as *activities which are performed in return for direct financial remuneration*.

Plan of chapters

In seeking to provide the reader with some answers to these complex questions, the book is organized into three stages of analysis. Firstly, it will be necessary to consider the basic elements through which we articulate our concept of work. In *chapter two* a brief etymology of the word 'work' is given in order to clarify the nuances of meaning which are commonly expressed within this general term and by the related terms 'labour', 'craft', 'house-work', 'job' 'occupation' and so on. Three *categories of definition* are then distinguished: anthropological, economic, and 'folk' or lay definitions. An examination of these categories of definition will illustrate how contemporary conceptualizations of work tend to revolve around a number of basic characteristics or themes. Without claiming that these themes are necessarily universal, it will be argued that the process of categorising some activities as work and some as non-work is achieved through the application of a number of *distinguishable criteria*. Typically, these include the understanding that work proper is a public activity, that it is done in return for financial reward, that it involves the application of physical and mental effort. If these criteria are changed, perhaps as a consequence of changes in productive technique, or if well-establish work-criteria are applied to 'old' activities, then it follows that the way in which some activities are defined as work and others not will also change. In contemporary society for example, the activity of conceiving and bearing a child as a surrogate mother, has resulted in the application of the criterion of direct financial remuneration to an activity which was not previously categorized as 'work' in this way.

These issues are taken a stage further in *chapter three*, where it is argued that one of the most useful and possibly universal explanations of the purpose, meaning and motivation for work, lies in what can be called the 'humanist' definition of work as 'productive activity'. The Marxian notions of species-being and species-powers, particularly as expressed in Marx's *Early Writings* are discussed, together with an analysis of their more recent representation in the work of Lucien Sève and André Gorz. Taking this as a starting point, the chapter goes on to describe a number of *fundamental principles of action* and four key expectations of work, which can be regarded as essential to any concept of work. In subsequent chapters, these principles and expectations, together with the work-criteria described in chapter two, will be used as a means of developing a more pragmatic understanding of the nature of the contemporary work paradigm.

The first part of the book concludes by developing a more specific definition of the work paradigm and of its internal dynamics in *chapter four*. This will establish an interpretative frame within which the subsequent discussion of past and present work paradigms can be understood. With regard to the conceptual aspects of the work paradigm, it will be suggested that all concepts of work contain a work-ethic which functions to provide an intellectual/moral justification of the prevailing organization of work. Within the work-ethic itself, a distinction should be made between ideas and beliefs which are 'authentic' in the sense that they accurately reflect and support the practical organization of work, and *ideological constructs*, which misrepresent these ideas and beliefs for other purposes. In subsequent chapters, it will be suggested that the contemporary (largely bourgeois-liberal/economistic) concept of work has become increasingly ideological (and therefore negative) *to the extent that it has failed to keep pace with fundamental changes in the material practice of work.* If it is the case that a serious disjuncture is occurring within the contemporary work paradigm, one issue which will certainly have to be addressed is how we might be able to bring our (pre-)conceptions about work 'up-to-date'.

With regard to the practical aspects of the work paradigm, it will be suggested that technical developments within the forces of production necessarily instigate particular forms of work-organization, which may result in changes in the relations of production. Whilst recognising that this remains a central issue particularly within Marxist scholarship, its treatment here will be more limited. 'Relations of production' will be used in a 'micro' sense to refer to the *co-operative relationships* which necessarily develop between individuals when undertaking a particular working activity. It will not be used in the more general 'macro' Marxist sense to denote *class relations*. When understood in this more restricted way, forces of production can be taken to be *inclusive of* relations of production. Changes in the pattern and organization of work can therefore be seen as a *joint consequence* of changes in *both* co-operative relationships *and* in productive technique; the latter are not necessarily *determined* by the former. The discussion of this issue will be used to develop the idea that each historical period - classical, feudal, industrial and post-industrial - can be characterized in terms of the emergence of a particular state of balance or equilibrium between the conceptual and practical dimensions of work. The satisfactory combination of these dimensions will be described as the work paradigm of a particular period.

Having put forward a revised theoretical model of the composition and dynamics of the work paradigm, and having made a number of suggestions as to the kind of analytical strategy might be most appropriate for testing its validity, the second part of the book goes on to see how useful this model is in helping us to understand the content and nature of past work paradigms. Focusing particularly on the conceptual aspect of the work paradigm, *chapter five* will describe the work paradigm of classical, pre-Christian and early Medieval society, and *chapter six* will describe the work paradigm of sixteenth and seventeenth European society. It will be shown that the categorization of activities as work, and the attribution of meaning to these activities is closely associated with wider aspects of the overall belief system of the society within which they occur. An important aspect of this association is the imposition of what can be called *principles of justification* upon the perceived acceptability of various forms of economic practice. This chapter includes a detailed discussion of Max Weber's *Protestant Ethic Thesis*, in which a particularly close association is made between a particular set of beliefs, namely ascetic Protestantism, and a particular set of working practices, namely acquisitive capitalism. Although Weber's interpretation provides one of the most useful accounts of the relationship between an economic practice and an incumbent ideology or concept of work, it will be argued that Weber's analysis remains ambiguous over the question of whether work paradigms are primarily determined by a particular belief system or by a particular practical organization of work.

The third part of the book turns our attention from the work paradigms of the past to that which has developed during the late-twentieth century. Of particular importance here, will be a description of recent changes in patterns of working, and an analysis of the impact of new 'technological paradigm' of 'flexibility' on the practical organization of work. These issues, together with current debates over the transition towards post-Fordism, are discussed in *chapter seven*. Finally, in *chapter eight,* and drawing upon the analysis developed in earlier chapters, a more critical discussion will be put forward as to whether the conceptual and practical aspects of our current work paradigm have become dislocated from each other. It will be argued that as we reach the end of the century, it is possible that this dislocation may result in what can be called a 'loss of legitimacy' within the current work paradigm, as increasing numbers of people find that their expectations of work are not being fulfilled. Adopting a more speculative tone, this chapter concludes with a discussion of whether a new concept of work might emerge as part of the process of re-establishing equilibrium within the current work paradigm. Drawing upon the theoretical perspective developed in the previous chapters regarding the interconnectedness of conceptual and practical aspects of the work paradigm, a number of proposals will be put forward as to how this paradox can be solved. It will be suggested that this disequilibrium is at least partly a result of the increasingly outdated nature of the present concept of work. If the definition of work depends upon the application of a number of relatively discrete criteria, it is reasonable to suggest that a change in criteria would result in a revised concept of work. If the somewhat restricted idea that work equals formal full-time paid employment were transcended by a more flexible definition, then it would be possible to legitimize a very much wider range of activities which are in some sense 'productive'. In the second place, a more broadly based concept of work might result in a *much reduced dependence* on the category of activities which currently fall into the rapidly diminishing category of work as 'formal paid employment'. Under these circumstances, the tendency for developments in productive technique to reduce the demand for some types of work might come to be seen as advantageous and beneficial. It would in other words, be possible to accept what has already become evident, that technological change has rendered our assumptions of work as full-time and life-long employment redundant. With regard to future developments, it will be argued that because of the *reciprocal nature* of the relationship between concepts and practices of work, and because new technologies offer an unprecedented degree of *flexibility and choice*, the process of technological innovation can and must once again become sensitive to the actual aims and intentions which individuals seek to fulfil through work.

2 Definitions and concepts of work

Any study of the meaning and purpose of 'work' must begin with the elementary problem of how this widely used term has been defined. Typically, and although it might be a somewhat subliminal process, our common sense or day-to-day idea of what work is, of what constitutes work, draws upon a number of assumptions. At their most basic, these assumptions are based upon or presume, a particular definition of work. This after all, is what language does; it allows us to communicate by applying concise and reasonably uncontested labels to things without the need for describing such and such a thing from scratch every time we want to refer to it. In the same way then, that if asked whether we have any pets, we spontaneously refer to our mental dictionary which tells us that 'pets' are domesticated animals which we might keep for pleasure, if we are asked whether we have done any work today, our mental dictionary conjures up a definition of what 'work' is. Although we might 'personalise' our definition of work, perhaps by giving precedence to activities which are closest to our own working activities (a labourer for example, might dismiss writing as not being 'real work'), the prevailing definition of work in a particular society at a particular point in time, is likely to be shared by a large majority of the population. The starting point then, for understanding concepts of work, is to understand how 'work' is defined.

In defining the word 'work', it is useful to consider the term both in terms of its linguistic origins, and in terms of how it has been used to distinguish between various categories of activities. Definitions of work and the categorization of particular types of activity as 'work' provide us with the basic outline of the concept of work. In discussing a number of past and present definitions of 'work', this chapter divides into two parts.

Part one distinguishes a number of basic elements in the definition of the word 'work'. A brief etymology is given in order to clarify the nuances of meaning which are commonly expressed within the general term 'work' and by the related terms 'labour', 'craft', 'house-work', 'job', and 'occupation'. These distinctions are then used to highlight a number of key *criteria* which have been used to distinguish between the realms of work and non-work.

Part two takes the discussion a stage further by considering a number of different approaches to the categorization of particular sets of activities as 'work'. The three categories of definition considered here are: anthropological, economic, and 'folk' definitions. It will be shown that a number of *themes* tend to recur in this process of categorization. When these themes are combined with the criteria set out in part one, they provide the basic building blocks of concepts of work. It will subsequently be argued that definitions and concepts of work, including contemporary concepts, are largely constituted through the application of the criteria discussed in this chapter. It is reasonable to suggest that although the content of the activities themselves may remain unchanged, a change in criteria, and perhaps more importantly, a change in the application of the criteria (i.e. a change in the inclusion or exclusion of an activity in the category of working activities) will effectively result in changes in the concept of work.

Part One - The definition of the word 'work'

Reference to the Oxford English Dictionary suggests the following definition of 'work':

> Something to be done, or something to do; occupation, business, task, function. Action involving effort or exertion directed to a definite end, especially as a means of earning a livelihood; regular occupation or employment. (*Shorter Oxford English Dictionary*, 3rd Edition, pp.2448-9)

Immediately a number of basic criteria of definition can be distinguished. Firstly, this definition of work encompasses a number of alternative terms used to denote the performance of an activity. Secondly, this activity is associated with the notion of payment or income. Thirdly, the basic assumption is made that this performance requires the discharge of physical and/or mental energy. Fourthly, there is the expectation that work is in some way useful or expedient, which is to say that working activities can be distinguished from non-working activities such as 'play' or 'leisure', on the grounds that their purpose tends towards some form of quantifiable material or practical gain rather than towards simple enjoyment or relaxation.

Taking the four elements action, payment, exertion and expediency one at a time, it will be useful first of all to disentangle the various shades of meaning between 'work' and the related terms 'labour', 'craft', 'housework', 'job' and 'occupation' which are commonly used to denote working activity. Raymond Williams suggests that 'work is the modern English form of the noun *weorc*, (Old English) and the verb *wyrcan*, (Old English), as our most general word for doing something and for something done' (Williams 1976, pp. 281-2). Work in this general sense can be distinguished from the term 'labour', which implies arduousness or 'toil', in the literal sense of doing something *laborious*: 'As a verb, *labour* had a common sense of ploughing or working the land, but was also extended to other kinds of manual work and to any kind of difficult effort. A *labourer* was primarily a manual worker' (Williams 1976, p.146). The notion of 'toil' or painful work derives from the Greek terms *ponos* meaning pain, toil, trouble or distress, and *eris* meaning strife. These can be distinguished from the alternative terms *ergon*, a general term for doing something, and *poiein* or *poiesis*, associated with both the activities and products of an artisan or skilled craftsman.[1] Further, as André Gorz argues, the notion of labour-as-toil can be associated with 'the need for Man to produce his means of subsistence "by the sweat of his brow"'. Thus labour can be defined as 'work carried out in order to ensure survival'. Gorz also wishes to maintain the distinction noted above between this realm of necessary activity, and the activities of craftworkers:

> Until the eighteenth century the term "labour" (travail, Arbeit, lavoro) referred to the toil of serfs and day-labourers who produced consumer goods or services necessary for life which had to be recommenced day after day without ever producing any lasting results. Craftworkers, on the other hand... did not "labour", they "produced works" (oeuvraient), possibly using in their "work" the "labour" of unskilled workers whose job it was to do menial tasks. Only day-labourers were paid for their "labour": craftworkers were paid for their "works" (oeuvre). (Gorz 1989, p.16)

In modern society, this notion of endlessly repeated labour or toil can be associated with domestic or 'reproductive' chores understood as activities 'which individuals undertake in order to complete tasks of which they, or their family, are the sole beneficiaries' (Gorz 1989, p.13). So for example, unpaid and self-directed 'house-work' can be distinguished from work which is carried out for direct remuneration, and from (craft-)work carried out for artistic purposes.

With reference to the notion of 'work' or 'labour' in Marx, and as Firth has pointed out, it is interesting to note that the German term *arbeit* can be translated into English as either 'work' or 'labour'. Firth suggests that 'work' denotes the 'expenditure of energy', but assumes that this expenditure 'does not give complete satisfaction in itself - as recreation may be thought to do - but is the pursuit of some further end'. The term 'labour' extends this notion, but in addition 'tends to carry the notion of more protracted activity, with emphasis on the more negative aspects of energy expenditure'. Thus 'one may speak of the satisfactions to be gained from work, but not so easily of satisfactions to be gained from labour' (Firth 1979, pp.178-9). In this sense, the translation into English of the term 'labour' in Marx acquires the pejorative sense of expropriative and exploitative activity with which it is commonly associated.[2]

A further important extension of the term labour emerged as part of the vocabulary of political economy during the nineteenth century, to encompass a more abstract or general category of 'socially necessary labour'. As Williams suggests:

> Where labour in its most general sense, had meant all productive work, it now came to mean that element of production which in combination with capital and materials produced commodities. This new specialized use belongs directly to the systematized understanding of capitalist productive relations. (Williams 1976, p.146)

This use of the term labour as a conceptual category within economics is discussed in part two below.

Finally, the emergence of the more recent terms 'job', 'occupation' and 'employment' should also be noted. The former originally denoted a particular or specific piece of work in the sense of doing a 'job of work'. Subsequently, as Williams has pointed out, the term has come to subsume other terms related to formal employment such as 'situation, position, post and appointment: What has then happened is that a word formerly specifically reserved to limited and occasional employment (and surviving in this sense, as a *price for the job*...) has become the common word for regular and normal employment' (Williams 1976, p.283). The terms 'occupation' and 'employment' can be regarded as alternatives for the word 'job', denoting formal and regular paid work. It is worth noting that the terms 'occupation' and 'profession' tend to carry a slightly more extended meaning in as much that they imply that the work-skills and credentials a person has, carry-over into their life more generally. Although a doctor or a nurse, a solicitor or accountant, a policeman or teacher, might not actually be able to exercise their skills outside their place of work, their professional identity is always with them. Their work is not just the job that they do, but is more fully the basis of their self-identity and social status. The preference amongst the middle-class for describing their work as an occupation or profession, clearly reflects a desire to mark a distinction between people whose work is 'just a job' and those whose work is much more than that. The fact that we are likely to modify our language when asking what work a person does, ("what job do you do" or "what is your profession") shows how readily we take account of the relationship between the work that a person does and their apparent social status. Table 2.1 summarizes the distinctions which can be drawn

Table 2.1: Defining the word work

Within the general term work, we can distinguish between work and:

labour defined as necessary or obligatory toil carried out by individuals to provide themselves and their dependants with the necessities of life

house-work, or 'reproductive-work' defined as necessary activities carried out predominantly within the private sphere and repeated on a cyclical basis to maintain the health and welfare of family members

craft defined as activities performed in pursuit of a particular end or 'product', and which require the application of various specific skills and abilities

Job, occupation or *employment*, as terms which denote the particular type or category of work in which a particular individual or group of individuals may be involved.

within the general term work and the related terms which are commonly used to denote doing something and something done.

The second element noted above, is that some form of payment, or reimbursement is given in return for the effort expended through work. This element brings us closer to the contemporary definition since this criterion is often decisive in denoting whether a particular activity does or does not constitute 'work'. A number of alternative methods of payment or reimbursement have been used at various times.[3] Referring back to the notion of labour as defined above, the idea of wage-labour has existed since the feudal period, where a simple 'unskilled' labourer or skilled day-labourer (or 'journeyman' from the French word for day, *journee*) would receive payment in cash or in kind in exchange for a days-worth of work or effort. Although the notion of payment in kind has persisted in a limited form up to the present day,[4] since the late eighteenth century, payment is almost exclusively associated with *money*. Work in other words, has come to be defined as *wage-work*:

> *Work* has not always existed in the way in which it is currently understood. It came into being at the same time as capitalists and proletarians. It means an activity carried out: for someone else; in return for a wage; according to forms and time schedules laid down by the person paying the wage; and for a purpose not chosen by the worker. (Gorz 1982, p.1)

The recent expansion of formal service-sector employment to encompass activities previously regarded as personal house-work or unpaid domestic labour, clearly illustrates the increasing use of the cash-payment criterion for distinguishing work from non-work. These activities may now be seen in terms of formal public employment rather than in terms of informal private house-work. As Wadel has pointed out:

> The care of children and of sick or elderly persons, *within a family setting*, does not seem to have been regarded in the past, as work proper (nor as leisure). However, the fact that these activities can now be bought on the market, or supplied by local authorities, coupled with the fact that more and more people make use of such professional services, seem to have led to a greater recognition and legitimation of them as work *even when carried out within the family setting*. (Wadel 1979, p.369, emphasis added)

These developments clearly imply that changes in the application of a particular criterion, (in this case that being paid in cash for undertaking domestic labour results in a renewed recognition of the usefulness and expediency of this type of activity), can result in significant changes in both the *perception* of the activity itself, and of the *status* of those who perform it. This suggests that changes in the definition of work can occur *without* prior changes in the nature and substance of the activity itself; *it is not the activity itself which has changed, but the perception that its worth and value justify direct payment.* I shall return to this point shortly.

The payment criterion draws our attention to two further characteristics of the concept of work in contemporary society. Firstly, since the early eighteenth century, 'work' has become associated with activities which are performed *outside* the home; work is a *public* rather than *private* realm of activity. In his analysis of the emergence of capitalist economic systems for example, Max Weber attaches great importance to this development as constituting a defining characteristic of 'modern' or 'rational' capitalism: 'The modern rational organization of the capitalistic enterprise would not have been possible without... the separation of business from the household, which completely dominates modern economic life' (Weber 1976, pp.21-2). Similarly, Gorz draws a distinction between ancient and modern societies in terms of the separation of these two spheres of activity:

> There is however, a fundamental difference between labour in capitalist society and labour in the ancient world: in the former it is performed in the public sphere, whilst in the latter it was confined to the private sphere. Most of the *economy* in the ancient city-state consisted in private activity performed, not in public, in the market place, but within the sphere of the family and the household. (Gorz 1989, p.15)

For Gorz, this is an important distinction, since 'freedom only commenced outside the private, *economic* household sphere. The sphere of freedom was the public sphere of the *polis*' (Gorz 1989, p.15). This association of freedom with the public sphere comes about for two reasons. Firstly, formal employment endorses the wider social participation or citizenship of the individual: *'The right to accede to the public, economic sphere through one's work is a necessary part of the right to citizenship'* (Gorz 1989, p.141, original emphasis). Work in other words, gives the individual access to an important source of public legitimation and status. Conversely, being outside work may result in the social displacement of the individual. Secondly, the opportunity to earn a living outside the home may change the dependent nature of relationships *between* members of that household; it has in other words, 'enabled personal relations to develop in their own right and become independent of that sphere' (Gorz 1989, p.141).

A second defining characteristic of the contemporary definition of work is that within the public sphere, further distinctions are made between *formal* work in the 'official economy' and *informal* work in the unofficial or 'black-economy'. Broadly speaking, the formal economy encompasses activities carried out under an agreed contractual arrangement, in a particular time and place, and which are 'declared' for the purposes of taxation. The informal economy encompasses activities which are performed without such arrangements, and are not 'declared'. 'Official' work in this sense, may also carry benefits for the individual through participation in government-run National Insurance schemes, and through membership of trade unions and staff associations which presume that the individual is 'officially' employed.[5]

The third element that 'work' involves some form of exertion or effort is relatively self-explanatory and does not require any particular elaboration here. Two related points should however be made. Firstly, it should not be assumed that the effort required to perform a particular task is exclusively or predominantly muscular. Clearly intellectual activity can result in considerable fatigue.[6] Secondly, the amount of effort required to perform a particular task may not necessarily be determined in terms of the visible product of the activity. In contemporary society, the rapidly increasing number of working activities concerned with handling electronic data, effectively renders the idea of classifying work on the basis of the product it produces redundant. It would certainly come as something of a shock to data-management personnel to be told that their activity is not work because they are not producing a tangible end-product. On this understanding, an activity can be regarded as 'productive' even if no discernible 'product' results from it.[7]

The fourth criterion that work should be seen to be in some way useful and expedient, raises a number of issues which are central to the humanist definition of work as 'productive activity'. A detailed discussion of the concepts of 'use' 'value' and 'worth' will therefore be reserved for the following chapter. Provisionally however, it should be noted that the criterion of perceived expediency has become one of the most elusive elements in defining activities as work. In economies where the production and consumption of commodities is immediate and direct, making judgements as to the use and value of a particular activity is relatively simple. If the action produces a commodity which satisfies a need then it is useful and expedient; if it does not, then it is pointless and wasteful. In rudimentary market economies the same general rule can be applied since income derived from the sale of surpluses is likely to be turned back into a needed commodity more or less immediately. In more developed market economies however, the geographical and temporal separation of production from consumption can make it much more difficult to assess the purpose and thus value of a particular activity. These developments alert us to the fact that the designation of an activity as work, on the grounds that it produces something 'useful' or 'valuable', can make the definition of work more or less conditional upon what is consumed and how it is consumed. It may in other words, be impossible to have anything other than a very transitory and provisional idea of what the use and value of working activities actually are. If this is the case, then arguably, notions of use and value might be seen to be particularly unhelpful as a means of defining work, or might tend to be displaced by other criteria which can be judged more easily. The contemporary criteria of work are summarized in the following table:

Table 2.2: Contemporary criteria of work

An activity is categorized as work proper if it:

is a purposeful expedient activity
requires mental and/or physical exertion
is carried out in exchange for wages or salary
is a public activity
is recognized as work for 'official purposes' such as taxation and insurance

Discussion

So far, we have looked at a number of criteria which are commonly used in defining work. These are that work involves action, that it is carried out in return for payment, that it requires physical and/or mental exertion, and that it is expedient or useful. Within the advanced capitalist economies, the definition has been further refined so that the (extrinsic) rewards for working are largely in terms of direct financial payment, that work is a largely public (rather than private) activity, and that it is conducted within the official (rather than unofficial) economy. So far so good. We have also noted however, that on closer examination, these criteria might be much more elusive and potentially unreliable than at first they might appear. This draws our attention to fact that effective application or 'operationalization' of each of these criteria, and therefore of the definition of work as a whole, depends upon the agreement of the population regarding those criteria. Definitions and perceptions of work are necessarily based upon a level of shared perception; in practical terms, a definition of work is only useful if it is shared by the majority of people living in a particular society. This raises the complex issue of the extent to which definitions of work are 'socially constructed'. Without undertaking an extensive discussion of the more fundamental debates which surround this point, we should acknowledge that since definitions of work form part (and a very important part) of the universe of understanding which mediates and mitigates our actions, we cannot ignore the charge that there may be no such thing as a 'universal' or objectively 'empirical' definition of work. Adopting a stringently phenomenological perspective for example, we might argue that criteria and definitions of work are somewhat superficial, and that what really counts are the wholly subjective and personal criteria which people 'choose for themselves' to apply to work; that there is a realm of meaning-attribution and subjective interpretation which essentially lies out of reach for the sociologist of work. Theoretically, we could go so far as to say that there are no concrete criteria for the definition of work: work can be defined as more or less anything that we chose to define it as. If we wanted, we could say that complete inactivity producing nothing tangible was 'work' while hyperactivity producing very large outputs was non-work.

Fortunately however, such a tumble into the never-never world of 'subjectivity' belies an unnecessary confusion about what it means to say that work is 'socially constructed'. There is a difference between something being 'socially constructed' in the sense of tending only to exist 'in the minds' of the population, and being 'socially constructed' in the sense that the attribution of meaning and significance to an activity, is subject to, and in some sense cases might be dependent upon, the *social dimensions* of the activity. When understood in this way, 'social construction' also acknowledges that the validity and utility of the criteria derive from the fact that other people explicitly acknowledge the usefulness of the criteria and agree to abide by them. It might be interesting to speculate about the entirely personal and subjective 'criteria' which particular individuals might apply to their activities, but we can only progress towards a more substantial understanding once we accept that definitions of work are social phenomena, which derive their usefulness from their practical operationalization in a shared social context.

From a practical point of view, the commonsensical reasonableness and actual use of the criteria described above, strongly suggests that these criteria, or some combination of them, *are* the criteria upon which the definition of work is based; for all practical purposes they *do* provide a fairly reliable practical basis for deciding whether a particular activity is or is not work. The reason for this is relatively straight forward. Work is not something we do for the sake of it, but is something we do consciously and purposefully; we work, and we are quite clear that we work, in order to provide ourselves with the necessities of life. Because the outcomes of work are so important to us (principally but by no means exclusively, in order to ensure survival), and because we are in competition with other similarly needful people, it is inevitable that the definition of work is formalized in some way. Agreeing what financial and other benefits an individual gets in return for work, and accepting that he or she is entitled to them, cannot be done unless we have an agreed definition of work. Indeed, an increasingly detailed division of labour, combined with decreasing resources (including the 'resource' of employment itself) may indicate that this process of formalization becomes more and more important. This is not to suggest of course, that criteria and definitions of work are set in stone. It will be useful to consider briefly a number of examples of how such perceptual change has taken place in the recent past.

Recalling the earlier reference to Wadel's observation that a process of marketization has rendered 'legitimate' a range of caring activities which were formerly regarded as private non-work, we can see that this reclassification of activities as work proper did not occur as it were spontaneously, but was closely associated with other developments in social attitudes and material necessity. Arguably, the re-legitimation of domestic labour as necessary and useful work, coincided with a growing change in attitude towards the economic and social position of women after 1945. This development represents a clear contrast with the situation in an earlier period when the formal employment of large numbers of urban workers in wealthy Victorian households, did not produce any such change of perception. For those 'in service', doing (other people's) domestic work did not carry a particularly high level of social recognition. In terms of changes in material necessity, it can be suggested that an increasing recognition today of the need to allow greater numbers of mothers access to formal employment may result in an expansion of nursery and other support facilities. As the number of people *formally employed* in providing these services increases, the perceived worth and value of these activities is also likely to increase. In this instance therefore, both a change in social perception (that domestic work is not low status), and the emergence of a practical economic need (increasing demand for nursery care), has resulted in the inclusion of a range of (largely unchanged) activities into the category of work proper.[8]

A similar process can be seen to have taken place around the criteria of 'official' and 'unofficial' working. Again the designation of an activity as 'official' or 'unofficial' may have little or nothing to do with the content of the activity itself. The activity of manufacturing and distributing narcotics for example, is very likely to be basically the same irrespective of whether the activity is classified as 'official' work or as 'unofficial' or 'criminal'. If a number of 'soft' narcotics were 'made legal', those who sell them to the public would be expected to pay tax on their earnings. A similar example can be seen in the case of terminating pregnancy. Depending on the law of the land, an abortionist might be regarded as a criminal or as a legitimate medical practitioner. In both these examples, the designation 'official' or 'unofficial' is made on the basis of institutional and legal precedent rather than on the basis of any particular consideration of the physics of the activity itself.

Voluntary work constitutes a further category of activities whose status occupies an ambiguous position amongst the criteria of work. While many of these activities fulfil the criteria of being orderly, productive, public and physically and mentally active, they don't qualify as work proper because they are not paid activities. Essentially, the designation 'voluntary' reminds us that most of the work we do is 'obligatory': the only real difference between the nanny and the unpaid baby-sitter, is that the latter can afford not to be paid for time spent on doing this 'work', or can at least choose to spend time on it, while the former *is working*.

The criterion public/private is a particularly useful illustration of the way in which both established and new types of activity have been both included and excluded from the category of work. Ostensibly, the public criteria implies that the activity is done outside the home. Clearly however, there are many activities which count as work although they are performed inside the home. The visiting hairdresser or cleaner for example, is clearly working although they do their work inside the home of the client. The activity counts as work, because the client's home is for all practical purposes a 'public' place form the point of view of the person doing the work. A further common example, relates to the large range of activities which are regarded as work proper even if the person doing them works entirely at home. While this range of activities is historically well-established (spinning and weaving, wet-nursing and so on), the advent of the electronic cottage and telecommuting may indicate that this form of working arrangement will become more and more common. The activities of these people is work proper because the commodities they produce are destined for the public market. Their mode of income is public even if their mode of production is apparently not. It is worth repeating the point, that in each of these examples, the classification of activities as work proper has very little to do with the nature of the activity, but a great deal to do with whether and in what ways the criteria are applied. The following table summarizes these characteristics of the criteria of work:

Table 2.3: Characteristics of the criteria of work 1
a certain ambiguity and arbitrariness accompanies the application of the criteria
for the criteria of work to be effective and useful in practical application, it is essential that the majority of the population agrees to adopt these criteria and to abide by their consequences
criteria of work are socially constructed in the sense that they reflect the social nature of work and the agreed social purposes of work

Part Two - Basic themes in the concept *work*

As noted in the introductory chapter, the concept of work, and the meaning and significance of activities described as work, play a central role in understanding the nature of a society. This is so both in the sense of defining the overall social structure, and in the sense of understanding how and why individuals attach meaning to particular aspects of their activity. As such, this concept has attracted a wide range of interpretations and definitions, not least because it encourages subjective and individual interpretations. It is however possible to distinguish between four basic categories of definition which emerge from alternative, and to some extent complementary academic disciplines, and to delineate a number of recurrent themes in the contemporary concept of work.[9]

1. Anthropological definitions of work

> Across cultures, those activities that are called "work" (or by the word which is translated as "work") change, and the component parts of work processes appear in different combinations and with different significance. A comparative perspective on work must therefore take into account not only what is done, how it is done and who does it, but also how and by whom it is evaluated. (Wallman 1979, p.1)

As this quotation emphasizes, anthropological approaches to work must take account of the fact that in common with many other concepts used in the comparative study of societies, the concept of work is problematic. In the first place, a concept which is applicable to one society at a particular point in time, may not be appropriate either within the same society at a different point in time, or in other societies at the same time. It is unlikely in other words, that developments in the concept of work will be universally applicable.[10] In this case a limited definition of work as a description of 'physical' activity may be appropriate. For example: 'Work is the application of human energy to things; which application converts, maintains, or adds value to the worker, the thing worked on, and the system in which the work is performed' (Wallman 1979, p.4). Considerable difficulties may subsequently emerge however, when moving beyond this descriptive definition, towards developing a means of measuring the differences and similarities between the working activities of different societies. As Schwimmer points out, where the Western concept of work is found not to be applicable, (for example if no equivalent linguistic term for the concept exists) alternative measures of 'economic' activity may have to be adopted: 'Economic anthropologists working in Melanesia have given up measuring labour force participation and concentrate instead on the concept of "time allocation" as a measure of socio-economic relationships;[11] "cost and value";[12] or price'[13] (Schwimmer 1979, p.300).

Aside then, from a very general descriptive definition of work as a form of physical activity, anthropological definitions must tend to be applicable only to the particular society for which the definition has been developed, and in accordance with the criteria of 'measurement' which are seen as appropriate in a particular context. Two further points can be noted. Firstly, anthropological research confirms that the significance and meaning which are attached to concepts of 'purposeful activity' within a given social system, are intimately bound-up with the wider conception of reality, or world-view of that society. 'Work' can in other words, be seen as an activity which greatly facilitates, and may indeed be constitutive of, social integration. Secondly, the measures which are chosen as being representative of, or applicable to, activities which would generally be described as work in Western cultures, predominantly tend to be framed in terms of *economic* criteria.

2. Economistic definitions of work

From a Western perspective, definitions of work are overwhelmingly associated with activities which are considered to be *economically expedient*. As noted in part one, the cash-payment and expediency criteria have become the most crucial criteria for distinguishing between work and non-work, and many definitions and concepts of work reflect this perception. So for example: 'Work is defined as all those activities which an individual is involved in on a regular basis and for which he [she] receives direct financial reward' (Fagin 1979, p.32). Similarly, Gorz defines 'work for economic ends' as 'work done *with payment in mind*. Here money, that is, *commodity exchange*, is the principal goal. One works first of all to "earn a living", and the satisfaction or pleasure one may possibly derive from such work is a subordinate consideration' (Gorz 1989, p.221, original emphasis). It is not surprising then, that the economistic definition and concept of work is constituted almost exclusively in terms of output; it is restricted in other words 'to activities one is paid for (paid work); such work takes place at specific places (work place) and at specific times (work time/working hours)' (Wadel 1979, p.369).

In his critique of the simplistic or stripped-down nature of economic definitions of work, Elkan has distinguished three categories into which 'almost everything in economics to do with work can be fitted':

> First, the relationship between work and output. Secondly, being in or out of work, i.e. being employed or unemployed. Thirdly, the allocation of time between work and leisure and the economic factors which determine it. (Elkan 1979, p.25)

This categorization reflects the emergence within economics of the notion of 'labour' as an abstract category; a quantum which is used as one element in the equation needed to calculate the costs and subsequent surplus derived from the production of commodities. To this extent 'the relationship between work and output was virtually the starting point of economics' (Elkan 1979, p.25).

As a consequence of this absorption of the notion of work-as-labour within political economy, perceptions of the purpose and value of activities have become heavily dependent upon the parameters of capitalistic economic rationality as a whole:

> We can thus say that the work concept among economists has become subservient to other concepts which they more easily handle professionally. These include those that can be quantified, like pay and product, and those which may be said to be the institutional basis of our kind of economy, like business organization and market. (Wadel 1979, p.367)

Indeed it is unlikely that modern economic rationality would have developed at all until the detailed division of tasks and the dominance of wage-labour, which this requires, had been established. In his analysis of the emergence of modern capitalism, Weber notes that 'the fifth requirement is free labour':

> People must be available who are not only legally in the position to do so but are also economically compelled to sell their labour on the market without restrictions. Only where in consequence of the existence of workers who in the formal sense voluntarily, but actually under the compulsion of hunger, offer themselves to work for a wage, can the costs of production be unambiguously determined in advance. (Weber 1983, p.110)

Similarly Gorz notes:

> It was essential for [the capitalist] enterprise to calculate and forecast labour costs accurately, since it was on this condition alone that the volume and price of the merchandise produced and the expected profit could be calculated. Without these forecast figures, the risk involved in making investments was too great. (Gorz 1989, p.21)

In turn, the need for rational calculability in the labour process led to a further abstraction of the whole notion of work; namely *the separation of the worker from the work done*. Gorz summarizes this process:

> To make the cost of labour calculable, it was necessary to make its output calculable as well. It had to be possible to treat it as a quantifiable material unit; in other words, to be able to measure it in itself, as an independent entity, isolated from the individual

> characteristics and motivations of the worker... it is this separation alone which made it possible to rationalise and economise labour, to make it produce surpluses in excess of the producers' needs and to use these growing surpluses to expand the means of production and increase their power. (Gorz 1989, pp.21/51)

This process of the abstraction or separation of activity from those engaged in it lies at the heart of Marx's analysis of the 'commodification of labour', and of the development of the notion of 'labour-power'. As Schwimmer notes:

> Work as a concept is based on the assumption that, from a certain viewpoint, all economically useful activities are fully comparable by a yardstick transcending their diversity, in other words, that labour has become a commodity and that the technical and administrative direction of that labour has become part of the same kind of commodity. (Schwimmer 1979, p.287)[14]

The emergence and subsequent dominance of the economistic definition of work clearly illustrates how material changes in the nature and organization of work (in this case the emergence of standardized machine manufacture and the expansion of the detailed division of tasks) have had a profound impact upon the way in which work is conceived. They also suggest that once a particular conception of work has become dominant, (in this instance that work is a rationally calculable form of activity, a commodity and cost of production) further developments in working practice may take place which are as it were 'sympathetic' to this view of work. The nature and implications of these processes for changes in the contemporary work paradigm, are extensively discussed the following chapters. At this point, it is useful to note a number of characteristics and limitations of the economic conceptualization of work.

Firstly, definitions of work which are framed solely in terms of economic categories tend to be somewhat *simplistic and specific*. Distinctions between work and non-work and between being in work or not being in work, become more or less cut and dried: 'In the advanced industrial countries... earning a living has come to be regarded as virtually synonymous with being employed, and if someone is *not*, then it is assumed that he must be *un*employed' (Elkan 1979, p.27, original emphasis). On this understanding, all those activities which take place *outside* the formal economy are not regarded as work proper, since their cost and yield cannot be calculated with sufficient accuracy.

Secondly, by evaluating usefulness and expediency in purely economic terms, economistic definition of work assess the worth and value of activities almost exclusively in terms of *extrinsic* outcomes or rewards. Since intrinsic satisfactions (both in terms of the pleasure which might be gained whilst working, and of being productively involved in activities outside work) are difficult to quantify or 'measure' objectively, the actions which give rise to them are not regarded as work proper. The predilection for mathematically quantifiable outcomes, necessarily leads to the exclusion of activities whose consequences are *subjectively* expedient.

Thirdly, it should be recognized that it is the *simplicity* of the economistic definition of work which has enabled it to remain relatively unaltered during periods of rapid development within the labour process. It has in other words, been able to absorb significant changes in the nature and organization of work whilst remaining relatively immune to such changes:

> Economists have had no difficulties in including new types of activity (as well as new occupational groups) under their work concept, so long as this activity is sold on the market. Thus, they have been able to incorporate as work, one of the major changes in modern society, i.e. the increasing division of labour, without changing or refining their concept of work. (Wadel 1979, p.367)

In summary, although the economistic definition of work may retain a degree of validity and utility when used within economics itself, this definition can only provide a very superficial means of conceptualizing the meaning and purpose of work in any more general sense. Outside the specific discipline of economics, we could agree with Wadel that the economic definition of work barely constitutes a definition at all:

> The main reason for this but moderate interest in the concept of work among modern economists is that they have come to operate with a very *simple* concept - so simple indeed that it needs no definition. The simplicity consists of treating work/labour exclusively as those activities that are sold on the market for a price. In short, work, for all practical and theoretical purpose, is paid work. (Wadel 1979, p.367).

3. The 'folk' definition of work

In view of the limitations of the economistic definition of work, Wadel has proposed the development of a 'folk work concept'. From this perspective 'work' is conceptualized as 'a socially constructed category' which recognizes that: 'Activities we term work in our own society are continuously changing: new types of activities are continuously included under the concept, while others are excluded' (Wadel 1979, p.365). This approach to the definition of work has a number of advantages. Firstly, a number of the *subjective* or *qualitative* aspects which may be associated with work can be more clearly specified; factors which economistic definitions tend to leave out of account. Ronald Fraser emphasizes for example, that work is essentially a *social* activity which is central to the development of a *communal* identity: 'Work, the capacity of acting humanely on the world, is a shared experience; for the majority of us it is done in common with others, for every one of us it is done, however privately, for others' (Fraser 1968, p.7). Indeed, as Erich Fromm has pointed out, co-operation with others is the pre-requisite for any social or cultural existence: 'In any conceivable kind of culture man needs to co-operate with others if he wants to survive, whether for the purpose of defending himself against enemies or dangers of nature, or in order that he may be able to work and produce' (Fromm 1942, p.16).

Secondly, and from the point of view of ontological development (defined as the purposeful and progressive development of individual capacities and abilities), this broader concept of work recognizes that the development of personal identity is crucially bound up with work: 'In the process of work, that is, the molding and changing of nature outside of himself, man molds and changes himself... he develops his powers of co-operation, of reason, his sense of beauty... the more his work develops the more his individuality develops' (Fromm, 1956(b), pp.177/178).

In his analysis of 'the need to work', Sayers summarizes a number of research findings which tend to confirm the importance of these less visible consequences and rewards of working. He notes for example, that research shows: 'the great majority want work and feel a need for work, even when they find it unsatisfying in all sorts of ways: dull, repetitive, meaningless.' These aspects are reflected by research into the negative effects of unemployment which 'have shown a lowering of self-esteem and morale, and increases in the suicide rate and the incidence of psychiatric treatment' (Sayers 1987, p.18).[15] In his analysis of white-collar work, C. Wright Mills also draws attention to a number of important factors which, particularly in contemporary society, are dependent upon or closely associated with work:

> Apart from the technical operations and the skills involved, work is a source of income; the amount, level, and security of pay, and what

one's income history has been are part of work's meaning. Work is also a means of gaining status, at the place of work and in the general community... work also carries various sorts of power, over materials and tools and machines, but, more crucially now, over other people. (Mills 1953, p.230)

These three features of work; income, status and power, are particularly interesting since they provide clear examples of those aspects of work which may combine both extrinsic and intrinsic motivations and satisfactions. The development of personality, the desire for self-expression, and the maintenance of a status differential between 'self' and 'other', are often articulated in terms of these features of work.

Thirdly, the folk concept also draws our attention to a range of activities which are closely associated with work, and without which work would not be possible, but which are not typically included within the category of work. These are activities which as it were, spill-over or surround actual working activities. Wadel describes these as 'hidden work', and we can divide these between activities which take place within work, and those which take place outside work. For Wadel, the former includes 'such things as social relations, technical and social skills, attitudes and values' and other necessary features of working life such as 'the maintenance of informal organization within formal organizations', 'the maintenance of community', 'informal political activities', and 'the hidden work of clients and professionals' (Wadel 1979, p.367/372ff). The latter includes the wide range of activities we undertake in preparing for work such as maintaining suitable clothes, the organization of non-work activities around the routine of work, and travelling to and from work. Although some aspects of this 'hidden' work might be remunerated in some way and could be regarded simply as part-and-parcel of work, others remain the sole responsibility of the individual, and are in a sense provided 'free of charge'.

On the basis of this discussion of alternative approaches to the definition of work, we can usefully add a number of additional items to the list of characteristics of the criteria of work given in Table 2.4 below:

Table 2.4: Characteristics of the criteria of work 2
a certain ambiguity and arbitrariness accompanies the application of the criteria
for the criteria of work to be effective and useful in practical application, it is essential that the majority of the population agrees to adopt these criteria and to abide by their consequences
criteria of work are socially constructed in the sense that they reflect the social nature of work and the agreed social purposes of work
concepts of work tend to be culturally specific
concepts of work form an essential and cohesive element within the overall world-view of society
activities which would generally be described as work in Western cultures, predominantly tend to be framed in terms of *economic* criteria.
concepts of work are essentially dynamic and organic

Summary

In part one, a number of distinctions have been made between the term work used as a general term for doing something or for something done, and a number of alternative but similar terms used to denote a particular type or realm of activity. Firstly, a distinction can be made between 'work' and *labour* defined as necessary or obligatory toil carried out by individuals to provide themselves and their dependants with the necessities of life. The predominantly public or private character of labour, and the methods of payment are determined by historical circumstances. Secondly, a distinction can be made between work and *house-work*, or 'reproductive-work' defined as necessary activities carried out predominantly within the private sphere and repeated on a cyclical basis to maintain the health and welfare of family members. Thirdly, a distinction can be made between 'work' and *craft* defined as activities performed in either the public or private sphere, in pursuit of a particular end or 'product', and which require the application of various specific skills and abilities. Finally, a distinction can be made between 'work' and *Job, occupation* or *employment*, as terms which denote the particular type or category of work in which a particular individual or group of individuals may be involved.

A number of basic criteria have then been described, which are typically applied in categorizing particular activities and sets of activities as work in the formal sense. These four criteria suggest a general definition of work as *purposeful activity which is seen to be in some way expedient, requiring mental and/or physical exertion, carried out in exchange for 'payment'*. The contemporary definition of work adds the two refinements that work is a predominantly public activity, and that payment takes the form of wages or salary.

With regard to the criteria themselves, it has been suggested that a certain ambiguity and arbitrariness accompanies the application of the criteria. A number of illustrations have been given which show that while the criteria of energy expenditure and purposefulness are reasonably reliable, in as much that these are features of *all* working activities, the criteria of official/unofficial, and of public/private have very little to do with the actual nature and substance of the activity. Rather, these criteria are applied much more arbitrarily; if one is involved in an officially legitimized public activity, then this qualifies as work proper almost irrespective of any other criteria which might apply. The key criteria, and at least in terms of the wider dimension of work, the most arbitrary, is the criterion of money payment. Although we can acknowledge that our common sense definition of work (and consequently our concept of work more generally) draws upon a range of identifiable criteria, the essential question is whether one gets paid for doing it. For all practical purposes, the payment criterion is *the criterion* for categorizing activities as work.

We have also noted, that for the criteria of work to be effective, for them to have a useful and practical application, it is essential that virtually the whole population agrees to adopt these criteria and to abide by their consequences. A definition of work which is not shared by the population, is, for all practical purposes, not a definition of work at all. This draws attention to the fact that definitions and concepts of work are socially constructed in the sense that they reflect the social nature of work and the agreed social purposes of work. This is highly significant, as it suggests that a widespread popular desire to effect changes in the criteria and definition of work, could actually bring a new definition of work into being. It can be tentatively suggested, that the likelihood of such change is dependent upon the nature of the criteria. If a particular criterion is arbitrary in as much as it bears little relation to the nature and purpose of the activity to which it is applied, then it might more likely that the particular criterion can be modified or replaced. If on the other hand, the criterion *is* closely related to the nature and purpose of a particular activity, then that criterion can be regarded as more or less absolute and therefore relatively permanent.

In part two, three alternative and to some extent complementary approaches to the categorization of activities as work have been examined, in order to outline a number of key themes in concepts of work. Anthropological accounts demonstrate that in many ways concepts of work tend to be culturally specific, and that the comparative measurement of working activities between different societies raises a number of difficulties. These accounts also suggest that the significance and meaning which individuals attribute to activities which may be described as work, form an essential and cohesive element within the overall world-view of society. The comparative analysis of societies, both historical and contemporary, would not be complete without some consideration of the processes of productive agency through which it is constituted.

The analysis of the economistic definition of work shows that this definition is somewhat simplistic, and tends to collapse the notion of work into an abstract analytic category; a category which is amenable to the economists' primary concern with the mathematical calculation of marginal costs, marginal revenue and productivity. From this perspective, a more sophisticated understanding of the intrinsic meaning and significance of work, other perhaps than as an aid to obtaining greater per-capita output, is seen as unnecessary or superfluous. This perspective does however emphasize that work is closely associated with expedient production. Work is a form of purposeful activity which is deliberately directed towards the production of commodities which are in some sense useful.

Perspectives which examine the phenomenon of work in a more holistic and qualitative way, are more able to avoid these limitations largely through a greater acknowledgement of the intrinsic worth and value of working activities. Work is recognized as providing individuals with access to important sources of social recognition and status, is a means through which individuals can express their own creativity, and may make a significant contribution to their psychological development. The folk concept of work also emphasizes the point made earlier, that definitions and concepts of work are essentially dynamic and organic rather than static and mechanical. This dynamism arises not only from changes in the practice of work, particularly those associated with technological innovation, but also from changes in perceptions of the meaning and purpose of work.

Finally, and regarding the nature of the relationship between concepts and practices of work, (the relationship that is, between the two aspects of the work paradigm), it has provisionally been suggested that this relationship is *circular and interactive* rather than *direct and linear*. The economistic definition of work used in political economy for example, emerged in response to the development of machine manufacture and the detailed division of tasks. Once established, this concept of work has had a considerable impact upon subsequent developments in productive developments and the organization of work. A particular concept of work in other words, may reflect back upon and thus influence subsequent developments in productive practice. The balance of influence between the practical and conceptual aspects of the work paradigm is investigated in the following chapters.

Notes

1. These distinctions have been developed in detail by Vernant 1965. Subsequently, this study has been drawn upon by Godelier 1980, and by Schwimmer 1979.

2. In discussing the alienation of labour, Marx writes for example that: 'The worker feels himself only when he is not working; when he is working he does not feel himself. He is at home when he is not working, and not at home when he is working. His labour is therefore not voluntary but forced, it is *forced labour*. It is therefore not the satisfaction of a need but a mere *means* to satisfy needs outside itself. Its alien character is clearly demonstrated by the fact that as soon as no physical or other compulsion exists it is shunned like the plague. External labour, labour in which man alienates himself, is a labour of self-sacrifice, of mortification.' (Marx 1975, *Early Writings* p.326, original emphasis)

3. It should be noted that the notions of 'income' and 'payment' in the form of currency are relatively modern constructs which emerge in

response to the development of markets. In societies where the exchange of surpluses is relatively unimportant when compared with the direct consumption of domestically produced commodities, or where one commodity is exchanged for another rather than for cash, the notions of cash-payment would be relatively meaningless.

4. For example coal miners, brewery workers, and workers in cigarette factories may receive a bonus in the form of the commodities they produce. The benefits or 'perks' of working in particular professions might also be considered a form of payment in kind. A bank or building society employee for example, might be eligible for a reduced rate of interest on their house loan.

5. For useful introductions to the form and characteristics of the 'black economy' see Harding and Jenkins 1989, and Dallago 1990.

6. Gramsci notes for example that: 'Many people have to be persuaded that studying too is a job, and a very tiring one, with its own particular apprenticeship - involving muscles and nerves as well as intellect. It is a process of adaption, a habit acquired with effort, tedium and even suffering.' (Gramsci 1977, p.42)

7. It should be noted that the difference between 'productive' and 'non-productive' labour has attracted considerable debate within Marxism. This debate has become particularly acute when the productive/non-productive criterion is invoked to establish who 'qualifies' as a legitimate member of the proletariat. For a discussion of this see: Marx 1954, *Capital I*, Part III; Poulantzas 1975; Olin Wright 1978, and Gough, I. 1972.

8. The issue of the perceived legitimacy of house-work has been widely discussed by both Feminists and Marxists in 'the domestic labour debate'. For a summary discussion of these issues see: Molyneux 1979; Dex 1985, and Hamilton and Barrett 1987. It is also interesting to note, that an increased acknowledgement of the need for *male* parents to be allowed time away from work to help look after new-born children may also indicate the extent to which the perceived status of these activities has increased. Indeed many of the characteristics of the so-called 'new man' relate directly to involvement in activities which are typically regarded as 'feminine'.

Other contemporary examples of changes in the perceived status and social worth of particular activities include the increasing stigma attached to jobs in the nuclear industry, while activities associated with the environment and conservation are attracting greater recognition and thus legitimacy.

9. The fourth category of definition, the 'humanist' concept of work is discussed in the following chapter.

10. Erik Schwimmer notes for example: 'One of my Orokaiva informants was categorical on this point: "The people of olden times did not take up work (*pure*) for it was only Jesus Christ who gave them work to take up."' (Schwimmer 1979, p.367)

11. See: Lawrence 1964.

12. See: Salisbury 1962.

13. See: Godelier 1977.

14. In his analysis of 'Wage-Labour and Capital', Marx illustrates this process of commodification: 'The capitalist, it seems, therefore buys [the workers'] labour with money. They sell him their labour for money. For the same sum with which the capitalist had bought their labour, for example two marks, he could have bought two pounds of sugar or a definite amount of any other commodity. The two marks, with which he bought two pounds of sugar, are the price of two pounds of sugar. The two marks, with which he bought twelve hours' use of labour, are the price of twelve hours' labour. Labour, therefore, is a commodity, neither more nor less than sugar. The former is measured by the clock, the latter by the scales.' (Marx 'Wage-Labour and Capital' (1849), in McLellan (ed.), 1977, p.249) For a detailed discussion of the displacement of 'natural rhythm' by 'clock time' which accompanied the development of industrial capitalism see Thompson, E.P. 1967.

15. Sayers is quoting from research reported by Jahoda 1979. The intrinsic and subjective aspects of work have received close attention in the research literature as 'scientific management', 'human relations', 'technological implications', 'orientations to work' and

'human resource management' have in varying degrees tried to ascertain the effects of these aspects on 'work satisfaction' and 'work motivation'. For examples of each of these approaches see: Taylor, F.W., 1911; Mayo 1933; Rohrer 1951 and Blauner 1964; Goldthorpe *et al.*, 1968, and Schein (ed.), 1987. For an extensive discussion of these issues see Ransome 1995.

3 The humanist definition of work

The previous chapter has described the basic criteria which are typically applied in categorizing particular activities as work in the formal sense. These suggest a general definition of work as purposeful activity which is seen to be in some way expedient, requiring mental and/or physical exertion, carried out in exchange for payment. The contemporary definition is refined so that work proper is an officially legitimated public activity, and that payment takes the form of direct monetary reward. These latter criteria tend be quite arbitrary in as much that they are used to distinguish between work and non-work on grounds which have very little to do with the substance and nature of the activity itself. It has also been noted that the effective practical application of a particular definition of work, is conditional upon agreement amongst the majority of the population that the definition is appropriate.

Having arrived at this definition, the next question we have to consider, is why is it that the majority of the population accepts this definition of work? Although there is a sense in which acceptance is a matter of habit, we have simply 'got used' to this definition, the underlying reason is that it reflects an identifiable set of expectations of work. We are motivated to accept this definition in the expectation that it will allow us to fulfil a number of our most fundamental needs. In considering the motives and expectations which underlie the attribution of meaning and purpose to working activities, we have to ask whether these attributions are largely individual and subjective, or whether they signify the existence of an underlying and perhaps 'universal' human predisposition for certain kinds of activity. This is an important point, because if the definition of work reflects the underlying motivation to work, and if this motivation is a manifestation of such a universal predisposition, then this predisposition could provide us with a concrete and potentially empirically verifiable means, for understanding the basis of *all* definitions of work. This could not only help us assess the extent to which a particular criterion of work is arbitrary in terms of underlying motivations and expectations of work, but also help us to understand 'the essential ingredients' of any new definition of work which might emerge in the future. In the context of the overall aim of our investigation into how the conceptual and practical aspects of the contemporary work paradigm interact, this knowledge could provide a very useful point of departure for understanding at least the first of these dimensions.

To this end, this chapter begins by describing a particularly useful account of the purpose, meaning and motivation for work, which develops out of Marx's characterization of mankind as a species-being. A description of this humanist concept as set out in Marx's *Early Writings*, and as subsequently developed in the work of Lucien Sève and André Gorz, is given in part one. It will be argued that all definitions and concepts of work are in fact based upon four fundamental *principles of work;* principles which become manifest through the concrete motivations and expectations which people have of work. The chapter concludes with a discussion of how these expectations are reflected in the criteria of work described in the previous chapter.

Part One - The meaning and purpose of work

From an historical perspective, discrete categories of activity, including activities defined as work, have been seen as a means of expressing the purpose of existence. In ancient societies for example, intellectual and contemplative activity was seen as the means by which humankind could attain the ultimate truths of existence. For early Christian society, work was seen as a means by which individuals could fulfil their destiny through the appeasement of the sins of Adam. During the Renaissance and following the Protestant Reformation, the meaning of human existence was defined in terms of the 'duty' of the individual to make the most of their natural skills through the reappropriation of nature. More recently, the concepts of man as 'homo faber' and 'homo economicus' have emerged which represent mankind almost exclusively in terms of work. Leaving aside the more philosophical aspects of this evolution, the particular point to be made regarding the role of work in this process of meaning-construction, is reflected in the contemporary definition of work provided by Godelier:

> So work refers at the same time to relations between people and nature and between people and their fellow beings. Understood as a relation to nature, any work process is a sequence of individual or collective acts designed to extract or detach from nature substances which either in their immediate form, or having undergone a variety of transformations in their forms and properties, become objects of use for human beings, *means of satisfying different needs*. (Godelier 1980, pp.107-8, emphasis added)

In general terms then, work can be defined as *acts undertaken in pursuance of the satisfaction of needs*.

This humanist definition is particularly useful as it focuses attention on the central fact that to a greater or lesser extent, all concepts of work derive from some understanding of what constitutes a 'need'. In turn, the definition of needs and the necessity to undertake activities which satisfy them, derive from a number of further assumptions about what it means to be a human being. Clearly the definition of 'needs' is fraught with difficulties, since the range of actions which could relate either directly or indirectly to the satisfaction of a 'need', is potentially very large indeed. Specifically with regard to the concept of work however, it can be suggested that drawing upon the Marxian concept of mankind as a species-being, the humanist concept of work goes some way towards resolving these difficulties. This concept brings such a resolution within reach because it tries to synthesise the existential problems of 'being' and 'doing'; it recognizes that the purposes and motivations we seek to fulfil through the activities we label work, derive from the same fundamental principles of action which underlie all other categories of action. If we can understand what motivates us to act in general, we can more easily understand what motivates us in our working activities. From this perspective then, work can be seen as a subset or subcategory of activity in general, rather than as a separate or distinct realm of activity which is as it were, cut off or detached from the general activity of the individual. Consequently, the motivation to work, and the attribution of meaning and purpose to work, can be seen as *essentially the same as the basic motivations and perceptions which underlie an individual's need to act at all*.

In his *Early Writings* under a section entitled 'Private Property and Communism', and following Feuerbach, Marx develops the concept of man as species-being:

> The immediate, natural, necessary relation of human being to human being is the *relationship* of *man* to *woman*... this relationship *reveals* in a *sensuous* form, reduced to an observable *fact*, the extent to which the human essence has become nature for man or nature has become the human essence for man.... It follows from the character of this relationship how far *man* as a *species-being*, as *man*, has become himself and grasped himself.... This relationship also demonstrates the extent to which man's *needs* have become *human* needs, hence the extent to which the *other*, as human being, has become a need for him, the extent to which in his most individual existence he is at the same time a communal being. (Marx 1975, p.347)[1]

This passage emphasizes that in essence, the human individual is a *social* being. There is a mutuality of existence inherent in species or human 'beingness': 'Society does not consist of individuals: it expresses the sum of connections and relationships in which individuals find themselves' (Marx *Grundrisse*; McLellan 1977, p.77). Ronald Fraser makes the same point: 'Work, the capacity of acting humanely on the world, is a shared experience; for the majority it is done in common with others, for every one of us it is done, however privately, for others' (Fraser 1968, p.7). These passages also emphasize that by acting in this social context, human beings constitute themselves and are themselves constituted. It is through action in other words *that we exist at all*:

> As individuals express their life, so they are. What they are, therefore, coincides with their production, both with *what* they produce and with *how* they produce. The nature of individuals thus depends on the material conditions determining their production. (Marx and Engels 1970, p.42)

The central importance of 'action' to human being and development has led Lucian Sève to conclude; 'every developed personality appears to us straight away as an enormous accumulation of the most varied acts through time' (Sève 1978, p.304), and citing Gramsci: 'Man is a process, and more exactly the process of his actions' (Sève 1978, p.308).[2] Gramsci goes on to develop this point:

> I mean that one must conceive of man as a series of active relationships (a process) in which individuality, though perhaps the

> most important, is not, however, the only element to be taken into account. The humanity which is reflected in each individuality is composed of various elements: 1. the individual; 2. other men; 3. the natural world.... Thus man does not enter into relations with the natural world just by being himself part of the natural world, but actively, by means of work and technique. Further: these relations are not mechanical. They are active and conscious. They correspond to the greater or lesser degree of understanding that each man has of them. So one could say that each one of us changes himself, modifies himself to the extent that he changes and modifies the complex relations of which he is the hub. (Gramsci 1977, p.352)

These observations argue forcibly that individual and thus social development *are dependent upon the exercise of species-powers through action.*

Having acknowledged the direct and reciprocal relationship between being and doing, and having suggested that for humans, this action is profoundly communal, Marx takes the analysis a stage further by describing how human action is qualitatively different from that of other animal species. He suggests that human activity is of a higher order than that of other animals, since humans not only act reflexively in response to physiological need (as other animals do), but uniquely, humans are able to act in accordance with their own *conscious preconceptions*:

> We pre-suppose labour in a form that stamps it as exclusively human. A spider conducts operations that resemble those of a weaver, and a bee puts to shame many an architect in the construction of her cells. But what distinguishes the worst of architects from the best of bees is this, that the architect raises his structures in imagination before he erects it in reality. At the end of every labour-process we get a result that already existed in the imagination of the labourer at its commencement. He not only effects a change of form in the material on which he works, but he also realises a purpose of his own that gives the law to his modus operandi, and to which he must subordinate his will. (Marx 1954, *Capital I*, p.174)

Through exercising these species-powers, principally the unique ability to preconceive in consciousness and to realize these preconceptions through co-operative actions with others, individuals are able to 'objectify' and thus create both themselves and their environment. Human action constitutes human-beingness, and the development of new actions and means of acting, constitutes the ontology of human development.[3] The key point to be grasped here, is that the motivation to act in the most general sense, is the means through which we manifest our species-being. Since as we have seen in the previous chapter, work is at root a form of action, there is no substantive or logical reason why we should not regard the motivation to work in the same terms as the motivation to act at all. To do otherwise would be to claim that there is a range of human actions which have nothing at all to do with human nature.

The humanist definition of work as productive activity is therefore useful for two clear reasons. Firstly, at the conceptual level, it provides a basis for understanding that in common with all categories of activity, work provides a context within which individuals can exercise their natural species-powers. The meaning and significance of work, and the motivation to work, both derive from this need to act in a purposeful way. Secondly, at the practical level, this concept provides a means of evaluating the quality of, and necessity for, a particular working activity. This takes us back to the criteria of 'use' and 'value' raised in the previous chapter. It was noted there, that in societies with a complex division of tasks, these criteria are particularly difficult to apply. The reason for this is twofold. Judgements about use and value are notoriously difficult to make. So much depends on prevailing circumstances, tastes, fashions and so on. Secondly, and partly because of this, other criteria which are easier to judge, tend to displace criteria of worth and value. This is especially so in the case of the payment criterion. It is much easier to categorize a particular activity as work proper if the individual gets paid for doing it, than to worry over whether the activity is in fact useful or valuable in any other respect. Indeed, for us, if an activity is paid for, then it is necessarily valuable *almost irrespective of any other 'use' or 'value' it might have.*

The humanist perspective also provides us with a broad basis upon which to asses those features of work which relate not only to the product, but also to the *act of doing*; the process of work as well as the product itself. If the work a person does, does provide them with an opportunity for individual creativity, social development, satisfaction in their work and so on, it can be regarded as 'valuable' and 'useful' to that person. If, on the other hand, work does not provide these outcomes for that person, then it can be described as *alienating work*. Marx describes the twin features of alienating work in terms of the commodificaion of labour:

> '... the object labour produces, its product, stands opposed to it as *something alien*, as a *power independent* of the producer.... In the sphere of political economy this realisation of labour appears as a *loss*

of reality for the worker, objectification as *loss of and bondage to the object*, and the appropriation as estrangement, as alienation [Entausserung].... So much does objectification appear as loss of the object that the worker is robbed of the objects he needs most not only for life but also for work. (Marx 1975, *Early Writings*, p.324)

Writing about the experiences of factory workers in the USA during the 1960s, Blauner describes alienation as:

A general syndrome made up of a number of different objective conditions and subjective feeling-states which emerge from certain relationships between workers and the sociotechnical settings of employment. Alienation exists when workers are unable to control their immediate work process, to develop a sense of purpose and function which connects their jobs to the overall organization of production, to belong to integrated industrial commmunities, and when they fail to become involved in the activity of work as a mode of personal self-expression. (Blauner 1964, p.15)

Initially, it could be objected that seeing motivations and expectations of work in terms of the general human need to be productively active, might not provide a sufficiently rigorous means of distinguishing between the necessity to engage in one activity rather than another. Doesn't the humanist perspective simply lead to the position that all activities are equally necessary and therefore equally valuable? In order to refute this objection, we need to return to Godelier's definition given above, that work can be understood as acts undertaken in pursuance of the satisfaction of needs. Although we must accept that the range of actions, and thus the particular needs to which they are directed, is potentially very large indeed,[4] a closer examination reveals that it is possible to prioritise between different needs; to see why some needs are in fact more important than others.

The Marxist debate on 'needs' has focused on distinguishing between different categories of needs. 'Vital' or 'basic' needs have been distinguished from 'existential', 'psychic' or 'acquired' needs, and arguments have been put forward to substantiate what should constitute a prescriptive social philosophy. Herbert Marcuse has argued for example that: 'The only needs that have an unqualified claim for satisfaction are the vital ones - nourishment, clothing, lodging at the attainable level of culture' (Marcuse 1964, p.19). Eric Fromm on the other hand, places much greater emphasis on the *psychic* needs of the human organism: 'Man's most intensive passions and needs are not those rooted in his body, but those rooted in the very peculiarity of existence' (Fromm 1955, p.20). Josephine Logan elaborates further on this position by pointing out that: 'Existential needs cannot be methodologically defined but most healthy human beings acquire needs beyond basic biological needs, and thus we might usefully term them "acquired needs"' (Logan 1985, p.12).[5]

Within psychology and sociology more generally, the broad assumption that people act in order to satisfy their needs, has provided the operational rationale for a considerable proportion of empirical research into 'work satisfaction' and 'work motivation'. Frederick Herzberg for example, distinguishes between two sets of needs which he associates with two views of mankind; the Adam concept and the Abraham concept. This distinction lies at the heart of his 'two-factor theory' of work satisfaction. He suggests that individuals have two fundamental sets of needs:

> The Human animal has two categories of needs. *One set stems from his animal disposition*, that side of him previously referred to as the Adam view of man; it is centred on the avoidance of loss of life, hunger, pain, sexual deprivation and on the other primary drives, in addition to the infinite varieties of learned fears that become attached to these basic drives. The other segment of man's nature... is man's compelling urge to realise his own potentiality by continuous psychological growth. (Herzberg 1968, p.56)

Similarly, Maslow has developed a 'hierarchy of basic needs' which broadly divides into two parts: deficiency needs, and growth needs required for 'self-actualisation'. In the first category he places physiological, safety, social and esteem needs, and in the second a number of 'syndromes' of higher needs for self-actualisation; 'the desire to become more and more what one is, to become everything that one is capable of becoming', which include cognitive and aesthetic needs (Huizinga 1970, p.23).[6]

From this brief account it is evident that a fair degree of consistency has been expressed over the types of needs that might motivate human behaviour in general and work as part of that behaviour. On the one hand, we have a set of basic physiological needs for food, clothing, shelter and so on. On the other, we have a more elevated set of needs for social and psychological development. It is still evident however, that it is impossible to make entirely satisfactory distinctions between different needs. How for example, could we distinguish between the physical and psychological benefits which are gained simultaneously from *the same* activity? Without wishing to enter into a detailed critique of the positions taken, it can be argued that it may in fact be unnecessary to categorize needs in this way; nobody is disputing the *existence* of a particular type of need but only the *definition* of the categories. Even if it were possible to define specific needs in an abstract sense, it would be extremely difficult to operationalize them for the purposes of empirical investigation.[7] We can however make progress if we approach the problem of the definition of human needs, and, perhaps more importantly, the issue of how and in what order they can or ought to be satisfied, in a slightly different way. Since it is undeniably the case that we must be alive in order to act at all, our greatest need must be to maintain our physical survival. Once this primary need has been achieved, we will then be in a position to administer to our more developed needs. We can therefore identify a clear sense of *priority* between different realms of activity:

> An animal only produces what it needs immediately for itself or its offspring; it produces one-sidedly whereas man produces universally; it produces only under the pressure of immediate physical need, whereas man produces free from physical need and only truly produces when it is free thus from. (Marx 1963, *Early Writings*, p.128)

'True' human production then, only develops in the context of *freedom from immediate physical need*. The satisfaction of this basic vital physiological need is the *prerequisite* for all other higher forms of activity, since without it people would not exist at all:

> The first premise of all human existence, and therefore of all history [is] that men must be in a position to live in order to be able to "make history". But life involves before everything else eating, drinking, a habitation, clothing and many other things. The first historical act is thus the production of the means to satisfy these needs, the production of material life itself. (Marx and Engels 1970, p.48)

Taking this as a starting point, we can now go on to consider how this primary need underlies all our other needs. Lucian Sève for example, distinguishes between 'concrete' and 'abstract' activity, emphasizing that the potential productivity of an activity both for the individual and for society as a whole, depends upon the type or nature of that activity. *Concrete activity* includes: 'all personal activity which relates to the individual himself, for example acts directly satisfying personal needs, learning of new capacities unconnected with the carrying out any requirements of social labour'. *Abstract activity* on the other hand relates to 'the personal activity of socially productive labour' (Sève 1978, pp.337/8), meaning activity which does not relate directly to individual needs but administers to social production 'outside' the individual. For Sève therefore, the superiority of concrete activity over abstract activity is highly significant since the former administers directly to the needs of the individual and allows personal development to take place in a productive and purposeful way. Furthermore, this process of development is potentially unlimited:

> From the highest point of view the expanded reproduction of activity and human needs is the result of the primordial fact that the real human essence consists not of an internal biological inheritance of hereditary psychic traits... but of an external social heritage capable of unlimited historical growth.... It follows from this that potentially, the process of individual assimilation of the human heritage is intrinsically inexhaustible. (Sève 1978, pp.322-3)

Abstract activity on the other hand, does not contribute directly to the development of capacities since it is extracted or expropriated from the individual worker in response to the superimposed needs of others, in the context of capitalist productive relations, to produce surplus value.

In his analysis of the role and nature of work in contemporary society, Gorz makes a similar distinction between 'autonomous' and 'heteronomous' activity. The former refers to: 'The non-market field of autonomous activity... in which the individual is the sovereign author of actions carried out without recourse to necessity, alibis or excuses' (Gorz 1982, pp.93/98). And later:

> I refer to those activities which are themselves their own end as autonomous activities. They are valued for and in themselves not because they have no other objective than the satisfaction and pleasure they procure, but because the *action which achieves the goal is as much a source of satisfaction as the achievement of the goal itself*: the end is reflected in the means and vice versa; I may will the end by virtue of the intrinsic value of the activity which achieves it and the activity by virtue of the value of the end it is pursuing. (Gorz 1989, p.165, original emphasis)

In contrast, the sphere of heteronomous activity 'is made up of socially predetermined and relatively impersonal tasks' (Gorz 1982, p.102):

> I term *sphere of heteronomy* the totality of specialized activities which individuals have to accomplish as functions co-ordinated from outside by a pre-established organization. Within this sphere of heteronomy

> the nature and content of tasks, as well as their relations to each other are hetero-determined in such a way as to make individuals and organizations... function like the cogs of a huge machine... which deprives the workers of any possibility of co-ordinating their activities through procedures of self-regulated co-operation. (Gorz 1989, p.32)

As part of his broader analysis, Gorz suggests that ideally, productive activity could be assured in practice through 'a dual organization of space into a heteronomous sphere subordinate to the sphere of autonomy':

> The former assures the programmed and planned production of everything necessary to individual and social life, with the maximum efficiency and the least expenditure of effort and resources. In the latter sphere, individuals autonomously produce non-necessary material and non-material goods and services, outside of the market, by themselves or in free association with others, and in accordance with their own desires, tastes or fantasies. (Gorz 1982, p.197)

Taking up the concept of work as productive activity, these analyses of different types of work (as concrete and autonomous or abstract and heteronomous) clearly imply that some working activities are *more necessary* and thus *more productive* than others, since the 'unlimited expansion of needs' and the development of the capacity to administer to them, *is predicated upon the physiological existence of the individual.* Individual and social development in other words, can only take place if people continue to exist; an existence which begins with the satisfaction of basic physiological needs.

Part Two - Fundamental principles and expectations of work

Principles of work

Having considered the nature of human action in general, and having described the basic motivators of this activity, we can now use this model to help us understand the basic motivations and expectations which people have of their working activities. To begin with, we can confidently state that all definitions, conceptualizations and practical organizations of work derive from and are essentially motivated by, four fundamental principles of action. Firstly, work reflects a number of assumptions about what it means to be a human being. If we accept the humanist characterization of human nature described above, we can say that *work constitutes a crucial manifestation of the basic human need for expression through action.* In this respect, work is no different in principle from all other forms of activity. The most basic motivator of work then, is simply our need to act in order that we can exist at all. Activities which are described as work can therefore be seen as part of activity in general, rather than as a separate or distinct realm of activity which is in some way separate from the general activity of the individual.

Secondly, and regarding the nature of that activity, we have acknowledged that our actions are guided by our innate capacity and predisposition for conceiving in advance what it is that we intend to do. In both our desire to achieve these goals, and in our desire to improve our capacity to act, *work is profoundly motivated by our desire to be creative.* In principle, and if we accept that the human capacity for creativity is unlimited, so too is our capacity for action.

Thirdly, we have recognized that in common with all activities, working activities are not random, but are *deliberately undertaken in pursuance of the satisfaction of recognized needs.* Through work, we expect to be able to fulfil various needs. Whilst it is extremely difficult to make conclusive statements about 'needs', and whilst we can claim that the performance of productive activity is a prerequisite for the satisfaction of needs however they are defined, we can say that levels of motivation are closely related to the priority we have about the needs we are trying to satisfy. In this sense, our needs form a continuum; the greatest need (and thus our strongest motivation) is to maintain physiological survival. Once this has been achieved, other acquired or more autonomous and personalized needs come into play. It is important to emphasize that this basic human need to provide ourselves with the necessities of life, remains a priority irrespective of the means of provision which apply at a particular time and place. Whether access to necessary resources is gained more or less immediately through direct consumption, or whether access is gained indirectly through participation in complex mechanisms of formal employment, the underlying motivation remains the same.

Fourthly, since all working activities are done either with other people or for other people, *work is necessarily a profoundly social activity.* Although a number of circumstances might affect the practical complexity and actual manner in which this sociability is manifest, the decisive factor is likely to be the available level of productive technique and the complexity of the division of labour. These fundamental principles of action/work are summarized in the following table:

Table 3.1: Fundamental principles of action/work
All concepts of work are based on the following principles:
work is a crucial manifestation of the basic human need for expression through action
work is an expression of human creativity
work is deliberately undertaken in pursuance of the satisfaction of recognized needs
work is a profoundly social activity

Moving from this relatively abstract level of analysis, we now need to consider how people manifest these principles in their actual and concrete expectations of work. To what extent, in other words, do people explicitly recognize these principles in their day-to-day expectations of work?

Expectations of work

A desire to understand the motivations and expectations which people express about the work they do, has provided the focus for a considerable body of empirical research in sociology, social psychology and industrial management. Whilst recognizing the possible limitations and shortcomings of this research,[8] and accepting that important variations may exist between different individuals and groups of individuals with regard to how they can best fulfil their expectations of work, there is clear empirical evidence that people explicitly acknowledge at least four key expectations of work. Whilst not including a detailed review of this empirical literature here,[9] a summary account shows quite clearly that people work in the hope that it will enable them to fulfil expectations for income, security, creativity and social interaction.

Summarizing their findings of the work expectations of workers in a food processing factory in 1966, Beynon and Blackburn conclude:

> Good pay and security of employment were seen by the men to be of basic importance in a job. Working conditions and opportunities for promotion were of additional importance.... Although not regarded as of prime importance, there was also a feeling that work should be worthwhile and interesting. (Beynon and Blackburn 1972, p.84)

In a further study of 1,000 male manual workers in 1970-2, the authors comment:

> We are struck immediately by the predominance of the intrinsic job aspects. Apparently, over half the workers remembered their best job for the work they were asked to do. Of these 144 remember its autonomy, 339 remember its interest, variety, skill or challenge.... The next largest group recall social relations at work, and of these 57 enjoyed the company of their workmates, 47 enjoyed the chance to meet people (i.e. not workmates), and 13 liked foremen or managers. Together these two categories comprise over three-quarters of the responses. (Blackburn and Mann 1979, p.154)

> We must realize that most workers want the same rewards: good pay, convenient hours, interesting work, friendly workmates and so on are attractions to virtually everyone. Thus orientations are not simply "wants" but entail priorities within the range of possible rewards. Furthermore, the possible levels of rewards are generally below what people would like in the abstract, in the sense that any increase would be an improvement. (Blackburn and Mann 1979, p.144)

Clear evidence of expectations for income, security, creativity and social contact are confirmed in a study of 276 blue and white-collar skilled craftsmen carried out in the United States by Mackenzie (1973). In response to an open-ended question about what they liked best about their jobs, Mackenzie reports:

> There were three main categories of response ...: extrinsic factors such as pay, or job security; intrinsic factors such as the challenge offered by the work, the feeling of pride and accomplishment in doing a good job; and, finally, the opportunities the job provided to meet and come into contact with other people, primarily workmates, but also clients or customers. (Mackenzie 1973, p.36)

Discussing the importance of social interaction in factory work as a whole, Blauner emphasizes that: 'It has been argued that the human contacts of the plant community are critical in making work which is otherwise alienating bearable for the mass-production workers' and that informal work groups provide 'a sense of belonging within the impersonal atmosphere of modern industry' (Blauner 1964, pp.24-5, referring to Blum 1953). Blauner also refers to research by Davis and Werling (1964), noting that: 'At the Bay chemical plant, Davis found that blue-collar employees ranked "friends at work" as that element of the total job situation which they most liked more consistently than ten other job factors, including interesting work, security, and pay' (Blauner 1964, p.146). Very similar findings were also reported by Walker and Guest (1952):

> Many X plant workers reported that the chance to talk and joke with others was one reason, although not necessarily the principal one, for liking their jobs. For a few it was probably the major compensation (aside from wages of course) in an otherwise totally unsatisfactory work situation. (Blauner 1964, p.114)

Looking at the intrinsic expectation that work is seen as providing opportunities for creativity, Mackenzie reports that: 'In reading the responses people gave to the question of what they liked best about their job, the words "challenge", "stimulating", "satisfaction" and "variety" came up with a monotonous regularity' (Mackenzie 1973, p.36-7). Mackenzie goes on to emphasize that this form of satisfaction is closely related to the nature of the work itself, and most importantly, that satisfaction with work as a whole, is closely related to this particular type of expectation. Commenting on the craft workers in his sample, he notes that:

> The intrinsic satisfactions inherent in craft jobs, rooted in the amount of freedom and control the craftsman has over his work situation, as well as in the nature of the tasks he is asked to perform, provide virtually *the* explanation of the degree of job satisfaction found amongst these blue collar workers. (Mackenzie 1973, p.41)[10]

The importance of intrinsic expectations about work and of the influence of particular types of work on levels of satisfaction, are clearly revealed in Goldthorpe *et al*'s study of 229 'affluent' workers in Luton in 1963. With regard to why respondents 'preferred their present job to other jobs previously held in the same firm', over 60 per cent gave intrinsic reasons, such as greater opportunities for skill, greater variety, and greater intrinsic interest, compared with 24 per cent giving extrinsic reasons, and 16 per cent who referred to the working environment. These preferences were also reflected in the reasons given by those who wanted to change their jobs, with 50 per cent of the process workers and machinists, and 77 per cent of the assemblers referring to intrinsic rewards, and 35 per cent and 17 per cent respectively referring to extrinsic rewards (Goldthorpe *et al.*, 1968, table 5, p.14, and table 7, p.17). Similarly, when those who expressed a desire to leave their firms where asked why this was so, 24 per cent referred specifically to a lack of intrinsic satisfaction (Goldthorpe *et al.*, 1968, table 11, p.27). In common with research already discussed, Goldthorpe *et al.*, also reported a close relationship between monotonous and uninteresting work tasks, and the experience of dissatisfaction with work more generally:

> Among our affluent workers generally, the experience of monotony, of unabsorbing work and of an excessive pace of work were all apparent sources of deprivation and of job dissatisfaction.... It could be said that, among our affluent workers, the performance of work tasks was accompanied by various, and in some groups fairly generalised, psychological or physical stresses. (Goldthorpe *et al.*, 1968, p.20)

The regularity with which these and other researchers have pointed to such a close relationship between uninteresting work and subsequent feelings of dissatisfaction, clearly suggests that in general, individuals do expect to be able to experience an at least minimal degree of self-fulfilment and creativity through their work.

Although Goldthorpe *et al.*, found that the Luton workers did not seem to attach any great importance to social relationships at work: 'Our affluent workers tend for the most part neither to anticipate, nor to experience any strong desire for, a high level of direct "social" satisfaction from the shared activities and relationships of their workplace' (Goldthorpe *et al.*, 1968, p.68), over 60 per cent of the couples who had moved to the town from elsewhere, did refer specifically to 'separation from kin and friends', 'poorer social life', and 'less friendly people' as specific *disadvantages* of moving to Luton (Goldthorpe *et al.*, 1968, table 69, p.153). It should also be emphasized that the apparently family-centred and privatistic orientation of the Luton workers may not necessarily reveal a deliberate *preference* for relative isolation, but may have been adopted as a *consequence* of a lack of meaningful relationships at work. Given such an inability to fulfil this expectation, it is not surprising that 'their major emotional investments... were made in their relationships with their wives and children, and these relationships were in turn their major source of social and psychological support' (Goldthorpe *et al.*, 1968, p.154). Once established, it is also unsurprising that 'the individual is the less able, and the less motivated, to enter into involvements which might interfere with his family life through placing seriously competing claims upon his time and energy' (Goldthorpe *et al.*, 1968, p.155).

These feelings of estrangement also tended to be reflected in a heightened instrumentality towards work more generally. In common with earlier studies, it is clear that the Luton workers also placed a particularly high premium on extrinsic rewards. In reply to a question about why respondents stayed in their present jobs for example, level of pay, good security and the nature of the work featured very highly, accounting for 35 per cent, 29 per cent and 10 per cent of reasons given respectively (Goldthorpe *et al.*, 1968, table 12, p.280). In addition, Goldthorpe *et al.*, report that typically, '"security" seemed to be thought of far more in relation to long-run income maximalization than to the minimum requirement of having a job of some kind' (Goldthorpe *et al.*, 1968, p,29). In this respect at least, the Luton workers could be seen as having a 'pecuniary' model of society, where expectations about what work is and what it provides tended to be seen only in terms of the 'cash nexus'. As Lockwood had earlier described it, work is seen as a deprivation 'which is performed mainly for extrinsic rewards; and "money-mindedness", the calculative exchange of labour power for maximum pay, is the predominant motive for remaining in the job' (Lockwood 1975, pp. 21-22).[11]

In an attempt to establish whether expectations for income, security, creativity and social contact remain constant over time, Brown *et al.*, (1983) undertook a largely quantitative comparative analysis of research carried out into work attitudes during the 1960s and 1970s. To begin with, these researchers considered evidence from a more recent study by Cullen *et al.*, (1980) of 411 men and women who had been looking for work in North London. Perhaps not surprisingly, their findings are very much in line with those discussed above. With regard to expectations about income, Brown *et al.*, report that over 60 per cent of respondents cited "more money" as one of their 'major priorities'. A further 43 per cent 'said they wanted to change the actual work they did', with 'professional and managerial workers [citing] the interest of the work itself as the main reason for taking a job' (Cullen *et al.*, 1980, pp.52/78; Brown *et al.*, 1983, p.27). Reporting the findings of their own study of 420 Newcastle-Upon-Tyne residents in 1979, Brown *et al.*, reach very similar conclusions:

> For both men and women wages were the feature most frequently cited as most important when looking for paid employment.... For men security ranked second to wages with interesting work third, but for women interesting work came a close second to wages with security relegated to fifth position after convenient hours and being near home. (Brown *et al.*, 1983, p.36)

They also report the continued importance of 'interesting work': 'Interest in the work itself was the most common reason for preferring the "best job" with responsibility second, whilst "boring work" and bad conditions were the major source of dissatisfaction with "worst jobs"' (Brown *et al.*, 1983, p.36).

Comparing these more recent findings with earlier research, Brown *et al.*, confirmed the importance and expected persistence of both extrinsic and intrinsic expectations of work,[12] concluding that: 'There do not appear to have been any clear changes in emphasis during the time period covered by these studies', and that 'we find it difficult on the basis of the evidence we have considered to argue a strong case for general changes over time in orientation or dissatisfaction in a job' (Brown *et al.*, 1983, pp.15/28). These findings clearly suggest that the expectations which people have of work have remained, and on the basis of available evidence, seem likely to remain relatively stable over time. There would not seem to be any pressing reason in other words, why the expectations which people currently have about work should not remain more or less the same for some time to come.

On the basis of this evidence it is possible to draw a number of relatively safe conclusions about the specific expectations which individuals have of work. In the first place it is clear that particular importance is attached to income, security, creativity and social interaction. Despite differences in the size and composition of these various samples, and despite variations in the methods used, these expectations are consistently reported as being centrally important.

Secondly, it is clear that levels of satisfaction with work tend to vary in direct relation to whether these expectations are or are not met. If for example, a particular work task is experienced as monotonous and unfulfiling, there is a high probability that individuals will, to a greater or less extent, find this experience unsatisfying and frustrating. In contrast, interesting and challenging work is likely to be associated with relatively high levels of satisfaction.

Thirdly, these studies suggest that expectations of work tend to be relatively consistent both for particular individuals across a number of situations, and over time. The fact in other words, that the expressed expectations and priorities of British factory workers in the 1970s share the same general features as those expressed by American factory workers in the 1940s, tends to suggest that the four basic expectations of work provide important bench marks against which satisfaction with work is invariably assessed. If this is the case, then it is not unreasonable to suggest that individuals will continue to express the same or very similar expectations for some time to come.

Having said this however, it must be acknowledged that particular expectations about what work is and what it provides do vary both in terms of the priorities of particular individuals, and in terms of the actual reality which surrounds them. To this extent, levels of satisfaction and therefore the degree to which particular expectations are or are not being met, have to take account of the weight of expectation itself. Blauner comments for example, that: 'Possibly it would be more appropriate to study the problem of freedom and self-expression in work among white-collar and professional people, whose higher education has awakened the aspirations for fulfilment and creativity that often lie dormant among the mass of less-educated manual workers' (Blauner 1964, p.ix). Discussing levels of satisfaction amongst textile workers, he suggests that these workers 'do not define repetitive, non-involving jobs as monotonous' simply because having 'very low estimates of their own abilities and possibilities', *'they do not expect* variety in work tasks or inherent interest' (Blauner 1964, pp.85/82, emphasis added). In addition to these different levels of *anticipated* satisfaction, evidence suggests that the *potential* for satisfaction is closely associated with the nature of the job itself. Goldthorpe *et al.*, suggest for example: 'There is evidence here that among the workers we studied it was this immediate relationship between men and their jobs which was the aspect of their work most capable of producing either some feeling of personal fulfilment or, on the other hand, some clear sense of deprivation' (Goldthorpe *et al.*, 1968, p.16).[13] Given these variables it is not surprising that different individuals and groups of individuals may attach greater significance to one expectation than to another. It has already been noted for example, that high wages are seen as a form of compensation for monotonous work, while some individuals are likely to place a high premium on intrinsic satisfaction, or on the companionship of their workmates, rather than on income alone.[14]

Overall then, and whilst acknowledging a degree of flexibility with regard to expectations of work, it is safe to suggest that people are motivated to work, and evaluate the satisfactions of work, in terms of a number of fairly precise expectations. The four key expectations are summarized below:

Table 3.2: Key expectations of work
People expect work to provide opportunities for:
Income
security
creativity
social contact

Discussion

This chapter has moved the discussion forward by illustrating how the humanist definition of work as productive activity provides a particularly useful model for understanding the purposes and motivations which people attach to their working activities. It has been argued that once working activities are seen as part of human activity in general, rather than as distinct from the general activity of the individual, it is possible to trace the motivations and expectations of work back to their origins in human nature. Whilst recognizing the potential difficulties of describing the purposes and motivations of work in such grand philosophical terms, the discussion in part two has strongly suggested that human action, and work as part of that action, does reflect our human predisposition to engage in creative purposeful activity with others. The purposefulness of this activity originates in our unavoidable requirement to satisfy our basic needs. Although the means of satisfying these needs has changed over time, our basic motivation to work remains the same; the means may change, but the end is constant.

The validity of the proposition that all concepts of work are based on the fundamental principles of action set out in Table 3.1 above, is amply confirmed by empirical evidence into work expectations. Almost without exception, empirical investigation repeatedly demonstrates that people go to work in the expectation that it will provide them with opportunities for income, security, creativity and social contact. If we compare the items listed in Tables 3.1 and 3.2 above, we can see a strong correspondence between the fundamental principles of action/work and the concrete and empirically demonstrable expectations which people have of work:

Table 3.3: Motivations and expectations of work	
Fundamental principles of action/work	**Key expectations of work**
work is a manifestation of the basic human need for expression through action	(ontological) security
work is an expression of human creativity	creativity/social contact
work is deliberately undertaken in pursuance of the satisfaction of recognized needs	income/security
work is a profoundly social activity	social contact/creativity

What this tells us, is that the various dimensions of our motivation to work are not random, but are concrete representations of our underlying motivation to act. In terms of understanding the concept of work, this analysis strongly suggests that a number of the key aspects of this concept at the very least remain constant over time, and may in fact be universal across and between different cultures. In the context of the current investigation, it may also provide a concrete basis upon which to predict with a high degree of certainty, which basic ingredients will have to be included in any future concept of work.

Finally, it will be useful to reconsider the criteria of work discussed in chapter two in light of the conclusions reached in this chapter. In the first place, we can note that in the same way that people's concrete expectations of work closely correspond with the fundamental principles of action/work, so too do the contemporary criteria of work set out in table 2.2 in the previous chapter:

Table 3.4: The contemporary concept of work

Principles of action	Work expectations	Criteria of work
work is a manifestation of the basic human need for expression through action	(ontological) security	requires mental/physical exertion
work is an expression of human creativity	creativity/social contact	purposeful expedient activity
work is deliberately undertaken in pursuance of the satisfaction of recognized needs	income/security	performed in return for wages or salary
work is a profoundly social activity	social contact/ creativity	public activity

In this combined table, it can be seen that the contemporary criteria of work listed in the right-hand column provide a more or less accurate reflection of both the expectations which people have of work (middle column), and of the principles which underlie all forms of human action (left-hand column). Looking at the first row of the table, the criterion that work requires mental and/or physical exertion reflects the expectation that work is a means towards establishing ontological security, which in turn reflects that principle that it is through action that we exist. In the second row, the criterion that work is purposeful and expedient reflects our expectation that work provides opportunities for creativity and social contact, which in turn reflects the principle that work is an expression of human creativity. In the third row, the principle that we work in order to satisfy our basic needs is reflected in the (general) expectation that work provides income, and hence the (contemporary/capitalist) criterion that work is something for which we get paid. Acquiring the income we need to satisfy our needs is essential to our sense of security. Finally, the fourth row shows a clear continuity between the expectation that work provides opportunities for social contact, and the principle that work is a profoundly social activity. This is at least partly reflected in the contemporary criterion that work is a public activity.

Whilst wishing to emphasize the evident continuity between the principles, expectations, and contemporary criteria of work, table 3.4 illustrates the highly significant point firstly that some of the criteria in the third column are not a 'perfect fit', and secondly, that there is a high degree of overlap between the rows of the table. The items listed in other words, are in some cases not mutually exclusive. An examination of these evident discontinuities provides us with a highly instructive means of reconsidering an important characteristic of the contemporary criteria of work noted in the previous chapter, namely their tendency towards arbitrariness and ambiguity.

Beginning with the lack of fit between some of the criteria across the rows, the first point to make is that some of these criteria are in a sense approximate to the expectations and principles from which they derive. A clear example of this, is the criterion that work is a public rather than a private activity. As was described in the previous chapter, the criterion that work is a public activity not only derives from the expectation that work is something we do with other people, but also from the additional criterion that the place of work is outside the domestic residence of the worker, and that the products of the work done are exchanged in the (public) market. Since it is clear that many people do (public) work 'at home', we can emphasize the point made earlier, that the designation that work is a 'public activity' does not actually relate to the substance or nature of the activity itself, but to the fact that the service or commodity provided is exchanged on the open market. On this understanding, it is perfectly possible for people to fulfil their expectation that work is something we do with other people (the expectation of social contact), and to enact the principle that work is a profoundly social activity, without necessarily having to work in a public place of work. Arguably, it is the destination of the service or commodity which matters, not whether the place of work is public or private.

This tendency towards arbitrariness is also reflected in the criterion which does not appear in table 3.4 at all, namely that work is recognized for official purposes such as taxation or insurance (see table 2.2). Whilst we can acknowledge that income tax provides the state with an essential form of income, and is therefore in a sense one of the ways in which the state 'works', the designation of an activity as work because it is officially recognized as such, bears almost no relation to either our expectations of work, or to the principles of action. Rather, this criterion is a manifestation of the system of income generation and exchange; it reflects one of the operational 'needs' or requirements of the economic structure itself. Presumably, if an alternative means of satisfying our heteronomous social needs were available, this particular criterion would be changed.

Throughout the discussion, particular importance has been attached to the criterion that work is something we do in return for income. Within the capitalist system, this income takes the form of wages or salary. Although the payment criterion accurately reflects the expectation for income, it is worth emphasizing again that financial income is not the only means through which we can adequately satisfy our basic needs. Following the general thrust of the analysis in this chapter, it can be argued that although for all practical purposes we do in fact require and actively seek financial income to fulfil our needs, in principle at least, this need not always be the case. It should be acknowledged that any revision or attempted redefinition of the criteria of work will have to face the fact that in contemporary society, the mechanisms of income distribution and the mechanisms of employment are almost one and the same thing. If, as is evidently happening, the availability of formal paid employment declines to a critically low level, the central problem will be how to provide people with an alternative source of 'income' through which they can satisfy their basic needs. Such a means may or may not include the notion of wages or salary as we currently understand it, or it may combine this with other means towards satisfaction.

The observation that income is not the only way in which we fulfil our needs, draws attention to the second issue noted above, that the items charted in table 3.4 are not mutually exclusive. The key point here, is that because we have a wide range of needs, any attempt to associate one particular need with one particular expectation of work is bound to be somewhat simplistic. This being the case, attempts to map particular expectations onto particular criteria of work are bound to be problematic. Moving across table 3.4 from left to right in other words, is likely in at least in some cases, to introduce an ever-increasing degree of ambiguity and arbitrariness. This draws attention to the multi-dimensionality of the concept of work in terms of the needs we hope to fulfil. It could be argued for example, that our expectation for ontological security can only be fully achieved if *all* the criteria of work in the third column are met. Is it not the case that both material and psychological needs have to be met if we want to feel secure? Similarly, opportunities for creativity might be heavily dependent upon opportunities for social contact and interaction. Engaging in social contact is after all a highly creative process. These considerations lead us back to the issue of the worth and value of activities discussed in part one above. Although it has already been acknowledged that such judgements are heavily influenced by the social perceptions of worth and value which prevail at a particular point in time, table 3.4 can be used as a kind of ready-reckoner for introducing at least some degree of continuity across judgements about the use and value of particular activities and their products. Broadly speaking, and according to these terms of reference, if an activity does provide a creative opportunity to fulfil an identifiable need, then that activity could be regarded as useful and its products valuable. If an activity is categorized as useful and its products valuable according to criteria which *do not* relate to the satisfaction of basic needs, then again within these terms of reference, we can legitimately describe the activity as unnecessary and its products of no real use or value.

This is not to suggest of course, either that these are *the only* terms of reference against which use and value can be assessed, or that a particular criterion cannot be judged to be non-arbitrary across a number of terms of reference. As the above discussion has shown, criterion of official recognition, public activity and monetary reward are, within capitalist economic systems, established as non-arbitrary according to terms of reference derived from the logic of economic rationality; terms which relate at least as much to the requirements of the economic system as they do to the needs of the individual. The point is, that if we want to reach a true understanding of the contemporary criteria of work, and most importantly of the necessity for particular activities and of the use and value of the products of those activities, we need to be clear which terms of reference are being brought to bear. If the evident needs of individuals are being subordinated to the requirements of the economic system, then we should be clear that this is the case. We may subsequently wish to debate whether this is or is not a good thing, but at least we know where we stand. The most fundamental error would be to try to disguise the terms of reference which are being brought to bear. The complexity of judging the arbitrariness or otherwise of the contemporary criteria of work, is at least partly a result of the fact that our criteria of work draw upon *a mixture* of terms of reference, some of which relate to individual needs and some to wider economic and political systemic requirements. It can also be observed, that within this mixture, the priority of one set of terms of reference over another may vary over time both in terms of individuals' expectations of work and in terms of the balance between human needs and systemic requirements; it is not simply a matter of one set always being dominant. During periods of relative economic prosperity for example, both employers and employees may tend to invest greater significance in the more intrinsic expectations of work because extrinsic rewards such as monetary income can be taken more or less for granted. Under these conditions, the balance of human needs and systemic requirements may also tend to be tilted in favour of the former, as systemic requirements for economic stability and growth are assured. In contrast, under conditions of economic down-turn, scarcity of formal employment is likely to oblige people to be far less concerned with the 'quality' aspects of work, than with the simple fact that a job means income. Similarly, systemic requirements might tend to displace human needs on the assumption that a weak economy is in nobody's interests. The increasing political and economic 'acceptability' of relatively high levels of structural unemployment in almost all advanced capitalist economies since the late-1960s, clearly illustrates the subordination of individual needs to the 'needs' of the economic system.[15]

A final important characteristic of the criteria of work which emerges from this discussion, is the possibility that the longevity of a particular criterion is related to its propensity for arbitrariness across a range of terms of reference. It might be the case for example, that a criterion which is non-arbitrary according to more than one (and possibly to all) terms of reference, will be retained more or less indefinitely. The criterion of mental/physical activity, of creativity and purposefulness, and of social activity for example, are, for the reasons given above, likely to be present *in all* concepts of work. In contrast, criteria which relate more or less exclusively to terms of reference which are in a sense 'beyond' or outside the needs of the individual, are likely to emerge and decay much more rapidly. Criteria of work derived from Soviet-style central planning for example, have passed away much more rapidly than those deriving from capitalist economic rationality. This tends to reinforce the point made earlier, that the degree of arbitrariness of the criteria is strongly related to the closeness of the criteria to the activity itself, rather than to the wider context within which that activity takes place. Put bluntly, criteria which minimize or disregard the basic principles of action, are much more likely to be arbitrary and thus short-lived, than those which do not. Building on the summary given in table 2.4 in the previous chapter, the following table summarizes a number of ways in which the potential arbitrariness of the criteria of work can be assessed according to the analysis presented here:

Table 3.5: Assessing the potential arbitrariness of the criteria of work

a certain arbitrariness accompanies the application of the criteria of work
criteria of work are not mutually exclusive in relation to the expectations which people have of work
criteria tend to approximate the expectations and principles with which they are associated
assessments of the arbitrariness of criteria of work have to be made in relation to the particular terms of reference from which they derive
a distinction can be made between criteria which relate to individual needs and those which relate to systemic requirements
more than one set of terms of reference can be in operation at any given time
criteria of work commonly derive from a mixture of terms of reference
the priority of one set of terms of reference over another, and therefore of the criteria to which they give rise, varies according to economic circumstances
the longevity of a particular criterion is related to its propensity for arbitrariness across a range of terms of reference
a criterion which is non-arbitrary according to more than one (and possibly to all) terms of reference, will be retained more or less indefinitely
the degree of arbitrariness of the criteria is closely related to the closeness of the criteria (and its terms of reference) to the activity itself, rather than to the wider context within which that activity takes place

A closer analysis of the potential arbitrariness of the some of the contemporary criteria of work will be developed in subsequent chapters. At this point, it will be useful to summarize some of the advantages of the humanist terms of reference described in this chapter. Firstly, they remind us that all human actions are closely related to the basic human drive to express its species being; human-beingness can only become manifest through action. Secondly, since work is simply one variety of action amongst many, we can understand the motivation to work in terms of the motivation to act at all. Thirdly, the humanist terms of reference allow us to get a grip on the difficult issue of how to assess the worth and value of activities, both in terms of the products of action, and in terms of the quality and satisfaction of the action itself. If an action produces a necessary outcome (commodity or service) in a way which provides the agent with an opportunity for creative self-expression, then it can be regarded as necessary. If not, then the outcome is likely to be unnecessary and therefore (in these terms at least) of little use or value, and the action which produces it is likely to be alienating for the agent. Fourthly, whilst acknowledging the difficulties of making concrete distinctions between different needs, the humanist concept illustrates that in practical terms, some needs are more necessary than others. Our first priority, and therefore our prior and most highly motivated actions, are directed towards satisfying our needs for the basic necessities of life. Subsequently, our actions are directed towards satisfying our developing needs for deeper social and psychological development.

Finally, and regarding the nature of the relationship between the conceptual and practical aspects of the work paradigm, the humanist terms of reference are useful in reminding us of the ends to which various practices of work are the means. Although these means have been manifest in a range of different types of economic organization, each of these types is at root a system for providing people with a means of gaining access to necessary resources.

Notes

1. The notion of species-being was first developed by Feuerbach. In *The Essence of Christianity* he notes: 'Man is in fact at once I and Thou; he can put himself in the place of another, for this reason, that to him his species, his essential nature, and not merely his individuality is an object of thought'. For the full text see Feuerbach 1957. For commentaries on Feuerbach's view of man see Engels 1934, and Kamenka 1970.

2. Sève is quoting Gramsci 1977, p.351.

3. Sève has developed a theory of personality formation based upon the dual concept of 'acts' and 'capacities'. He defines these in the following way: 'Every act is on the one hand, the act *of an individual*, an act of his biography, a self-expression; but on the other, is the act of a determinate social world, an expression *of objective historical conditions*' (Sève 1978, p.311, original emphasis). 'I call capacities the ensemble of "actual potentialities" innate or acquired, to carry out any act whatever and whatever its level' (Sève, 1978, p.313). Sève goes on to argue that the constitution of the personality is dependent upon the relationship between an individual's acts and his or her capacities. The development of personality in other words, depends upon the ability to act in accordance with a set of developing capacities: 'These two aspects of dialectical acts-capacities relations do not only express the fact of their belonging to an identical cycle of activity in which they appear as a moment; they also lead us to consider the individual's total activity as necessarily dividing into two basic sectors, maintaining strictly defined relations with each other. I call *sector I* of individual activity the set of acts which produce, develop or specifically determine capacities. I call *sector II* the set of acts which, only making use of the capacities already existing, produces some effect which the exercise of these capacities makes it possible to attain.' (Sève, 1978, pp.322-3)

4. Durkheim suggested for example, that the human predisposition for new appetites makes the notion of need almost limitless: 'For beyond the indispensable minimum which satisfies nature when instinctive, a more awakened reflection suggests better conditions, seemingly desirable ends craving fulfilment. Such expectations however, admittedly sooner or later reach a limit which they cannot pass. But how determine the quantity of well-being, comfort or luxury legitimately to be craved by a human being? Nothing appears in man's organic nor in his psychological constitution which sets a limit to such tendencies. The functioning of individual life does not require them to cease at one point rather than at another; the proof being that they have constantly increased since the beginning of history, receiving more and more complete satisfaction, yet with no weakening of average health.' (Durkheim 1952, p.247)

5. For a more detailed discussion see: Soper 1981, Fitzgerald 1977, and Plant *et al.*, 1980. For a full explication of the dispute on this topic between Marcuse and Fromm see: Fromm 1955, Marcuse 1956, and Fromm 1956(a). For a discussion see Ransome 1987.

6. See also Maslow 'A theory of human motivation', in Vroom and Deci, (eds.), 1970. For a discussion of these views as they relate to the investigation of 'work attitudes' see Warr and Wall, 1975.

7. Aside from the difficulties of developing an appropriate experimental design, any 'lack of satisfaction' is likely to be experienced in profoundly personal and therefore subjective terms. In the second place, since many needs are expressed simultaneously, it would be very difficult to determine which need was or was not being satisfied at any particular moment. The empirical investigation of needs may therefore be helpful to the extent that it highlights the problematic nature of needs, but it is unlikely to be conclusive. For example, writing about American white-collar workers in the early 1950's, C. Wright Mills was uneasy about the findings of job satisfaction surveys, which indicated higher satisfaction, interest, and enjoyment amongst professionals and executives: 'Such figures tell us very little, since we do not know what the questions mean to the people who answer them, or whether they mean the same thing to different strata' (Mills, C.W. 1953, p.229).

8. Rose has suggested for example: 'The problems an investigator chooses, and his method of investigating them, are always influenced by the ideas of the scientific community with which he identifies, and by the needs of the people who fund his work' (Rose 1975, p.86). Similarly Fox notes that: 'research in this field is beset by pitfalls. The replies people give for example, to structured questionnaire surveys can give us much useful information, but the surveys have to be carefully and imaginatively devised if they are to illuminate the complex, multi-layered, and sometimes apparently contradictory body of attitudes we bring to work in general and our own job in particular.' (Fox 1980, p.164)

9. For such an account see Ransome 1995, ch.2.

10. Elsewhere Mackenzie notes that: 'There is clearly a close relationship between the frequency with which people describe the satisfaction of their job in intrinsic terms and the fact that the majority of respondents described their jobs as being "very interesting"' (Mackenzie 1973, p.36). These findings tend to confirm those reported by Blauner. Comparing levels of dissatisfaction between automobile workers and factory workers in general, Blauner reports: 'The proportion who complained of monotony was 61 per cent among the unskilled male auto workers, 27 per cent among the low-skilled, 16 per cent among the medium-skilled, and only 6 per cent among the skilled workers. The regular and consistent relationship between rising skill level and increased job interest is common to factory industries in general.' (Blauner 1964, p.116)

11. When asked about their future aspirations for example, the Luton workers clearly focused on increased material prosperity: 'From group to group it can be seen that clearly the most widespread kinds of aspirations held by our affluent workers were those which related to increased consumer capacity and to higher standards of domestic living. And most important of all, it would appear, was the simple aspiration to have more money to spend and more goods and possessions. In all groups, around 3 men out of 5 saw this as their major objective for the years ahead' (Goldthorpe *et al.*, 1968, p.136 and table 63, p.137).

12. Brown *et al.*, note for example, that of the studies which asked about which aspects of a job were considered to be 'important' or 'desirable: '"Good wages" or "economic rewards" more generally, were almost invariably given the highest priority and/or the most frequent mention in this context' (Brown *et al.*, 1983, p.28), and that while extrinsic considerations are not 'the sole considerations of importance', and however much they may have been 'the prime considerations' for some, 'a range of other considerations influenced job preference and job choice'. They conclude that: 'No one type of such considerations was dominant, but the nature of the work itself and social relations at work appeared fairly frequently as characteristics favourably viewed, and conditions as a reason for liking or disliking a job' (Brown *et al.*, 1983, p.16).

13. Mackenzie reaches a very similar conclusion: 'We must focus on the *nature of the job itself* in explaining both the relatively high level of satisfaction found amongst the craft workers and the relatively low level expressed by the clerks' (Mackenzie 1973, p.41).

14. Goldthorpe *et al.,* comment for example: 'Thus work which offers relatively high intrinsic rewards may not in fact form the basis of a powerful tie between the worker and his employment because of countervailing dissatisfactions and grievances; and, conversely, work which by its very nature entails severe deprivations for those who perform it may nonetheless offer extrinsic - that is, economic - rewards which are such as to attach workers fairly firmly to the employer who offers this work' (Goldthorpe *et al.,* 1968, pp.31-2).

15. For a full discussion of the possible impact of mass unemployment on social stability, see Ransome 1995.

4 The work paradigm

A central feature of the concept of work which has emerged in the previous chapters, is that essential aspects of this concept are shared by the majority of the population. This is so both in the sense that criteria of work can only be of practical value if most people agree to their use and to live by the consequences of their application, and in the sense that work is necessarily an activity we do with other people. It has also been suggested however, that while at this level, perceptions of the meaning and purpose of work reflect the immediate daily concerns which people have for satisfying their needs, the concept of work also involves other more generalized beliefs about society. The concept of work in other words, reflects important aspects of the overall belief system of society. Whilst the concrete application of principles and criteria of work in daily working practice inevitably provides an important basis for stability within the economic structures of society, the question remains as to whether people's more generalized ideas and beliefs about society are also reflected in the concept of work. If these ideas and beliefs constitute an important part of what we can call the work-ethic, what is the role of the work-ethic, and what status should be attached to the ideas it contains?

Taking the conceptual and the practical aspects of the work paradigm in turn, this chapter develops a more specific definition of the work paradigm. The first part of the chapter will describe its 'ideational dimension'. It will be suggested that specifically with regard to the work-ethic, a useful distinction can be drawn between generalized aspects of the world view which are 'authentic' in the sense that they put forward an expedient and useful interpretation of the purposes and practices of work, and 'ideological' concepts which tend to put forward a partial or incomplete interpretation.[1] A number of suggestions will then be put forward as to how it might be possible to tell the difference between these two types as they occur within the work-ethic.

Turning to the practical aspect of the work paradigm, the second part of the chapter, looks briefly at the nature of the relationship between the methods, techniques or 'forces' of production, and the co-operative relationships with which a particular organization of work is associated. It is important to clarify the character of this relationship, since claims about the manifestly social or communal nature of working activities inevitably have implications for the nature of the working relationships between particular individuals and groups of individuals. It should be emphasized however, that although this remains a central issue within Marxist discourse, its treatment here will be strictly limited. In the present context, 'relations of production' are understood as referring to the patterned inter-relations of individuals to one another within the context of a more or less specific working practice. No direct attempt will be made to resolve the complex issues surrounding the association of relations of production with general 'class' relationships. It will be argued that, used in this more limited sense, forces of production can be taken to be *inclusive of* relations of production.[2] The analysis presented in this chapter will help us to develop a fairly rigorous understanding of the mechanisms or 'internal dynamics' of the work paradigm which can then be used to analyse a number of examples of particular work paradigms in the following chapters.

Part One - Ideas, ideologies and the work-ethic

To begin with then, if an important constituent part of the concept of work is a work-ethic of general beliefs about society and our role within it, there is a clear implication that by participating in the organization of work individuals are endorsing these wider beliefs. Participation in the world of work in other words, also requires participation in the wider belief systems of society. Two aspects of this possibility require closer examination. Firstly, and accepting that the work paradigm does include a work-ethic of generalized beliefs, it is important to consider the extent to which the work-ethic is actually and actively held by the majority of the population. Secondly, we need to consider whether the contents of the work-ethic, the ideas of which it is made, do have a significant bearing on people's beliefs about work. Should we accept in other words, that the variety of different generalized beliefs and systems of beliefs which may make up the work-ethic, are equally useful in a practical sense, or are some of them more useful than others?

To the extent that members of a particular social structure participate in the same labour process, and to the extent that they apply similar if not identical criteria of work, it is inevitable that up to a point, the concept of work does reflect a common understanding and possible acceptance of wider social beliefs. In this sense, the concept of work constitutes an important part of what Durkheim called the 'collective conscience' of society. In *The Division of Labor* for example, he defines this as:

> The totality of beliefs and sentiments common to the average citizens of the same society forms a determinate system which has a life of its own; one may call it the collective or common consciousness... it is diffused in every reach of society [but] nevertheless it has specific characteristics that make it a distinctive reality. (Durkheim 1933, pp.79-80)

In a similar vein, using the concept of hegemony, Antonio Gramsci develops the idea that social stability is closely associated with the presence of a system of shared beliefs. Gareth Williams has defined this as a 'socio-political situation' in which:

> The philosophy and practice of a society fuse or are in equilibrium; an order in which a certain way of life and thought is dominant, in which one concept of reality is diffused throughout society in all its institutional and private ramifications. (Williams, G. 1960, p.587)[3]

The nature and extent of this form of apparent 'ideological consensus' within society has attracted a good deal of attention, much of it focused on the suggestion that a 'dominant' minority maintains control over the means of access to necessary resources because the majority are willing to assimilate and accommodate the ideas it puts forward. Referring to Abercrombie and Turner's classic text *The Dominant Ideology Thesis* for example, Conrad Lodziak summaries some of these 'dominant' ideas:

> Thus Abercrombie *et al.* refer to the ideologies of accumulation - those ides that help to justify profit; managerial ideology - ideas that help to justify income inequality and socioeconomic status; ideologies of state neutrality and welfare - ideas that legitimate the authority of the state and the system of liberal democracy; plus particular elements of bourgeois culture that encourage a respect for hierarchy and deference to authority, and that promote individualism and nationalism. (Lodziak 1995, p.27)

Although persuasive, considerable doubt has however been cast on the view that the majority of the population does in fact adhere to such a system of shared beliefs. In his summary of research on this topic, Mann concludes for example, that although 'a significant measure of consensus and normative harmony may be necessary among ruling groups *it is the absence of consensus* among lower classes which keeps them compliant' (Mann 1982, p.391, emphasis added). Similarly, Fox comments that:

> It is impossible to describe the world of work as being shaped and regulated by a unitary, homogeneous, and consistent social meaning in terms of its values, objectives, and priorities. It takes its shape from a variety of pressures, and for this reason is a patchwork of diverse values and purposes displaying many contradictions and inconsistencies. (Fox 1980, p.143)[4]

Rather then, than there being a single apparently coherent set of beliefs, a number of different and in some cases rather conflictual attitudes tend to be held by different groups. Specifically with regard to work for example, these might include particular beliefs about gender and class differences suggesting that particular forms of work should only be performed by 'men', and that deference dictates that some aspects of work should be carried out by 'the properly qualified'. Phillips and Taylor have noted for example that: 'Skill definitions are saturated with sexual bias. The work of women is often deemed inferior simply because it is women who do it. Women workers carry into the workplace their status as subordinate individuals and this status comes to define the work they do' (Phillips and Taylor 1986, p.9). Similarly, in a study of the attitudes of agricultural workers in Suffolk, Newby reports one respondent as suggesting that: 'There'll always be a boss and there'll always be workers. It's a good thing - if everybody was all the same nobody would say what has to be done. No work would get done. You've got to have someone with money to work for' (Newby 1976, p.392).[5] These beliefs might also be used as a basis for justifying various strategies aimed at excluding or restricting the access of rival groups to necessary resources.[6] In concluding his analysis of the presence of a 'dominant ideology', John Thompson is quite explicit:

> It cannot be plausibly assumed that there is a core set of values and beliefs which are widely shared and firmly accepted by individuals in modern industrial societies, and which thereby bind individuals to a common normative framework, for it seems likely that most core values and beliefs are contested and that there is a fairly high degree of disagreement and disaffection. If social reproduction were

> dependent on a generalized acceptance of core values and beliefs, then the ongoing reproduction of the social order would seem very improbable indeed. (Thompson, J.B., 1990, p.88, quoted in Lodziak 1995, p.36)

On the basis of the discussion put forward in the previous chapter, the view taken here, is that while it is critically important not to confuse the idea of the ideology of the dominant group with the assumption that this ideology necessarily 'dominates' all other ideologies and other social groups,[7] it nonetheless seems highly probable that at the practical level of daily life, to the extent that individuals participate in *the same labour process*, and to the extent that they hold *largely similar* expectations of work, these expectations are likely to provide the basis for a degree of common understanding. Indeed it would be true to say that any configuration of productive practices, and particularly those involving a complex division of labour, *necessarily* depends upon the fact that the majority of the population expresses at least minimal agreement with regard to their expectations of work. Whilst recognizing therefore, the limitations of postulating ideational consensus at the level of what Mann calls normative acceptance ('where the individual internalises the moral expectations of the ruling class and views his own inferior position as legitimate'), an at least minimal degree of agreement does exist with regard to expectations of work, *at least at the level of pragmatic acceptance* 'where the individual complies because he perceives no realistic alternative' (Mann 1980, p.375).[8] To the extent that compliant participation in the mechanisms of employment is conducive to economic and social stability, people are in effect endorsing in practical terms, a particular organization of the productive forces. It does not follow from this however, that at a more 'abstract' level, individuals necessarily share or participate in the wider beliefs contained within the work-ethic, or that these beliefs necessarily originate amongst so-called dominant groups. It is important to maintain a clear distinction between the concrete practical aspects of the concept of work (articulated through the shared principles of work and criteria of work described in the previous chapter), and the more diverse ideas which may be contained within the work-ethic. Participation in the mechanisms of employment, does not necessarily or inevitably require acceptance or even recognition of the contents of the work-ethic:

> Individuals may act in a manner that accords with normative expectations *without themselves subscribing to the values and beliefs which underlie the norms*.... There is no necessary correlation

between symbolic action and non-symbolic behaviour; between speech and action; intention and actuality; motives or purposes and institutionalized social arrangements or social behaviour. (Marshall 1982, p.65, emphasis added)

In terms of the role of the work paradigm in maintaining social stability, we can therefore say that any configuration of productive practices, and particularly those involving a complex division of labour, necessarily depends upon the fact that the majority of the population expresses at least minimal agreement as to the purpose and practice of work. If this threshold of practical agreement is not maintained, then it is likely that the division of labour would be seriously threatened as individuals would no longer be willing or able to participate in it. A serious disruption of the mechanisms through which individuals seek to fulfil their expectations of work, meaning in effect the mechanisms of formal employment, would inevitably constitute a considerable threat to economic and thus social stability.[9] At the more abstract level of the work-ethic however, it is highly debatable whether and to what extent such stability is dependent upon popular agreement. In principle, there is no reason why the same practical organization of work cannot be associated more or less successfully with quite different work-ethics, or why a multiplicity of work-ethics cannot co-exist.[10] What we have in common, is a shared set of expectations of work combined with a pragmatic acceptance of a particular means of satisfying these expectations. In a sense, participation in a particular work-ethic is coincidental to this overriding concern.

Having reached this conclusion however, and as the discussion in the following chapters will show, the wider ideas contained in the work-ethic cannot be reduced to the four basic expectations of work described in chapter two. We should not overlook the fact that wider ideas about society *do have* an important bearing upon the concept of work. Indeed some of these ideas and beliefs are specifically designed to do so.[11] This brings us to the second issue raised above, namely *what role* do these beliefs play in maintaining the concept of work?

A reasonable initial assumption would be that the work-ethic provides a form of intellectual and moral support or justification for the concept of work as currently constituted. That the work-ethic forms a necessary link between the daily practicalities of work and less immediate concerns both about the way work is organized and how this organization fits within the social structure, and about other beliefs about the meaning and purpose of life in general.[12] If this is the *function* of the work-ethic, and assuming that we do not wish to accept that the work-ethic is composed of an entirely incoherent and benign set of ideas and beliefs, then it is important to consider *where* these have come from, and *what status* should be attached to them. Is it possible to distinguish between ideas which are 'legitimate' and 'authentic' with regard to the practicalities of work and those which are not?

Taking these issues one at a time, it seems likely that the work-ethic is made up of a mixture of ideas coming from two basic sources. In the first place, wider beliefs are likely to emerge as part and parcel of the general process of human creativity. In this sense, wider beliefs about the meaning and purpose of work, form an additional category of our expectations of work. Whilst we expect work to provide income for example, we might also see work in terms of some kind of moral obligation, or perhaps as a means of spiritual salvation. Whilst we expect work to provide social contact, we might also believe that we have a duty to help provide commodities and services for or on behalf of other people. Whilst we expect work to provide the basis for material survival, we might also see it as essential to a less clearly defined but none the less significant sense of psychic or spiritual development.

In the second place, the work-ethic includes a number of ideas and beliefs which although loosely affecting the population as a whole, originate either from past beliefs or from beliefs which are held by a minority. These ideas and beliefs might in effect be a composite of fragments of beliefs rather than a single coherent 'big idea'.[13] This is the most difficult aspect of the work-ethic to define, because if the work-ethic performs a justificatory and legitimating function, it inevitably raises the question of *whose interests* are being represented through these ideas. While we can accept a particular individual's belief in spiritual salvation through work as a choice they have made for themselves, it is more difficult to accept ideas whose authorship is unclear.

A number of examples of these personal and general idea-elements and of their influence will be discussed in some detail the following chapters. In order to provide a suitable analytical framework for this analysis, it will be useful at this point to differentiate between two types of collections of ideas which are involved in the composition of the work-ethic. The term 'ideology' will be used to denote collections of ideas and beliefs which tend to be based upon an incomplete or partial understanding of the work paradigm. In general terms, it can be suggested that the clearest indication of the 'ideological tendency' comes from the prioritising if economic systemic requirements over the personal aspirations and needs of individuals. In order to emphasize the sense in which these ideas and beliefs are 'imposed' or 'superimposed' onto the work-ethic, the term ideology will be attributed a largely negative meaning.

By way of contrast, the term 'ideational understanding' will be used to denote collections of ideas, which individuals inherently develop as part of the process of making sense of their activity; an understanding which is neither necessarily incomplete nor negative. It is worth noting the full meaning which Jorge Larrain attaches to the notion of an ideational level of understanding:

> If one wants to uphold both a negative concept of ideology and the idea of an all encompassing level of consciousness, then the solution is to propose a superstructure of ideas or 'ideational superstructure' which contains both non-ideological and ideological forms of consciousness. The superstructure of ideas refers to a global societal level of consciousness, whereas ideology is only a restricted part of the superstructure which includes specific forms of distorted consciousness. (Larrain 1983, pp.172-3)[14]

Following this definition, general ideas and beliefs attached to working activities, constitute a broad ideational level of understanding which is simply part and parcel of our social consciousness. These ideas may or may not be based on a thorough understanding of the practical reality of work. Within this overall superstructure of ideas, particular sets of ideas and beliefs which are both incomplete *and are used by particular groups for their own advantage*, may be regarded as constituting a subset of ideological ideas.

Having proposed an analytical distinction, we need some kind of concrete basis upon which to put it into operation. For the purposes of the following discussion, the notion of 'authenticity' will be used to distinguish between ideological and non-ideological ideas and beliefs about work. 'Authenticity' refers to the extent to which particular ideas and beliefs do or do not accurately reflect both the expectations which people have of work, and whether in practical terms, they are conducive to the effective operation of the work paradigm as a whole. This reflects the earlier assumption that the function of the work-ethic is to reinforce the perceived legitimacy of the current organization of work. If the work-ethic fails to provide such a justification, or if this justification is made on grounds which have little or nothing to do with the practicalities of work, then it can be described as inauthentic and thus potentially ideological. This approach is an extension of the method of analysis developed in the previous chapter for assessing the arbitrariness of various criteria of work.

There it was suggested that arbitrariness tends to emerge if the criterion fails to acknowledge the basic principles of action and expectations people have of work. Such an assessment can be made on the basis of an objective analysis of whether work does or does not provide individuals with opportunities to satisfy their needs. Here it is being suggested that the authenticity of a particular idea or belief about work can be assessed on the basis of not only of whether it fully to acknowledges the expectations which people have of work, but also of whether it actively supports the practical organization of work.

While as already noted above, it must be acknowledged that all individuals are prone to making inauthentic claims through the work-ethic, and that not all ideas about work are necessarily based on a thorough understanding of the practical reality of work, the extent to which an idea or belief becomes overtly ideological (as opposed that it, to being benignly or accidentally inauthentic), *depends upon the degree to which it fails to complement the current organization of work.* Although in other words, all ideational understanding has the potential to become ideological, some aspects of the work-ethic *are more ideological than others.* In the context of capitalistic economic practices, these ideologies tend to be most actively pursued by members and representatives of the economically advantaged minority who base their understanding of reality at the level of appearances only, and thus propagate a partial understanding of reality in order to further their own particular interests rather than the interests of all individuals.[15] Since this group stands to gain the most from the preservation of the labour process in its current form, it would not be surprising to find that many of the ideas and beliefs put forward in the work-ethic are likely to be focused at the level of systemic requirements rather than individual needs; it is the system which really matters, not the individuals who work within it. Although capitalism provides a particularly clear example of how the work-ethic might be manipulated in this way, it is likely that all forms of economic organization are vulnerable to a similar process of ideological manipulation, since there will always be one group of people who stand to benefit from the maintenance of the status quo. It is not just capitalists in other words, who will invoke the support of a particular work-ethic in order to preserve things as they are. The crucial point is that the prioritising of systemic requirements (albeit motivated out of self-interests) is inevitably accompanied by an emerging gap between the claims of the work-ethic and the reality of work in practice. It is important to emphasize this point, as it will subsequently be suggested that the contemporary work paradigm has entered a period of instability *precisely because* the current concept of work, and important aspects of the work-ethic it contains, have failed to keep pace with recent developments in productive technique. Our work-ethic in other words, has been stranded in the past. As a consequence of this, new working practices which fully take account of the inherent flexibility of the technology have been slow to emerge. In turn, this has resulted in a considerable disruption of traditional patterns of work as new innovations tend to be introduced in a somewhat piecemeal and incoherent way. The overall effect has been to generate a very high and rising level of actual and perceived job insecurity throughout the economy as more and more people are becoming less and less confident about the sustainability of formal paid employment.

Table 4.1: The work-ethic
The work-ethic provides an intellectual/moral basis for justifying and legitimizing the current concept and organization of work.

The work-ethic is composed of ideas and beliefs coming from two main sources:
   1 - an additional category of expectations of work
   2 - fragments of past ideas and beliefs

We can make an analytical distinction between two basic types of ideas and beliefs:
   1 - general level of ideational understanding
   2 - ideological ideas and beliefs

Use notion of authenticity to distinguish between these two types:
   do they represent a clear understanding of the practical reality of work? - *if yes:*
   they can be regarded as authentic - *if not:*
   do they prioritise systemic requirements over individual needs? - *if not:*
   they can be regarded as benignly inauthentic - *if yes:*
   are they deliberately misrepresentative in pursuit of minority interests? - *if yes:*
   these ideas and beliefs are likely to be ideological

If as is evidently the case, economic stability and social stability more generally, are dependent upon the willingness of the population to participate in the mechanisms of employment as currently constituted, and if this willingness is dependent upon people's confidence that these mechanisms can provide them with a reliable means of satisfying their needs, then loss of confidence could result in a severe disruption of the labour process. Table 4.1 above summarizes the analytical approach to the work-ethic discussed thus far.

It will be useful to elaborate a little on some of these points by looking briefly at examples both of how some aspects of the work-ethic tend to become divorced from the working practices they claim to support, and of how events in the world of work may have a knock-on effect upon ideas and beliefs about the nature of society more generally. Firstly, ideas associated with a particular organization of work tend to become quite deeply embedded not only within the practical organization of work itself, but also within the justificatory function of the work-ethic. Once a high level of inter-dependence has emerged between ideas about work and the way it is organized, it would not be surprising to find that changes in this arrangement are likely to be seen as a threat to the status quo of work. Consequently, the prospect of changing tried an tested practices is likely to be strongly resisted. A clear example of this, is the high level of suspicion amongst the British Trade Unions about the introduction of new working practices during the 1980s. For them, established patterns of work provided a level of relative stability on the basis of which they could consolidate their economic and political position. The introduction of new working practices inevitably undermined these taken-for-granted assumptions and expectations, and was therefore strongly resisted. The animosity which developed between the electricians' union the EETPU, and the Trade Union Congress during the late-1980s, precisely illustrates the conflict which emerged between the union status quo and the 'new unionism' which accepted the need to embrace the new technology. On the employers side, the implementation of new working practices also threatened established mechanisms of authority, as earlier demarcations between, for example, different management functions and hierarchies were to be replaced by new forms of lateral rather than vertical control. Looking at changes in the structure of employment more generally, the significant and continuing increase in part-time working, together with important changes in the contractual arrangements of employees, has had a considerable impact both upon patterns of work and upon people's attitude towards it. It would not be surprising to find that many people are strongly resistant to the idea that opportunities for life-long full-time employment are rapidly becoming a thing of the past. In the context of the present discussion, and from the point of view of those employers and employees who are willing to 'embrace the new technology', the ideas and beliefs of those who are resistant to change will inevitably be seen as conservative and reactionary. In practical terms, it is difficult to reach any other conclusion than that *they are* conservative and reactionary. To this extent, and whilst recognizing that they have not always been so, these now out-dated ideas and beliefs can be labelled inauthentic or ideological precisely because they are no longer in harmony with the world of work as it now is. How else could we describe ideas and beliefs which increasingly bear very little relation to the reality which surrounds them?

A second important aspect of the question of the authenticity or otherwise of work-ethics raised above, relates to the possibility that the authenticity of a particular idea or belief about work depends on the extent to which it supports particular rather than universal interests. This refers us back to the earlier suggestion that ideas and beliefs which correspond more or less closely with people's basic expectations of work are more likely to be authentic than those which relate to systemic requirements. Since however it is absurd to suggest that 'the system' somehow expresses ideas and beliefs as if it had a voice of its own, we need to recognize that these ideas and beliefs tend to be articulated by those individuals and groups of individuals *whose interests are most closely associated with the maintenance of the economic structure in a particular form*. While in principle there is no reason why the economic structure should not be developed and maintained in such a way as to reflect everybody's interests, the reality is that through history, some groups have supported the development of a particular manifestation of the productive forces in a way which is very much to their own advantage. In capitalist society for example, those who own and control the means of production have a very strong vested interest in maintaining a particular manifestation of the structures of employment and the organization of work. Inevitably, this vested interest is reflected in the development and dissemination of a work-ethic which both overtly and covertly justifies and legitimates this organization of work. In order then, to reach a full understanding of the role of the work-ethic and of how it might or might not be open to change, we need to acknowledge the influence of vested interests. This is not to suggest that the work-ethic is only affected by wider political pressures, since as we shall see in the following chapters, technological and other factors are potentially much more important. Nor is it to suggest that it is only the 'capitalist class' that has manipulated the work-ethic in order to maintain a position of economic superiority. The basic point, is that all work-ethics, whatever their political predisposition, are influenced more strongly by some groups in society than by others. The real significance of this difference is the extent to which their ideas and beliefs devote a disproportionate amount of effort to 'singing the praises' of a particular organization of the productive forces, rather than to recognizing and accepting the real needs and expectations which people have of work. There is only so much weight that the work-ethic can carry. If it is unduly burdened with responsibility for justifying and legitimizing the requirements of the system, then there will not be enough spare capacity to accommodate and articulate real human needs.

In noting that the work-ethic may be co-opted for minority interests, we should be careful not to suggest either that all ideas and beliefs about work are ideological, or that all those individuals who adopt these ideas and beliefs are suffering from false consciousness. Rather, the development of an ideational understanding of work is constitutive of a more general phenomenon of consciousness, important parts of which are held in common by all individuals precisely because they work in the same labour process. It is likely in other words, that there are significant similarities between employers' and employees' perceptions of work, precisely because they literally 'work together' and because their motivation to work derives from the same predisposition to provide for their own and their dependants' needs. What we can say though, is that when trying to assess the authenticity of the work-ethic, those ideas and beliefs which support particular interests/systemic requirements, are *more likely* to be ideological than those which support 'universal' interests. A work-ethic which contains a high proportion of the former, is more likely to be an ideological work-ethic.

The role of the work-ethic in sustaining perceptions of justification and legitimacy, is inevitably affected by the tendency for the work-ethic to contain a mixture of authentic and inauthentic ideas and beliefs. It can be suggested that during periods of transition in the organization of work, various groups might call upon the work-ethic to span the emerging gap between what went before and what is to come. In this sense, the work-ethic may act as an ideational bridge to sustain people's confidence in the utility of the work paradigm when this confidence is under threat; it may be used to fill the vacuum as one set of justifications and legitimations is superseded by another. What this means in effect, is that when the work paradigm enters a period of change, the threshold of perceived legitimacy, meaning the extent to which people are willing to accept a particular organization of work as valid and expedient, tends to be raised necessitating an increased concentration of ideational or ideological persuasion on the part of those who stand to gain the most from it. In Britain during the 1980s for example, the increasing threat posed by the marginalization of large sectors of the workforce through unemployment was dealt with in precisely this way. At the ideational level, vigorous attempts were made to reinstate central aspects of the Protestant work ethic, particularly its emphasis upon the individual as opposed to the collective, through strong appeals to so-called 'Victorian values'. These pressures were precisely matched within the economic sphere by a radical adoption of the monetarist doctrines of the free market developed by Hayek and Friedman. At the same time, 'the rule of Law' was invoked in an attempt to restore the basic premise of bourgeois economic rationality, that the law provides the basic foundation of authority within society. At the practical level, strict controls were placed on the trade unions aimed specifically at shifting the balance of economic and political power back towards the employers.[16] In a similar vein, and again in light of the restructuring of work, the British Labour Party has engaged in a considerable ideational effort to comfort people by suggesting that restructuring should be accompanied by a return to collective values and the reinstatement of 'social justice'. Both these examples demonstrate how the work-ethic is invoked to restore confidence in the economy.

In general terms, it can provisionally be suggested that the need for an ideationally persuasive work-ethic is determined by the overall character of the organization of work. This need arises firstly to the extent that individuals have become distanced from immediate means of satisfying their needs, and secondly by the degree of choice of occupation available to them. In medieval society for example, 'obedience' and 'natural law' were sufficient to maintain a rudimentary work-ethic. The proximity of physical danger and the likelihood of starvation provided the primary basis of, and motivation for, working. To this extent, the motivation and compulsion to work was not something which required a particularly high level of intellectual justification or legitimation on the part of the common peasant. Not to work would simply result in starvation. In contrast, the emergence of a highly developed division of labour, has in itself generated the need for a much more robust work-ethic. Once individuals are predominantly employed as wage earners, the relative freedom of choice available to them in terms of how they may ensure access to the means of survival, increases the pressure on the part of those who effectively control access to resources to 'convince' those who seeking such access of the need to work, and to continue to work, in particular ways. As Anthony has argued:

> An ideology of work is redundant when the labour force can be conscripted and coerced at will. In conditions of a freer labour market an ideology has to be developed in order to recruit labour and then in order to motivate it by persuading it that its tasks are necessary or noble. (Anthony 1977, p.22)

Finally, it is important to stress that the work-ethics develop out of, and only have power in terms of actual and 'real' experiences of working in particular ways. The ideas and beliefs they contain, whether authentic or inauthentic, do not have 'power' in themselves beyond the extent to which they are materially articulated. By the same token, new or modified aspects of the work-ethic only emerge and become recognisable when the material conditions upon which they depend, and which they reflect, have become available.[17] It is for this reason that the relationship between the conceptual aspect of the work paradigm (of which the work-ethic is a constituent part), and its practical aspect, is dialectical and reflexive rather than directly causal and linear.

To summarize the discussion in this part of the chapter, it has been suggested that the work-ethic forms an important part of the concept of work. The work-ethic is composed of various ideas and beliefs about the wider meanings and purposes of work, and performs the function of justifying and legitimizing the particular organization of work to which it refers. Within the work-ethic, we can distinguish between ideas which are authentic and ideas which are not. Authenticity refers to the extent to which particular ideas or beliefs firstly acknowledge and reflect the expectations which people have of work, and secondly, of whether they are actually relevant to the practicalities of work. Ideas which have little bearing on the realities of work and which represent minority (self-) interests are likely to be inauthentic and ideological. In the same way that criteria of work tend towards arbitrariness to the extent that they are based upon terms of reference which relate to systemic requirements rather than to the needs of individuals (and therefore refer to characteristics which have very little to do with the nature of the activity itself), we can begin to suggest that as the general meanings and purposes put forward in the work-ethic become more and more abstract, they are prone to become increasingly ideological to the extent that they loose sight of the basic expectations and purposes of work of the kind described in the previous chapter. It can further be suggested, that the more abstracted or distanced these ideas are from the immediate experience of individuals, the smaller will be the proportion of the population that believes them, and/or the less enthusiastically are they likely to be held.

Part Two - Forces and relations of production

Any discussion of the practical aspect of the work paradigm necessarily has implications for the nature of the relationship between what Marx called the forces and relations of production. Before proceeding to a discussion of how these relationships have developed in particular historical periods, it will be useful to specify briefly to how these terms are being used here.

As Alex Callinicos (1985) has pointed out, a certain initial imprecision can be detected in the use and significance which Marx attaches to the terms forces and relations of production, an imprecision which is subsequently resolved through his delineation of antagonistic class relations presented in the *Grundrisse* and in *Capital*. It will be helpful to follow Callinicos' analysis before stating the position taken here. Callinicos suggests that:

> Contrary to interpretations which treat the versions of historical materialism in *The German Ideology* and *Capital* as identical, the former work suffers from serious conceptual ambiguities, most importantly a persistent confusion of *technical* and *social* relations. (Callinicos 1985, p.48, emphasis added)

He goes on to suggest that in Marx's earlier works two central analytical concepts are developed: 'productive forces (*Produktioweise*)' and 'form of intercourse (*Verkehrsform*)' (Callinicos 1985, pp.48-9). 'Productive forces' 'involves two elements': 'the "productive powers" of man', understood as 'the productivity of labour permitted by the existing level of development of technique', and a second element, 'developed in line with Marx's stress on the social nature of production' which is that:

> the technical organization of the labour process requires a certain "mode of co-operation" among the producers. This arises from the specific *technological imperatives* of production, irrespective of the nature of the prevailing social relations. (Callinicos 1985, p.48/9, emphasis added)

From this analysis, Callinicos suggests that 'productive forces' thus defined, 'presents no serious difficulty, and points toward Marx's discussion of the labour process in *Capital*' (Callinicos 1985, p.49). However, Marx uses the second element of 'forms of intercourse':

> to embrace social relations generally, trade and commerce, along with class and property relations... [and thus tends] not only to embrace all social relations promiscuously, but it appears to include elements such as the organization of transport which might be regarded more properly as part of the productive forces. (Callinicos 1985, p.49)

On this reading, Marx fails to distinguish clearly enough between the technical and social aspects of productive forces, in order to be able 'to justify treating the development of the productive forces as the source of historical change' (Callinicos 1985, p.49). It is not clear in other words, whether the motor for historical development can be attributed primarily to developments in the 'technical forces' of production rather than to the social forces.

Again according to Callinicos, 'Marx resolved this "unclarity" by introducing in *The Poverty of Philosophy* (1847), the concept of the relations of production (Produktionsverhaltnisse):

> These relations are constituted at the level of production; however, they do not, unlike the productive forces, consist in a specific technical organization of the labour process, but are rather "social relations based on class antagonism. These relations are not relations between individuals, but between worker and capitalist, between farmer and landlord, etc." (Callinicos 1985, p.49; Marx *Collected Works* 6:159)

In *Capital* this concept was further consolidated 'where the forces and relations of production form an articulated unity, the mode of production':

> The relations of production in class societies are "the specific economic form in which unpaid surplus-labour is pumped out of the direct producers" (Marx: *Capital III*: 791) They are, therefore, in the first place relations of exploitation. The mode of appropriation of surplus labour depends upon the specific social from in which the direct producers are combined with the means of production. (Callinicos 1985, p.50)[18]

On this understanding, the former implication that the relations of production are determined by the forces of production is reversed;

historical development is primarily determined by changes in the relationships between the classes: 'The transformation of the labour process involved in the introduction of mass factory production [and by implication any other form of technical innovation] is attributed to the prior "formal subsumption of labour under capital"' (Callinicos 1985, p.51). In his discussion of the processes of the feudal economy and of the part played by technical innovations, (for example, 'the use of the iron-plough for tilling, the stiff-harness for equine traction, the water-mill for mechanical power, marling for soil improvement and the three-field system for crop rotation'), Perry Anderson follows this order of analysis. He points out that:

> It was precisely only the formation and consolidation of *new social relations of production* which could set them to work on a general scale. It is only after the crystallisation of a developed feudalism in the countryside that they could become widely appropriated. It is in the internal dynamic of the mode of production itself, not the advent of new technology which was one of its material expressions, that the basic motor of agrarian progress must be sought. (Anderson 1974, p.183, original emphasis)

Whilst acknowledging the usefulness of Callinicos' analysis, and whilst recognizing that the main thrust of his argument relates to the development of Marx's philosophical position, it can be suggested that a degree of ambiguity can still be detected in Marx's use of the terms forces of production and relations of production. It seems clear that particularly in *Capital*, Marx places the antagonistic contradictions which inherently pertain to capitalist forms of productive relations at the centre of his analysis. Without wishing to take issue with this position here, it can be suggested that the precise nature, direction and degree of 'determination' which exists between available levels of technological innovation, and the forms of co-operative activity associated with them, remains unclear. Referring again to the reference from *The German Ideology* cited by Callinicos above that:

> A certain mode of production, or industrial stage, is always combined with a certain mode of co-operation, or social stage, and this mode of co-operation is itself a "productive force". Further, that the multitude of productive forces accessible to men determines the nature of society, hence, that the "history of humanity" must always be studied and treated in relation to the history of industry and exchange. (Marx and Engels 1970, p.50)

If 'mode of production' is taken to be inclusive of 'mode of co-operation', and if 'mode of co-operation' (subsequently labelled 'relations of production') itself constitutes a 'productive force' then arguably, forces and relations of production become conflated precisely because they may be regarded as indistinguishable in reality. Thus the process of causality between forces and relations would seem to be dialectical and recursive, not direct and linear.

Similarly, reference to *The Poverty of Philosophy*, in which Marx makes a number of references to this process as it relates to the forward dynamic of human development, may not fully resolve this issue. A number of examples will emphasize this point:

> Till now the productive forces have been developed by virtue of this system of class antagonisms.... Thus in the history of society we see that the mode of exchanging products is regulated by the mode of producing them. Individual exchange corresponds also to a definite mode of production which itself corresponds to class antagonism. *There is thus no individual exchange without the antagonism of classes.* (Marx 1977, pp.196/8, emphasis added)

> In acquiring new productive forces men change their mode of production; and in changing their mode of production, in changing the way of earning their living, *they change all their social relations*. The hand-mill gives you society with the feudal lord; the steam-mill, society with the industrial capitalist. (Marx 1977, p.202, emphasis added)

> Is not this as good as saying that the mode of production, the relations in which productive forces are developed, are anything but eternal laws, but that they correspond to a definite development of men and of their productive forces, and that *a change in men's productive forces necessarily brings about a change in their relations of production?* (Marx 1977, p.210, emphasis added)

The first quotation supports Callinicos' reading of Marx with regard to the subsequent supremacy of relations of production as determining forces of production. The second two quotations however seem to contradict the first, at least to the extent that the ascendancy of 'forces' over 'relations' once more remains ambiguous. If 'in changing their mode of production... they change all their social relations', and if 'a change in men's productive forces necessarily brings about a change in their relations of production', then Marx could be interpreted as suggesting that the forces of production do in fact have a determining influence.

In the context of the present discussion of the practical aspect of the work paradigm, the position taken is that at least within the context of particular working practices, the forces and relations of production are conflated to such a degree that they may be seen as *inclusive of one another*. A productive force in other words, is seen as being made up of both a particular instrument (tool, machine, computer etc.), and a particular pattern of working relationships. To this extent, relations of production understood as wider social or class orientations, need not be seen as having a determining influence over particular technical developments. This should not be taken to mean that new technologies are not developed and implemented in such a way as to take advantage of the patterns of working relationships which already exist. In his analysis of the development of hierarchy within capitalist production for example, Marglin argues that:

> Neither of the two basic steps in depriving the workers of control of product and process - (1) the development of the minute division of labour... and (2) the development of the centralised organization that characterises the factory system - took place primarily for reasons of technical superiority. Rather than providing more output for the same inputs, these innovations in work organization were introduced so that the capitalist got himself a larger share of the pie at the expense of the worker. (Marglin 1974, p.49)

The more general point which is being made here, is that in principle, technological change can be introduced which is not governed by pre-existing relations of production. Although in contemporary society, this introduction may imply the decay of capitalistic relations of production, this decay is not necessarily a prerequisite for such change.

Summary

The first part of this chapter has outlined in largely theoretical terms, how different types of ideas and beliefs are combined in the work-ethic. It has been suggested that some ideas are authentic in the sense that they are based upon a genuine understanding of the practical reality of work and are therefore supportive of the effective operation of working practice. In contrast, other ideas and beliefs tend to be based on a partial understanding, a tendency which is reflected in the extent to which they focus more abstractly on systemic requirements. Although it should be accepted that many ideas and beliefs about work are at least to some extent inauthentic, the extent to which inauthentic ideas and beliefs become ideological is reflected in the extent to which they support minority rather than universal interests. In this sense, and in common with all categories of ideas and beliefs about society, the work-ethic can be used as a means of preserving the status quo. In more general terms, the function of the work-ethic is to provide an intellectual/moral justification for the organization of work in a particular form. This justificatory and legitimizing function may become especially important when for example, developments in productive technique, or changes in the international dimensions of economic exchange, require significant modifications to be made in the organization of work. It is at this point also, that the ideological tendencies of the work-ethic may become particularly apparent, as it is likely that changes of this kind will be strongly resisted by those groups who have a vested interest in maintaining the status quo. The corollary of this, is that during periods of economic stability, the work-ethic remains very much in the background. In Gramscian terms, the work-ethic, and indeed the concept of work more generally, forms an important part of social hegemony. It functions as a kind of intellectual/moral umbrella under which people can feel protected and secure.

The second part of the chapter has briefly outlined how for our present purposes, the forces of production can be taken to be inclusive of the relations of production. This is an important point because some interpretations of the historical development of the labour process, particularly those which follow Marx's analysis in *Capital*, strongly suggest that this development is primarily driven by antagonistic class relations. If this is the case, then it is difficult to attribute anything other than secondary importance to developments in productive technique. The position taken here, is that the implementation of new techniques cannot be separated from developments in the working relationships necessary for their introduction. To this extent, relations of production are in effect a productive force.

If we combine the two parts of the analysis in this chapter, we can define the work paradigm as combining a particular concept of work with a particular organization of work in practice. In this sense, the work paradigm of society is analytically the same as the combination of conception and execution which characterizes all human action. In the same way that an individual has an idea of what he or she intends to do, and then develops the means to do it, so too does society as a whole. Again following Gramsci, the work paradigm can be seen as hegemonic in that through a combination of material force - the basic compulsion to satisfy survival needs, and of a minimal level of ideational/moral consent - the ideas and beliefs of the work-ethic and of the concept of work more generally, a particular manifestation of the labour process comes into being and is seen to be legitimate. Combining this analysis with elements from the previous chapters the following table summarizes the essential components of the work paradigm:

Table 4.2: The work paradigm	
Conceptual aspect	*Practical aspect*
principles of work	forces of production
expectations of work	*made up of:*
criteria of work	techniques of production
work-ethic	relations of production

Having set out a theoretical framework for understanding the work paradigm and its internal dynamics, we are now in a position to see how useful this framework is for analysing particular work paradigms.

Notes

1. It is important to emphasize that the discussion of ideology given here will be limited to the notion of an ideology of work. No direct attempt will be made to consider the wider debates which surround the role of ideology understood in a more universal sense. For an introduction to these debates see: Centre for Contemporary Cultural Studies 1978; Larrain 1979; Thompson, J.B. 1984 and 1990, and Eagleton, T. 1991.

2. For a discussion of these wider issues see Poulantzas 1975; Wright, E.O. 1978; Parkin 1979, and Giddens 1980.

3. For a detailed discussion of Gramsci's notion of hegemony see Ransome 1992, chapters 4 and 5.

4. For a detailed analysis of this topic see Abercrombie *et al.*, 1980.

5. Similar prejudice may also be expressed about alleged racial differences. For a discussion of race at work see Braham *et al.*, 1981

6. For example, Frank Parkin has referred to 'two generic forms of social closure', namely usurption and exclusion. He has defined these: 'The distinguishing feature of exclusionary closure is the attempt by one group to secure for itself a privileged position at the expense of some other group through a process of subordination... it is a form of collective social action which, intentionally or otherwise, gives rise to a social category of ineligibles or outsiders.' 'Usurption is that type of social closure mounted by a group in response to its outsider status and the collective experience of exclusion.... What is entailed in all such cases is the mobilisation of power by one group or collectivity against another that stands in a relationship of dominance to it.' (Parkin 1979, pp.45/74) For a discussion of Parkin's analysis, see Ransome 1988.

7. Lodziak notes for example that: 'The dominant ideology is not dominant because a majority have adopted it, or even most of it. It is dominant in two senses. First, the values and beliefs of members of the dominant groups are dominant, not by virtue of their appeal to the majority but simply because members of dominant groups occupy positions of power that enable them to enact their values and beliefs. The consequent materialisation of dominant ideas forms the material context in which everybody lives and shapes the ideological climate. Second, some ideas are dominant in the sense that they serve the interests of dominant groups, irrespective of whether or not they are actually held by dominant groups.' (Lodziak 1995, p.38)

8. Fox comments for example, that: 'For the most part, then, work for the majority is little more than an irksome precondition for the real business of living. Most people in our society accept, in the main, a personal meaning in their work which accords well (i.e. is "congruent") with the social meaning embodied in the present design

of work and the predominant meaning projected by public communications.' (Fox 1980, p.151)

9. For a discussion of this point see Ransome 1995.

10. In contemporary British society for example, a number of different religious and cultural groups are all able to participate successfully in the labour process. It would be foolish to deduce from this however, that they all share the same ideas and beliefs about the meaning and purpose of work.

11. The classic example of this is Max Weber's *Protestant Ethic Thesis*. This is extensively discussed in chapter six.

12. This is after all why these ideas and beliefs are described as an 'ethic' defined as 'a moral principle or set of moral values held by an individual or group'.

13. This emphasizes the important point that even the most basic work-ethic is likely to accumulate through time. In this sense, work-ethics do not suddenly appear ready formed, but tend to evolve in response to other economic and social developments.

14. For example as Lukács has noted: 'When bourgeois thought "transforms the different limbs of society into so many separate societies" it certainly commits a grave theoretical error. But the immediate practical consequences are nevertheless in harmony with the interests of capitalism. The bourgeoisie is unable in theory to understand more than the details and the symptoms of economic progress.' (Lukács 1968, p.74) Lukács is quoting Marx 'The Poverty of Philosophy', (Marx 1977, p.203). It should be added that although the capitalist labour process has rendered bourgeois analysis particularly vulnerable to ideological tendencies of this kind, the same tendency can be seen in all groups who hold a dominant position within the labour process. In feudal society for example, Lords and Masters were not reluctant to co-opt the products of the labour process for their own ends.

15. In this sense and as Larrain notes: '"ideational" means "of or pertaining to ideation or the formation of ideas (OED)"' (Larrain 1983, n.14, p.251).

16. For an exposition of the philosophy of the 'new right' see: Friedman 1962; Friedman and Schwartz 1963, and Hayek 1980. For a critique of this position see: Bosanquet 1983, and King 1987. For a discussion of 'Thatcherism' see: Hall and Jacques (eds.), 1983, Gamble 1988, and Jessop *et al.*, 1988.

17. This does not of course preclude the elaboration of imaginative or speculative ideas about what might become possible in the future. The point is that these imaginings can only become 'real' when they are realised in practice.

18. The full reference to Marx is: 'The specific economic form in which unpaid surplus-labour is pumped out of direct producers, determines the relationship of rulers and ruled, as it grows directly out of production itself and, in turn, reacts upon it as a determining element.' (Marx 1959, *Capital III*, p.791)

5 The work paradigm of Classical and Medieval society

Having put forward a revised theoretical model of the composition and dynamics of the work paradigm, and having made a number of suggestions as to the kind of analytical strategy which might be most appropriate for testing its validity, the next task is to test the model by looking at a number of examples of how it does or does not help us to understand work paradigms of the past. Focusing particularly on the conceptual aspect of the work paradigm, the first example focuses on the work paradigms of classical, pre-Christian and early Medieval society. The second example, discussed in the following chapter, is the work paradigm of sixteenth and seventeenth European society. It will be shown that the categorization of activities as work, and the attribution of meaning to these activities is indeed closely associated with wider aspects of the overall belief system of the society within which they occur. An important aspect of this association is the development and implementation of three distinct types of what can be called *principles of justification* within the work paradigm. Although containing a strongly intellectual/moral dimension, these principles are very much concerned with the practical operation of the labour process. A number of issues raised in this chapter will be carried over for discussion in the following chapter. In the final chapter, this method of analysis will be used as a means of understanding why the contemporary work paradigm has entered a period of disequilibrium.[1]

It will be useful to begin with a brief description of the principles of justification mentioned above. The term 'justification' refers to the sense in which people are prepared to accept that the practicalities of work, and the products of work are being carried out and used in a proper and expedient way in the context of prevailing economic and social conditions.

Although as already noted, these principles may draw heavily on conceptual aspects of the work paradigm, they are most important in their practical application; their effect is felt in the practice of work. In this sense, the principles of justification can be seen as forming a bridge between the work-ethic in its function as a mechanism for legitimatizing at the intellectual/moral level, a particular organization of work, and the practical aspects of the work paradigm. The 'rules' and 'regulations' of a particular belief system are transposed onto the rules and regulations which govern the organization of work and the conduct of economic affairs. We can usefully distinguish three types of principles. Firstly, a number of principles have been developed within the work paradigms of the past, which are concerned with establishing active agreement as to the *worth* and *value* of the ends to which work is the means. It can be suggested that to a large extent, the perceived worth of a particular working activity might be far less dependent upon criteria of intrinsic worth and usefulness such as those discussed in chapter three, than upon largely extrinsic criteria which are as it were, attributed to it by association. As with the criteria of work in general, perceptions of the worth and value of work and its products are heavily dependent upon the terms of reference or wider beliefs which are being used. In a monastic community for example, menial labour and its products might be attributed a high value because of their association with spiritual virtue. The notion of spiritual value emerges out of a particular set of religious beliefs. In contrast, menial labour in a colonial community might be attributed a low value because if its association with military defeat and conquest. The imperialist belief system would include the belief that people who are defeated in battle are only fit for menial work. As the following discussion will show, these terms of reference are likely to change over time.

Secondly, various *principles of limitation* have been established in an attempt to determine acceptable limits to accumulation and wealth. The acceptance of such limits is necessary, since without them, both the ends and means of work would become limit-*less* and thus, presumably, insatiable. This is a particularly important principle, as it tends to carry with it a burden of responsibility for social inequality. If, as is often the case, some individuals in society are considerably more wealthy than others, and if this wealth tends to provide the holder with disproportionately high levels of social and political 'authority', then it is necessary that the holding of such wealth is seen to be legitimate. As with the principle of worth and value, perceptions of acceptable limits to wealth have varied quite considerably over time.

Thirdly, and on the assumption that a multitude of individuals are pursuing similar ends by similar means, *principles of conduct* have been put forward in order to ensure that individuals have equal opportunities and equivalent access to necessary resources. It is of course debatable whether such a high degree of equality ever has or could ever been achieved. The point is, that in order to avoid the mutual destructiveness of what Hobbes called 'the war of all against all' and in order to provide some sense of security in the conduct of economic affairs, an at least minimal degree of agreement is required with regard to how economic ends can be achieved. In his analysis of the forced division of labour in capitalism, Durkheim makes a similar observation:

> Let us suppose that men enter into life in a state of perfect economic equality, which is to say, that riches have entirely ceased being hereditary. The problems in the environment with which we were struggling would not be solved by that. Indeed, there will always be an economic apparatus, and various agents collaborating in its functioning. (Durkheim 1933, p.30)

At a more abstract level, it may be sufficient that most people at least *feel* that the conduct of economic affairs is being regulated by some form of overall agreement as to what is and what is not acceptable. The sense of outrage that some people might express when it is revealed that a particular person or organization has not been acting within these limits, indicates the extent to which people do have this feeling.

Each of these principles of justification are based upon some form of mutually agreed *legitimate authority* which can be invoked to sanction illegitimate or unacceptable conduct. It can be suggested that a transition has taken place from dependence upon the authority of divine will, and the principles of 'sufficiency' and 'moderation' which this prescribes, towards dependence upon the authority of the Law, and upon the principles of scientific logic and economic rationality. To a large extent, the principles of justification and the balance between them, are heavily influenced by the prevailing type of legitimate authority. Although in contemporary society for example, some aspects of economic conduct are still 'regulated' by religious beliefs and thus reflect the authority of a Christian or non-Christian God, it is increasingly the case that regulation stems from an acceptance of national and international law. Those who are accused of transgressing these regulations would have redress either to religious texts or to litigation. In each case the form of sanction which might be invoked would be quite different. The following table summarizes these principles of justification:

Table 5.1: Principles of justification

1. principles of the *worth and value* of work and its products
2. principles of *limitation* on the acceptability of accumulation and wealth
3. principles of *conduct* to determine what means are suitable for achieving 1 & 2
4. *legitimate authority* to which decisions about the above can be referred

Part One - Classical and pre-Christian concepts of work

For the Ancient Greeks the pursuit of *truth* was considered to be the overall and commanding purpose of human existence. Thus activities through which this quest could be conducted, namely art, philosophy and political rhetoric, were regarded as the ultimate goal of human activity; a goal which freed the individual corporeally and more importantly, spiritually from the vagaries and uncertainties of the exterior material world. From this perspective, other forms of activity such as manual labour, acquired a pejorative connotation since it 'draws the soul away from the roots of virtue in the soul of whosoever submits to it' (Tilgher 1930, pp.6-7).[2] Within this overall pejorative attitude towards 'labour', the Ancient Greeks and Romans did however make some distinctions between different occupations. Agriculture for example was seen as more worthy an occupation than that of the artisan and craftsman since the former enabled men 'to provide for their needs without having to depend on others', while the latter 'was forced to depend on his customers in order to live and prosper' (Godelier 1980, p.171). This position was particularly significant with regard to the relative *political rights* of individuals. Under such circumstances as Sabine suggests: 'Citizenship is frankly restricted to a class of privileged persons who can afford to turn over their private business - the sordid job of earning a living - to slaves and foreigners' (Sabine 1951, p.81; Anthony, 1977, p.16).

Two significant points arise here; firstly, the early association of *occupation and perceived social status*, and secondly the perceived desirability of *self-sufficiency*. With regard to the first point, and as

Godelier points out, with the increasing use of slave labour during the fourth century BC,[3] agricultural occupations increasingly came to be seen as 'unworthy of free men'. Thus:

> *The evolution of representations* of agriculture and craftsmanship, and *the transformation of the status of those engaged in them*, were linked to the evolution of the ancient economy towards ever more intense use of slaves and servile labour. (Godelier 1980, pp.171-2, emphasis added)

This is a clear example of how relative social status and occupation are both intimately bound up with one another, and are at the same time dependent upon material developments in the economic structure; in this example the expanded use of slave labour in agriculture. Similarly, and as an extension of this attitude towards occupational status, an overall social synthesis was achieved since: 'The cultural, political, and economic strata of this society coincided; those at the bottom have least culture, least authority and least economic power, and vice versa.' (Anthony 1977, p.25). In this way, the *occupational hierarchy* and the *hierarchy of social status* became mutually supportive and tended to validate or justify each other. Both are regarded as 'natural' since they reflect the fundamental beliefs noted above regarding the supremacy of contemplative and intellectual pursuits.

Paradoxically however, reference to the more humanitarian aspects of this belief system caused some difficulty. For Roman society in particular, the position of slaves, indeed the whole notion of slavery as a mode of production, increasingly came to be seen as at variance with other aspects of Roman philosophy regarding the 'equality of men'.[4] By extolling the virtues of equality, this belief system inevitably came into conflict with the practice of slavery. In Roman society, a partial solution to this dilemma was sought in the advocacy of different 'levels' of law and legal jurisdiction: 'By distinguishing *ius civile*, the customary law of the state; *ius genitum*, municipal law; and *ius naturale*, natural law, it was possible for a particular case to be both legal and illegal at the same time' (Anthony 1977, p.24). Without wishing to go further into the issue of the development and significance of the Roman legal system,[5] the point to be grasped, is that the perception of work and the status and worth attributed to it became intricately bound up with a hierarchy of higher ideals and priorities which were enshrined in law. Material subjugation at the base was at least partially justified by those 'above' through reference to these 'higher' ideals. It can be argued that a justificatory process of this kind has played an important part in the development of work paradigms ever since. Put crudely, an attempt is made to mitigate the necessity for menial, repetitive and largely unrewarding working activities by appealing to higher or supra-human priorities; priorities which as it were lie beyond or outside mortal comprehension. Obedience or adherence to this overarching belief system at the level of mundane daily activity, is ensured through the establishment of a number of principles of conduct initially reinforced by, and subsequently constituted by the practices of the Law.

With regard to the second point - the perceived desirability of self-sufficiency and of freedom from the activities of others - the notions of wealth and accumulation were also accepted with varying degrees of caution, since ultimately wealth was the means by which individuals could free themselves from both present and future obligations of directly earning their own living. As Tilgher notes, a number of alternative positions emerged with regard to the desirability and legitimacy of accumulated wealth. At one extreme, Antisthenes (c.450-360 BC) put forward the view that 'wealth and virtue were wholly incompatible', while Cicero (106-43 BC) and Seneca (c.55 BC-40 AD) 'allowed the wise man to possess even to seek riches but only as a means for exercising social virtues such as generosity, magnificence and the like' (Tilgher 1930, pp.9-10). This raises for the first time, the problematic issue of the justification of wealth and of the means by which this may lawfully and 'morally' be achieved; an issue which re-emerged in a particularly vigorous form during the Protestant Reformation.

For ancient society a solution to this difficulty was sought in the consideration of *use-values*. As Godelier emphasizes: 'the making of an object was not conceived in antiquity as a transformation of nature' rather, 'the form of an object was defined by its use and its utility was defined in turn by need' (Godelier 1980, p.171). Thus the causal origin of a product was not the craftsman or artisan, but the need for which the object had been made. On this understanding: 'Human beings were not aware of acting (praxis) when they made things, but rather when they used them' (Godelier 1980, p.171). This association of 'usefulness' with 'worth' and 'value' can be seen as an early awareness of a difficulty which persisted through the medieval period and up to the present day, namely the problem of the indirect accumulation of value or 'usury'.[6]

For Aristotle, all forms of usury were examples of misuse since a secondary impulse, namely the desire for unlimited wealth, had displaced the use for which the objects had originally been produced. Thus 'the proper and improper use of a thing distinguished, more precisely, between what the Greeks regarded as proper and improper work:

> To work for oneself was praiseworthy, even for a soldier and a gentleman to engage in what we would regard as menial manual labour was perfectly honourable. It was not the nature of the task which was significant, it was the purpose of the task. (Anthony 1977, p.18)

In classical society therefore, a clear distinction exists between the production and consumption of objects, a distinction which is at least partially resolved in terms of use-values rather than in terms of exchange-values. Assessments of the worth and value of a particular type of work were therefore made primarily on the basis of whether its product was useful. Similarly, and as an extension of this, the acceptability and legitimacy of accumulation and wealth were determined in terms of whether there was any valid purpose in possessing wealth. At the same time, the materialist conception that through work, man and nature are simultaneously transformed lies outside the classical conception of work. In Anderson's words: 'Both agricultural and artisannal work were essentially deemed "adaptations" to nature, not transformations of it; they were forms of service' (Anderson 1974, p.27).[7]

Part Two - Early Christian and Medieval concepts of work

The notion of work as painful toil re-emerged in early Hebrew society, but with the significant additional understanding that this was the necessary price mankind had to pay for their 'Fall from Grace'. Work 'is accepted as a penalty, as an expiation through which man may atone for the sin of his ancestors and reconquer his own lost spiritual dignity'; a way of bringing mankind 'back to the cosmic unity and harmony which reigned when man was first brought into being by divine activity' (Tilgher 1930, pp.11/13). As noted in chapter three, this understanding of work as a necessary penance has been described by Herzberg as the 'Adam concept of man':

> Two millenia of teaching have convinced many men that when Adam was cast out of the Garden mankind was doomed, warped and bound to a lifetime of pain. This notion of man's sinfulness conceives of the whole purpose of existence as a sentence of suffering for Adam's fall. (Herzberg 1968, p.16)

In contrast to this somewhat pessimistic view, Herzberg suggests that a second concept of man emerged following Abraham's 'covenant' with God:

> The second definition of man, as epitomised in the Abraham concept of man, can be interpreted as meaning that man is capable, that he had been given innate potential, indeed so much potential that God had chosen him to be His emissary on earth. In addition, man came to know God by translating his God-given attributes into ethics and laws to govern human behaviour. (Herzberg 1968, p.16)

Following the teaching of Jesus of Nazareth, a further significant change took place in the conception and purpose of life and therefore in the concept of work. Jesus taught that death represented the passage of the individual from an earthly to a heavenly life; a life of paradise in the presence of God akin to the state which had existed before Adam's misdemeanours. In contrast to the more elitist and scholastic priorities of Jewish theology, the Christian doctrine placed much greater emphasis on the notion of 'qualifying' for heavenly salvation as a direct consequence of more mundane aspects of earthly conduct; conduct which was largely exemplified through *work*. Earthly life had a new purpose: 'Man had two forms of existence, one his earthly body and its life; the other his eternal soul. The salvation of man's soul was now the objective rather than the goal of man's human endeavour' (Herzberg 1968, p.18). Physiological survival in other words, was represented as a means to an end other than an end in itself.

It is clear from these accounts that the whole realm of human earthly activity, including working activities, is seen as intimately bound up with heavenly purpose; the former finding justification and validity in the perception of the latter. Under such circumstances, working activities tended to be contextualized within a higher order of priorities, and, on the whole, were seen as subordinate to them. Whilst this perception remained relatively unchallenged, the perceived legitimacy of the social structure and of the role of work within it, remained relatively stable. Inevitably however, the naivety of this belief system became more and more evident, as appreciation of the earthly and concrete benefits of economic activity, increasingly came to be seen as at least as attractive as heavenly and spiritual rewards. During the medieval period, and as both Tilgher and Herzberg have pointed out, a considerable re-evaluation and reorganization of the Christian Church became necessary; a re-evaluation which included the notion of work itself: 'The Church now became the custodian of a complex theology that was to provide sanctions for current behaviour as well as for future goals' (Herzberg, 1968, p.19). These new priorities received close attention in the writings of Thomas Aquinas (1225-74), where occupational position was adopted as a foundation for social legitimacy:

> From now on, in the Scholastic synthesis, work appears as a natural right and duty, the sole legitimate base of society, sole legitimate foundation for property and profit. (Tilgher 1930, p.40)

Predictably however, this allocation of the various occupational strata and consequently of the social status which pertained to them, was not man-made but God-given:

> social classes and professions are divine and immutable forms of society; they existed before labour which does not create them, *but must adapt itself to the already existing forms which they offer.* (Tilgher 1930, pp.40-41, emphasis added)

Further still, in view of the divine ordination and orientation of these positions, it became the *duty* of the political and spiritual leaders of society to ensure that individuals did not attempt to trespass beyond the position or 'station' to which they have been allocated. This can be seen as an appeal to a hierarchy of social and divine ideals similar to the development of the three components of Roman Law noted above.[8] In his account of the correspondence between developments in religious outlook and economic practice, Tawney has described this perspective in terms of a 'functional theory of society':

> Society, like the human body, is an organism composed of different members. Each member has its own function, prayer, or defence, or merchandise, or tilling the soil. Each must receive the means suited to its station, and must claim no more. Within classes there must be equality; if one takes into his hand the living of two, his neighbour will go short. Between the classes there must be inequality; for otherwise a class cannot perform its function or... enjoy its rights. Lords must not despoil peasants. Craftsmen and merchants must receive what will maintain them in their calling, and no more. (Tawney 1960, pp.22-3)

Tawney's description is particularly interesting as it draws attention to the manner in which 'Natural Law',[9] the law of nature and of men, gradually displaced the overtly rigid 'Divine Law' of an earlier period, and in its turn, constituted a modified principle of justificatory legitimation in response to altered material circumstances. As Tawney points out:

> By lifting the weight of antiquated formulae, they cleared a space within the stiff framework of religious authority for new and mobile economic interests, *and thus supplied an intellectual justification for developments which earlier generations would have condemned.* (Tawney 1960, p.30, emphasis added)

This flexibility continued to develop, as the intensification of economic activity forced the Church to develop much more explicit guidelines both towards the rigidity of occupational position and especially towards its prime motivator, *accumulated wealth*, while at the same time seeking not to undermine the now firmly established principles of equality, natural law and 'sufficiency':

> Man has a natural control over material things; for he can, in virtue of his reason and will, make use of material things for his own benefit, as though they were intended for this purpose.... Therefore the division and the appropriation of property, which proceeds from human law, must not hinder the satisfaction of man's necessity from such goods. Equally, whatever a man has in superabundance is owed, of natural right, to the poor for their sustenance. (Aquinas, *Summa* Qu 66, arts.1 and 7; D'Entreves 1970, p.86)

Space does not allow a full analysis of the lengthy doctrines espoused by Thomas Aquinas and others on these topics. It is possible however to outline the basic principles which were developed with regard to work. In the first place, the principle of *use* and of use-values re-emerges. In the *Lectio* for example, Aquinas notes: 'The art of acquiring money is subordinate to the art of using money, not so much by way of providing material for it as by way of providing tools for it. For money and every kind of wealth are merely economic tools' (Aquinas, *Lectio* v., p.348; Jarrett 1968, p.154). On this understanding, and following the views noted in part one above, *the purpose of an activity provides a natural limit to that activity*. If 'the object of the art of making money is merely the making of money, and to this there can be no limit' (Aquinas, *Lectio* v., pp.390-391; Jarrett 1968 p.155), this activity is unnatural and possibly even evil. If on the other hand, as Jarrett points out, the purpose of the activity 'was to secure enough money to live on, and to help forward the good of his neighbour', then the individual 'was lawfully engaged in his profession' (Jarrett 1968 p.155). In the second place, *the manner* in which working activities were carried out was crucially important: 'All work must be pursued with discretion, adapted with prudence to each one's needs and capacities, and not overstepping the times and days appointed by divine law or just human law' (Jarrett 1968, p.175). Thirdly, and with regard to the more specific problem of usury and commercial trade, Aquinas was obliged to confront the problem of 'abstract' financial gain. In cases of direct personal credit, the borrower was entitled to keep the full proceeds of his loan: 'The proceeds of money taken in usury are due to the person who acquired them... on account of his own industry... wherefore he has more right to the goods acquired with usurious money than to the usurious money itself' (Aquinas *Summa*, QQu 78, art.3, obj.3). Since however, in cases where money was lent 'to a merchant or craftsman so as to form a kind of society', the lender *does not transfer the ownership of his money to them*, and so accepts the possibility of inconvenience or loss (perhaps through shipwreck or piracy), the lender 'may lawfully ask for or even exact something else besides the money lent... *it is not unlawful in lending money to anyone, to demand some sort of compensation as a condition of the loan*' (Aquinas, *Summa*, QQu 78, art.2 obj.1/5, emphasis added). Gradually therefore the pursuit of profit became more and more legitimate:

> Now it is lawful to desire temporal things, not indeed principally, by placing our end therein, but as helps whereby we are assisted in tending towards beatitude, in so far, to wit, as they are the means of supporting the life of the body, and are of service to us as instruments in performing acts of virtue. (Aquinas *Summa*, QQu 83, art.6, obj.4)

Accumulating surpluses could therefore be regarded as legitimate on the condition, or at least in the expectation, that they could be used to support good neighbourliness. At the same time, the constraining nature of divinely allocated social position began to soften in order to allow individuals to benefit from increased social status as the result of their economic endeavours. Upward social mobility in other words, became both an acceptable and legitimate *benefit* of economic activity and consequently one of its *aims*.

Gradually the stability and cohesion of medieval society was shaken as changes took place in the economic sphere. With the displacement of payment in kind by wage-labour during the twelfth and thirteenth centuries, the workforce became increasingly mobile as wage-labour gradually displaced payment in kind. Producers could now obtain a proportion of their income through the sale of surplus at market:

> Work could begin to be taken seriously, particularly as markets began to develop. Nabholtz argues that it was becoming both possible and worth-while for the tenant to put more work into his own holding because increasing mobility made it easier for him to sell his surplus produce in a town market; the transition from a self-sufficient to an exchange economy was taking place. (Anthony 1977, p.31)

The collapse of the feudal economy and the emergence of mercantile capitalism was inevitably accompanied by further developments in the perceived meaning and purpose of work. During and after the European Renaissance work came to be seen much more *positively* as a means by which individuals could gain access to personal independence and choice. In combination with the growth of urban markets, the spread of international commerce and the emergence of increasingly complex organizations of business and trade, these new feelings of self-assurance found ample opportunity for expression as economic activity acquired a distinctively 'entrepreneurial' character. Deeply embedded within the ethos of this period of dramatic expansion and growth in all spheres of activity, was the central idea of *man as creator*; an active purposeful and interventionist view of mankind which largely overthrew the passive, humble and subservient attitude of mankind towards itself propagated through earlier religious doctrine. By the turn of the sixteenth century it must have seemed as if human ingenuity and creativity were almost limitless; a limitlessness which was amply demonstrated by the unprecedented expansion of *economic* organization and prosperity:

> For it was the mastery of man over his environment which heralded the dawn of the new age, and it was in the stress of expanding economic energies that this mastery was proved and won.... Heralded by an economic revolution not less profound than that of three centuries later, the new world of the sixteenth century took its character from the outburst of economic energy in which it had been born. Like the nineteenth century, it saw a swift increase in wealth and an impressive expansion of trade, a concentration of financial power on a scale unknown before.... The outburst of capitalist enterprise in mining and textiles; the rise of commercial companies, no longer local but international, and based, not merely on exclusive privileges, but on the power of massed capital to drive from the field all feebler competitors; a revolution in prices which shattered all customary relationships; the collapse of medieval rural society in a nightmare of peasants' wars; the subjection of the collegiate industrial

organisation of the Middle Ages to a new money-power; the triumph of the State and its conquest, in great parts of Europe of the Church - all were crowded into less than two generations. (Tawney 1960, pp.67-70)

Summary

For ancient society, the overall purpose and meaning of life was the contemplation of truth. In order that this should be possible it was necessary for society to be maintained in a state of balance and equilibrium. To this end, the divisions between citizens metics and slaves were perceived as part of a natural order: 'For he that can foresee with his mind is naturally ruler and naturally master and one that can do these things with his body is subject and naturally a slave' (Aristotle *Politics I*, p.1252a; Calvert 1982, p.27). The activities of these various groups were consequently perceived in the form of a *hierarchy* wherein the vast majority of working activities were considered to be of very little intrinsic value especially since their usefulness was only revealed at the point of consumption. Further, as noted above, the correlation between occupation and social status was firmly established, a correlation which has persisted to our own time.

In Hebrew and early Christian society, the meaning and necessity of work was established through religious teaching as essentially a form of *penance*. With the growth and spread of the idea of a heavenly hereafter, the notion of corporeal existence and material sustenance achieved through work, came to be seen as a temporary state of affairs. The overriding purpose of existence was to ensure the salvation of the spirit beyond the limitations of earthly life, an assurance which could in part be achieved through diligent fraternal labour.

During the medieval period this attitude towards work was initially maintained and then gradually modified, as the church came to terms with less profound issues particularly the organization and conduct of economic practices. The monastic orders of St Augustine and St Benedict were a direct attempt to provide, by example and through teaching, a set of principles of conduct by means of which individuals could ensure that their activities would be pleasing to God. By the mid-thirteenth century religious teaching was forced to confront the ethics and morality of economic gain in a still more forthright manner. The legitimacy of upward social mobility, achieved through accumulated wealth was increasingly sanctified by the Church, and consequently the purpose of work, for some strata of society at least, was no longer seen as being tied directly to divine allocation but as being a justifiable means of self-advancement.

Following the Renaissance, the structure of feudal society collapsed under the pressure of economic change. The dramatic expansion of European influence stimulated by the rapid discovery and exploitation of other parts of the world, led to the influx of new and seemingly endless sources of powerful economic wealth. As a consequence, new principles and structures of economic and social justification were developed, structures which depended upon, and were stimulated by, new attitudes and practices of work. Work came to be seen as the means by which individuals could express their destiny as beings who could literally *recreate* the world.

Notes

1. It should be emphasized that although some of the characteristics of the work paradigms discussed here can be seen as the forebears of the contemporary concept of work, the following discussion is not intended to provide a definitive 'history' of the Western work ethic. Rather, these glossed accounts are put forward in order to illustrate the usefulness and applicability of the general analytical framework developed here.

2. Tilgher's account of the development of the nature and perception of 'work' has become something of a standard reference for this topic. Unfortunately, some authors have tended to accept this account somewhat uncritically. See for example: Rose 1985, ch.2; Parker 1972, ch.3; Mills, C. W. 1953, ch.10, and more indirectly, Anthony 1977, ch.1.

3. For a detailed account of these developments see Hammond 1959, p.520ff.

4. For example, Stoic philosophy maintained that: 'Because men and God share in the power of reasoning there is an affinity between them; men are the children of God therefore they are brothers. *Because they are brothers all men are equal*, except for innate

differences between wise men and fools.' (Anthony 1977, p.23, emphasis added)

5. Anderson for example, stresses its significance in establishing the notion of 'absolute property': 'The great decisive accomplishment of the new Roman law was thus, appropriately enough, its invention of the concept of 'absolute property' - dominium ex jure quiritium. No prior legal system had ever known the notion of an unqualified private property.' (Anderson 1974, p.66)

6. The term usury is here taken in Tawney's words as: 'A summary name for all kinds of extortion: not only the taking of interest for a loan, but the raising of prices by a monopolist, the beating down of prices by a keen bargainer, the rack-renting of land by a landlord, the sub-letting of land by a tenant at a rent higher than he himself paid, the cutting of wages and the paying of wages in truck, the refusal of discount to a tardy debtor, the insistence on unreasonable good security for a loan, the excessive profits of a middleman.' (Tawney 1960, p.153)

7. An example of this attitude emerges in the pastoral poems of Virgil: 'What makes the cornfields happy, under what constellation/ It's best to turn the soil my friend, and train the vine/ On the elm; the care of cattle, the management of flocks,/ The knowledge you need for keeping frugal bees; - all this/ I'll now begin to relate....' (Virgil, *Georgics*, Book 1, lines 1-5)

8. This attitude has been particularly persistent. During the Don Pacifico Debate in the House of Commons in 1850 Lord Palmerston noted: 'We have shown the example of a nation in which every class in society accepts with cheerfulness the lot which Providence has assigned to it; while at the same time every individual of each class is constantly striving to raise himself in the social scale... by preserving good conduct, and by the steady and energetic execution of the moral and intellectual faculties with which his creator endowed him.' (Palmerston 1850, Don Pacifico Debate, House of Commons. Quoted in Neale 1983, p.27) Or in the words of the familiar hymn: 'The rich man in his castle, the poor man at his gate, God made them high and lowly, and ordered their estate.'

9. Thomas Aquinas defined Natural Law in the following way: 'Now in human affairs a thing is said to be just, from being right, according to the rule of reason. But the first rule of reason is the law of nature.... Consequently every human law has just so much of the nature of law, as it is derived from the law of nature. But if in any point it deflects from the law of nature, it is no longer a law but a perversion of law.' (Aquinas *Summa*, Qu 95, art.2)

6 The work paradigm of sixteenth and seventeenth century European society

The examples in the previous chapter have illustrated how concepts of work evolve in response both to changes in economic and social structure, and to changes in the overall belief systems of particular societies. Adopting the strategy outlined in the first part of the book, this evolution can be usefully characterized in terms of the periodic revision of principles of worth and value, of the acceptability of various limits to productive activity and of notions of legitimate conduct reinforced by agreed sources of authority. It was also shown that the rapid acceleration of economic activity which accompanied the transition from the feudal economy to mercantile and later to 'modern' capitalism, required a particularly forthright re-evaluation of these principles. Although it is clear that developments in the conceptual aspects of the work paradigm are closely related to developments in economic practice, the question remains as to whether and to what extent either of these elements plays the leading role. In Roman society for example, the fact that aesthetic activities were highly valued, was contingent upon the availability of slave labour to provide the necessities of life. In medieval society on the other hand, it could be argued that the stability of the social structure depended upon the willingness of the population to accept that their respective roles were part of a divinely ordained higher order. The first example implies economic determination, the second a form of hegemonic or ideological consent.

Perhaps the best known attempt to establish the direction of causation between a particular belief system and a specific type of economic practice, is Max Weber's seminal essay *The Protestant Ethic and the Spirit of Capitalism*, where it is argued that a close association or 'affinity' pertained between the development of 'modern' capitalism in Northern

Europe and America during the sixteenth, seventeenth and eighteenth centuries, and the spread of the belief system of ascetic Protestantism. Although Weber's interpretation provides one of the most useful accounts of the relationship between an economic practice and an incumbent concept of work, it will be argued that Weber's account is somewhat ambiguous with regard to the direction of causation of between the conceptual and practical aspects of the work paradigm. In taking the work paradigm of sixteenth and seventeenth European Society as our second example, it is highly instructive to consider Weber's analysis in some detail. The first part of the chapter outlines the basic principles of the Protestant work-ethic. This is followed in part two by a critique of Weber's position. Part three provides a discussion of the issues which have emerged from the examples described in this and the previous chapter. The chapter concludes with an assessment of the usefulness of the analytical framework of the form and internal dynamics of the work paradigm developed in the earlier chapters.

Part One - The Protestant work-ethic

In the wake of Weber's thesis on the interconnectedness of a Protestant or Puritan belief system and a capitalistic work ethic, a great deal of discussion has emerged ranging from theological exegesis of the works of Luther and Calvin on the one hand, to empirical analysis of the material 'pre-conditions' of a capitalistic economic system on the other.[1] Many questions have been raised concerning the incidence of capitalistic enterprise in predominantly Catholic countries, the historical peculiarities of alternative Protestant doctrines and subsequent differences in the rate of growth of the business enterprise to which they may have given rise, and more recently with regard to how Weber's thesis may or may not provide an adequate model for the analysis of 'developing' countries especially in the Third World.[2] The view taken here, is that whilst accepting the affinity between certain religiously founded behavioural ethics and the ethics appropriate for capital accumulation, Weber tends to overstate the importance of the former. To this extent, the parallel analysis offered by R.H.Tawney in *Religion and the Rise of Capitalism* may provide a more decisive account. Space does not permit an adequate examination of the rival positions taken by these authors. It will however be useful to note in summary form, three of the broad criticisms that Tawney has made and which will re-emerge during the following discussion:

[Firstly] The development of capitalism in Holland and England in the sixteenth and seventeenth centuries was due, not to the fact that they were Protestant powers, but to large economic movements, in particular the Discoveries and the results which flowed from them.

[Secondly] Weber ignores, or at least touches too lightly on, the intellectual movements which were favourable to the growth of business enterprise and to an individualist attitude towards economic relations, but which had little to do with religion.

[Thirdly] Weber appears greatly to over-simplify Calvinism itself... he apparently ascribes to the English Puritans of the seventeenth century the conception of social ethics held by Calvin and his immediate followers. (Tawney 1960, pp.319-320. n.32)[3]

Broadly speaking, the influence of the Protestant ethic can be seen as operating simultaneously in two ways; 'as a *code of ethics* for the conduct of everyday life and as a *sanction* which operates to compel the faithful to adhere to these ethical norms' (Marshall 1982, p.70, emphasis added). As in previous historical periods, the coercive authority of the sanction is provided by the threat of spiritual damnation. For Martin Luther (1483-1546), this code of ethics was seen as operating through the agency of all individuals rather than being restricted to an elite group of clerics and monks. Thus for the first time, the distinction between the mass of the population, the *praecepta*, and the priesthood, the *consilia* was set aside in favour of a *universal* concept of the brotherhood of man. As long as individuals performed their duties diligently they could gain heavenly reward *irrespective* of the particular form of activity in which they were involved. As Weber points out, this resulted in:

> The valuation of the fulfilment of duty in worldly affairs as the highest form which the moral activity of the individual could assume... The only way of living acceptably to God was through the fulfilment of the obligations imposed upon the individual by his position in the world. That was his calling. (Weber 1976, p.80)

However, despite the fact that the principles of justification by faith and of the 'calling' are universally available irrespective of one's social position and occupation, the allocation of occupation is still seen as a divine prerogative; a prerogative which reinforced the notion that one's calling was a *duty*: 'The perseverance of the individual *in the place and within the limits which God has assigned to him was a religious duty*' (Weber 1976, p.160, emphasis added).

Although Luther's teaching can be interpreted as representing a liberalization of religious precepts, it should be emphasized that particularly with regard to economic affairs, many of his views were extremely conservative. It would therefore be a mistake to imply that Luther saw himself as the spiritual mentor of an emerging bourgeoisie. As Tawney points out: 'International trade, banking and credit, capitalist industry, the whole complex of economic forces... seem to [Luther] to belong in their very essence to the kingdom of darkness which the Christian will shun' (Tawney 1960, p.94). Evidence of Luther's belief in the need to maintain a rigid social hierarchy can be found in the way in which he rejected the claims of the peasantry for an end to villeinage:

> This would make all men equal and so change the spiritual kingdom of Christ into an external worldly one. Impossible! An earthly kingdom cannot exist without inequality of persons. Some must be free, others serfs, some rulers, and others subjects. (Luther, *Ermahnung zum Freiden auf die zwolf Artikel der Bauerschaft in Schwaben* (1525), in *Werke*, vol.18, p.327; Tawney 1960, p.93)

By contrast, John Calvin (1509-64) did direct his attention more explicitly towards the consequences of changing economic practices. The exponents of Calvinism:

> Addressed their teaching... primarily to the classes engaged in trade and industry, who formed the most modern and progressive elements in the life of the age.... In doing so they naturally started from a frank recognition of the necessity of capital, credit and banking, large-scale commerce and finance, and the other practical facts of business life. (Tawney 1960, p.104)

Awareness of these material developments was however still framed in terms of divine prerogative, a prerogative which was summarized in the notion of predestination. According to this principle: 'Certain individuals he chose as his elect, predestined to salvation from eternity by "his gratuitous mercy, totally irrespective of human merit"; the remainder have been consigned to eternal damnation, "by a just and irreprehensible, but incomprehensible judgement"' (Tawney 1960, p.108, quoting Calvin, *Institutes of the Christian Religion*, (1838 translation), p.128-9 (bk.3, ch.21, para.7).

At first sight this position seems paradoxical, since if the fate of the individual's 'eternal spirit' is predetermined and thus lies entirely beyond their own influence, then what is to be gained from pursuing earthly toil in a Godly manner, why not simply lead a life of pleasure and idleness?

Calvin emphasized however, that precisely since there can be no certainty of salvation, each individual should as it were 'prove' his or her election by leading an exemplary life on earth. Moreover, this proof could not simply be demonstrated by 'abstract' faith in the possibility of salvation hereafter, but through concrete action in the present: 'Faith had to be proved by its objective results in order to provide a firm foundation for the *certitudo salutis* [the certainty of salvation]. It must be a *fides efficax* [a productive faith], the call to salvation an effectual calling' (Weber 1976, p.114). Although 'good works' could not guarantee salvation, intense worldly activity was nonetheless indispensable 'as a sign of election': 'They are the technical means, not of purchasing salvation, but of getting rid of the fear of damnation' (Weber 1976, p.115). Through frenetic devotion to one's calling in other words, the individual is provided with a means of demonstrating both to oneself and more importantly to others, the certainty of one's conviction in salvation.

The originality of this revitalised work-ethic lay not so much in acceptance with one's lot in life and faith in the possibility of spiritual salvation, principles which as shown above have existed throughout history, as in the substance of the psychological sanction of damnation. A sanction which was to a large extent self-administered: 'If one does not behave according to the strict observances of the Calvinist precepts for Godly living, then one can take it for granted that this is a sure sign that one is of the damned' (Marshall 1982, p.76).[4] It followed from this, that success in one's working life provides a measure of one's likely membership of the elect. If this success is measured in terms of financial gain, then conveniently: 'The earning of money within the modern economic order is, so long as it is done legally, the result and the expression of virtue and proficiency in a calling' (Weber 1976, pp.54).

With regard to the product of this freneticism, and the application of limiting principles to it, 'accumulation of riches' was not in itself seen as a danger to the likely salvation of the spirit. Rather it was 'their misuse for purposes of self-indulgence or ostentation' which was severely criticised. Calvinist doctrine thus extended previous elements of Christian ideology, and put forward refined principles of limitation regarding trade, profit and usury, limitations which were to a large extent increasingly liberal and directly sympathetic to the activities and aspirations of the entrepreneurial bourgeoisie. Space does not allow a detailed discussion of the advice offered by Calvin on the subject of usury, profit and trade, advice, which Tawney suggests 'was not strikingly original' (Tawney 1960, p.106).[5] What Calvin did do however was:

> *To change the plane on which the discussion was conducted*, by treating the ethics of money-lending, not as a matter to be decided by an appeal to a special body of doctrine on the subject of usury, *but as a particular case of the general problem of the social relations of a Christian community, which must be solved in the light of existing circumstances*. (Tawney 1960, p.107, emphasis added)

Two central points emerge at this point. Firstly, there is the notion that work and the way that it is carried out represents one's providential duty, and secondly that religious guidance in these matters had become primarily concerned with the practicalities of economic expediency. With regard to the first point, Weber does not hesitate to draw the conclusion that:

> In truth this peculiar idea, so familiar to us to-day, but in reality so little a matter of course, of one's duty in a calling is what is most characteristic of the social ethic of capitalistic culture and is in a sense the fundamental basis of it. It is an obligation which the individual is supposed to feel and does feel towards the content of his professional activity, no matter in what it consists, in particular no matter whether it appears on the surface as a utilisation of his personal powers or only of his material possessions (as capital). (Weber 1976, p.54)

Further, and most importantly, since the enjoyment of wealth is considered sinful evidence of one's non-election, the only legitimate use for excess revenue is as a reinvestment to perpetuate the cycle of future demonstration of worldly success and thus heavenly salvation. Having 'proved' one's election in the present in other words, surplus capital could be 'saved up' to ensure the saving of one's soul in the future. For the entrepreneurial businessman of the seventeenth century therefore, any surplus profit was immediately put back into the business itself: 'The idyllic state collapsed under the pressure of a bitter competitive struggle, respectable fortunes were made, and not lent out at interest, but always reinvested in the business' (Weber 1976, p.68). As a consequence, perceptions as to the present and immediate needs of the individual (and therefore as to the ends to which work is the means), tended to be superseded by the perception of future needs. Since the apparent need to ensure salvation is paramount, and since personal salvation and the need to 'sanctify' the world in God's name are inherently limitless (presumably one cannot be saved too much) then both work and the surpluses it produces can be seen as without limit. For Weber, it is this coincidence within the Protestant Ethic between frenetic activity and an ascetic attitude towards the wealth it tends to generate, which lies at the heart of the 'elective affinity' between Protestantism and capitalism:

> When the limitation of consumption is combined with the release of acquisitive activity, the inevitable practical result is obvious: accumulation of capital through ascetic compulsion to save. The restraints imposed upon the consumption of wealth naturally served to increase it by making possible the productive investment of capital. (Weber 1976, p.172)

With regard to the second point - that religious guidance is essentially concerned with practical expediency - it is important to stress that Weber is not suggesting that this religious ethic translates directly into a capitalistic 'spirit'. Rather, he emphasizes that it is *the daily material conduct* of the former, *subsequently detached from its theological origins*, which provided a new set of principles of conduct which were essentially conducive or 'sympathetic' to the capitalistic organization of economic practice. Although therefore, as Weber notes, 'the usefulness of a calling, and thus its favour in the sight of God, is measured primarily in moral terms:

> Above all, in practice the most important criterion, is found in private profitableness... the faithful Christian must follow the call by taking advantage of the opportunity. (Weber 1976, p.162)

It will be useful at this point, to outline the most important principles of conduct which define the 'Protestant Work Ethic' and demonstrate its emphasis on the *practical expediency* of economic conduct.[6] The first and perhaps most important principle of conduct is the great emphasis placed on making good use of *time*: 'Waste of time is thus the first and in principle the deadliest of sins. The span of human life is infinitely short and precious to make sure of one's own election' (Weber 1976, p.157). Consequently, activities which demonstrate the wasting of time are regarded as particularly sinful: 'Loss of time through sociability, idle tale, luxury, even more sleep than is necessary for health... is worthy of absolute moral condemnation' (Weber 1976, p.157-8). This theme of time well spent is reflected in the prescriptive advice of Benjamin Franklin quoted by Weber. For Franklin, punctuality, as a social habit and as a demonstration of good intent particularly in the repayment of debts, is very significant. This significance however rests not in its own *intrinsic* worth but *instrumentally as a means of gaining credit*: 'He that is known to pay punctually and exactly to the time he promises, may at any time and on any occasion, raise all the money his friends can spare' (Weber 1976, p.49).

Secondly, and related to the above, is the principle of *industriousness*. From a Protestant perspective each individual can be regarded as an embodiment of potential activity seeking an opportunity to express itself: 'Loose no time; be always employed in something useful; cut off all unnecessary actions' (Franklin 1874, p.229). To be idle therefore, not only represents a 'cost' in terms of resources which might be consumed through 'idleness',[7] but more significantly, it represents a far greater cost in terms of earnings *which have not been achieved*: 'He that idly loses five shillings' worth of time, looses five shillings, and might as prudently throw five shillings into the sea' (Weber 1976, p.50). The same principle is equally true of leaving one's capital idle since, as Franklin reminds us: 'Remember that money is of the prolific, generating nature. Money can beget money and its offspring can beget more and so on.... The more there is of it, the more it produces every turning so that the profits rise quicker and quicker (Weber 1976, p.49).[8]

A third pair of principles relate to the need for *thrift* and *frugality*. Like the wasting of time, the wasting of other resources inevitably demonstrates a lack of foresight, a flippant disposition, and may be seen as an insult to God for not putting 'His gifts' to good use: 'Make no expense but to do good to others or yourself; i.e. waste nothing' (Franklin 1874, p.229). Clearly these characteristics are a consequence of the general attitude of self-denial and abstemiousness noted above. It is important to note that this principle also extends to include the 'resource' of human labour power, wherein employees may be regarded instrumentally as a 'cost' to be accounted for. Indeed for Macpherson, this principle of dehumanision through the market largely defines the 'possessive society' as against the more traditional form of the 'customary or status society':

> If a single criterion of the possessive market society is wanted, it is that man's labour is a commodity, that is, that man's energy and skill are his own yet are regarded not as integral parts of his personality, but as possessions, the use and disposal of which he is free to hand over to others for a price. (Macpherson 1962, p.47)[9]

Finally, Weber emphasizes that modern economic practice must be conducted in a thoroughly 'rational' manner.[10] In addition to the growing belief that 'science' could provide a new set of guiding principles for human development and prosperity,[11] the notion of rationality was adopted in the business sphere to denote that the modern business enterprise should conduct itself in a scientific, logical and highly organized calculative form:

> In the last analysis the factor which produces capitalism is the rational permanent enterprise with its rational accounting rational technology and rational law, [complemented by] the rational spirit, the rationalisation of the conduct of life in general and a rationalistic economic ethic. (Weber 1983, p.128)

Part Two - A critique of Weber's position

It was suggested at the start of this chapter, that Weber's analysis of the coincidence of capitalism and ascetic Protestantism remains ambiguous with regard to the priority of conceptual over practical developments in the work paradigm of 'modern' or 'rational' capitalism. The point to be emphasized here, is that many of the characteristics of this work paradigm, may rely less upon religious principles than upon the dictates of material expediency; a form of expediency which includes, at least amongst its strongest advocates, the desire firstly to create and subsequently to preserve the organization of work and the conduct of economic affairs in a form which supports their own material interests. To this extent, the incorporation of these principles into a specific work-ethic, and the subsequent use of this work-ethic as a means of justifying a new work paradigm, is vulnerable to the charge of inauthenticity described in the previous chapter. It can be suggested in other words, that although an ascetic Protestantism may have provided a useful means of justifying and legitimating a particular organization of work, the latter was not *determined* by the former. This interpretation can be supported by showing firstly, that the religious precepts which are claimed to underlie the principles of conduct listed above, *are not only tangential but largely contrary* to the realities of capitalistic economic practice, and secondly, that the principles themselves may only realistically be associated *with that sector of the population who stood to gain substantially from it*; namely property-owning bourgeois entrepreneurs.

On the first point, it is not being suggested that the principles of conduct of ascetic Protestantism have not as it were 'existed'. The point is that once a particular set of institutional practices have been established, a development which may or may not also be sympathetic towards a particular understanding or interpretation of reality, these practices exercise coercive power and 'authority' over individuals *irrespective* of whether those individuals adhere to the more abstract ideals and values which were instrumental to their development. Again quoting Marshall:

> Individuals may act in a manner that accords with normative expectations *without themselves subscribing to the values and beliefs which underlie the norms*.... There is no necessary correlation between symbolic action and non-symbolic behaviour; between speech and action; intention and actuality; motives or purposes and institutionalised social arrangements or social behaviour. (Marshall 1982, p.65, emphasis added)

Furthermore, once these original ideas and interpretations, religious or otherwise, have been integrated into real material institutions and structures, their residual influence may be limited to the extent to which they can be used by those social groups which benefit from them, to justify these institutions and practices *retrospectively*. With regard to an ideology of work, it may be very difficult as it were, to 'deconstruct' such a belief system and to separate out the *original* ideas from their *subsequent* embellishments.[12] Weber himself makes this point with regard to the *instrumental worth* of aspects of the Protestant value system when he notes that the whole point, the 'essence' of maintaining a display of personal integrity has very little to do with *the intrinsic worth* of 'honesty, punctuality, industry and frugality' and so on, but has a great deal to do with the *appearance* of credit-worthiness. Once this end has been achieved any extended display of virtue is pointless:

> A logical deduction from this would be that where, for instance, the *appearance* of honesty serves the same purpose [i.e. to gain credit] that would suffice, and an unnecessary surplus of this virtue would evidently appear to Franklin's eyes as unproductive waste. (Weber 1976, p.5)

Similarly, Weber acknowledges that the original religious basis of the capitalistic 'ethic' had not only been set aside but may have come to be seen as a hindrance to economic practice:

> In fact [the capitalist system] no longer needs the support of any religious forces, and feels the attempts of religion to influence economic life, in so far as they can still be felt at all, to be as much *an unjustified interference* as its regulation by the state. *In such circumstances man's commercial and social interests tend to*

determine their opinions and attitudes. (Weber 1976, p.72, emphasis added)

On the second point of criticism - that the principles which underpinned the Protestant ideology of work are largely associated with property-owning bourgeois entrepreneurs - a number of points can be made. In the first place, considerable caution is needed in attributing the scholarly, theological and intellectually elite ideas discussed above to the lay population as a whole. To a large extent, the perceived legitimacy of the capitalistic organization of work and apparent acceptance of the principles of value, conduct and limitation associated with it, may have arisen less on the basis of adherence to a system of religious and spiritual beliefs than through the pressure of primary material necessity. Looking again at the examples discussed in the previous chapter, there is no doubt that in medieval society, the ideas of St Augustine, Thomas Aquinas and others may well have penetrated into the consciousness of lay individuals, and that the monastic orders did provide a practical example of appropriate daily conduct. Similarly as Anderson points out, during the medieval period: 'The Church, which in Late Antiquity had always been directly integrated into the machinery of the imperial State, and subordinated to it, now became an eminently autonomous institution within the feudal polity' (Anderson 1974, p.152). In addition, the magnificent architectural and technical achievements represented by church buildings provides ample material 'evidence' of the power of religious institutions during this period. Despite this, it can be suggested that for the average peasant in feudal society, the teaching of the Church may have had very little impact on their own understanding of reality, and in the present context, upon the purpose and meaning of work. It can be argued in other words, that in the face of physical danger, disease and starvation the majority of the population would have had neither the time nor inclination to participate in relatively abstract analyses of the meaning and purpose of work.[13]

Space precludes an adequate analysis of the realities of peasant existence within medieval society.[14] Two examples can however be given. Firstly, as Miller and Hatcher point out, the average peasant or villain was primarily motivated to work for simple existential reasons:

> The peasant's prime endeavour was, if not to achieve self-sufficiency, at least to supply himself with the main necessities of life from his own land.... The primary motive of peasant farming [was] an enterprise directed towards the self-supply of the family group. (Miller and Hatcher 1978, pp.161-4)

Secondly, 'social, economic, political, even legal relations were rooted in personal dependence' (Miller and Hatcher 1978, p.x.); a structure of interdependence which extended into the economic sphere since 'services and obligations were also based on the giving and receiving of land, so that the 'man's dependence on his lord was reinforced by the fact that, in relation to that lord, he was also a dependent tenant' (Miller and Hatcher 1978, p.x).[15] Anthony has summarized the impact of this system of essentially *structural dependence* upon the motivation to work:

> The network of obligations, rights, and protections ran through the whole society. The economic relationships were such as to stress *not effort or zeal or initiative, but the simple performance of obligations*. Work was necessary in order to ensure the survival of the family, and as a kind of tax due to the lord. There could be little point in working harder or more productively because, as the market economy was rudimentary, there would be nothing to do with the surplus. The taskmaster was, as is always the case with those who work on the land, not so much a man as nature itself; what was done had to be done according to a rhythm dictated by the natural cycle. (Anthony 1977, p.30)

Returning to the sixteenth and seventeenth century example, Weber's account is a least to some extent dependent upon a similar tendency to attribute the aspirations and life chances of the educated entrepreneur to the population as a whole. Throughout his account attention is focused almost exclusively on the attitudes and motivations of the upwardly mobile entrepreneur, whilst an analysis of the position of the undifferentiated mass of the working classes is largely absent. Aside from the fact that at least during the late eighteenth and early nineteenth centuries, Methodism rather than Protestantism had become one of the dominant belief-systems of the propertyless masses,[16] the assumption seems to be that these workers more or less adhere to the same beliefs and interpretations of their bourgeois employers; that they too perceive of their work as a duty and an obligation. Weber comments for example: 'The treatment of labour as a calling became as characteristic of the modern worker as the corresponding attitude towards acquisition of the businessman' (Weber 1976, p.179), and that: 'The power of religious asceticism provided [the bourgeois business man] with sober, conscientious, and unusually industrious workmen, who clung to their work as to a life purpose willed by God' (Weber 1976, p.177). However, in his analysis of the use of piece-rates Weber seems to contradict himself by concluding that: 'A man does not "by nature" wish to earn more and more money, but simply to live as he is accustomed to live and to earn as much money as is necessary for that purpose' (Weber 1976, p.60).[17] This predisposition towards *satisfaction* rather than *accumulation* presents a distinct problem to the progress of capitalism: 'Whenever modern capitalism has begun its work of increasing the productivity of human labour by increasing its intensity it has encountered the immensely stubborn resistance of this leading trait of pre-capitalist labour' (Weber 1976, p.60).[18] This reference to 'pre-capitalist labour' implies that the modern or 'post'-capitalist worker has experienced a transformation in his creative and moral consciousness in response to the demands of modern economic practice. Significantly however, the explanation which Weber gives of this process of transformation, a transformation which is necessary for the continued participation of the worker, is not framed in terms of intellectual or moral incorporation, but in terms of *material necessity*:

> People must be available who are not only legally in a position to do so but are also economically compelled to sell their labour on the market without restrictions. Only where in consequence of the existence of workers who in the formal sense voluntarily, *but actually under the compulsion of hunger,* offer themselves to work for a wage, can the costs of production be unambiguously determined in advance. (Weber 1983, p.110, emphasis added)[19]

In the context of such evident material compulsion, it seems unlikely that the majority of the working population of this period would have seen work primarily as a form of religious devotion in a calling or as a means of extolling the virtues of bourgeois economic conduct. It is more likely that work would have been seen as a strictly *necessary* activity which must be carried out in order to obtain even the most basic level of physiological survival. Nor indeed are the pressures of this evident structural necessity limited to the experiences of the propertyless mass. As Weber notes: 'In a wholly capitalistic order of society, an individual capitalistic enterprise which does not take advantage of its opportunities for profit-making would be doomed to extinction' (Weber 1976, p.17). It would seem in other words, that under some circumstances at least, spiritual salvation may not have been a substitute for basic necessities and capital accumulation.

Part Three - Discussion

Focusing on the conceptual aspect of the work paradigm, and taking the discussion in this and the previous chapter together, a relatively consistent pattern of development can be seen in the formation of work-ethics and concepts of work. The main features of these developments can be summarized using the principles of justification relating to perceptions of purpose and value, acceptable limits, and appropriate conduct outlined above.

Firstly, with regard to the perception of the overall meaning and purpose of work, it has been shown that within perspectives which see 'work' as primarily ordained by God, the perception of work has passed through a number of stages: firstly being seen as a *punishment*, secondly as an *obligation*, and finally as a *duty*. As the influence of this underlying belief-system declined through processes of secularisation, reference to supra-human aims and justifications gave way to more directly *self-justifying* perception, wherein work was seen as a demonstration of *human potential* rather than as a reflection of *divine will*. This transition was accompanied by a decline in the perceived dependence upon a hierarchy of beliefs and values sanctioned by the assumption of divine will at its apex, in favour of a much more *instrumental* interpretation of the meaning and purpose of work. By the eighteenth century, the view that work forms an essential part of an overall 'cosmic synthesis' had been displaced by a more modern view of work as largely *independent and self-determined* activity carried out by *individuals*.

The displacement of divine authority by 'natural' and legal authority, was accompanied by the more general separation which took place between the affairs of the body and of the spirit, a development which runs parallel with the more general separation of the institutions of the Church from those of the State. In discussing moral attitudes during the Industrial Revolution Tawney suggests for example:

> It was not that there was any relapse into abnormal inhumanity. It was that the very idea that the Church possessed an independent standard of values to which social institutions were amenable had been abandoned. The surrender had been made long before the battle began. The spiritual blindness which made possible the general acquiescence in the horrors of the early factory system was not a novelty, but the habit of a century. (Tawney 1960, p.193)

With regard to the attribution of worth and value to work and its products, considerable changes have also taken place. In classical and medieval society, general attributions of worth and value, and decisions as to the relative value of particular types of work, were largely resolved in terms of the immediately recognisable and concrete dominance of use-values over exchange-values. Towards the end of the medieval period however, a reversal of this process of assessment took place as rapidly expanding internal and external markets led to the development of new mechanisms of trade and exchange. A central feature of these new mechanisms was the actual and perceptual separation which began to emerge between the production and consumption of commodities, a separation which tended to undermine the attribution of the value of commodities in terms of their *usefulness* in favour of their value within the process of *exchange*. The displacement of use-values by exchange-values also had a profound impact upon the perceived *limits* of work, since the ends to which work was directed, and thus decisions as to whether sufficient work had been done, could no longer be determined in terms of the satisfaction of immediate needs. An increasingly fluid and abstract concept of worth and value in other words, had undermined the earlier and relatively concrete assessment of how much work was *necessary*, by developing the idea that if the accumulation of exchange values was potentially limitless, then so too was the amount of work that needed to be done. In his well known description of the activities of the putter-out, Weber emphasizes how the displacement of use-values by exchange-values, and of sufficiency by limitless potential played a central role in the transcendence of 'traditional', 'parasitical' or 'opportunist' capitalism, by 'modern' 'rational' capitalism.[20] Despite the fact that in earlier forms of capitalism 'the form of the organization was in every respect capitalistic' involving the 'use of capital' and 'rational book-keeping', the enterprise remained traditional since the business man was content to lead his life at a relatively relaxed pace, setting aside any surplus profit he might make to ensure a leisurely retirement. The modern entrepreneurial businessman on the other hand, rejected these notions of comfort and sufficiency in favour of continuous accumulation:

> The old leisurely and comfortable attitude towards life gave way to a hard frugality in which some participated and came to the top, because they did not wish to consume but to earn, while others who wished to keep on with the old ways were forced to curtail their consumption. (Weber 1976, p.68)

For the entrepreneurial businessman of the eighteenth century therefore, the purpose and motivation of work was seen as being less concerned with local production for the satisfaction of immediate needs, than with the desire to expand the enterprise in a much more universal and limitless way. Consequently, notions of 'necessity', 'satisfaction' and 'moderation' were displaced by the calculation of supply and demand, prices and wages, and the management of liquid capital; a quest which for the fortunate credit-worthy minority, could be seen as virtually limitless.

The emergence of these new principles in the attribution of meaning and value, of acceptable limits, and of appropriate conduct within the new work paradigm of modern capitalism, also required some re-evaluation of the basis of authority against which these principles could be seen to be *legitimate*. As noted above, three basic forms of legitimate authority were accepted during the classical and medieval period: God, Natural Law, and Human or Positive Law. So for example, in Roman society, the difficulties of reconciling the practices of slavery with the notion of the fundamental equality of men, were partly solved through the implementation of a three-tier legal structure. During the medieval period, difficulties over the legitimacy of accumulated wealth and upward social mobility were largely mitigated by invoking notions of sufficiency, moderation and charity. By the turn of the seventeenth century, the accumulation of wealth increasingly came to be seen as wholly acceptable, as long as the practices which gave rise to it *fell within the Law*. In terms of the practicalities of daily economic conduct, appeals to 'higher authority' become more or less redundant since they no longer represented a source of meaningful coercive authority. As Tawney notes:

> The process by which natural justice, imperfectly embodied in positive law, was replaced as the source of authority by positive law which might or might not be the expression of natural justice, had its analogy in the rejection by social theory of the whole conception of an objective standard of economic equity. The law of nature had been invoked by medieval writers as a moral restraint upon economic self-interest. By the seventeenth century a significant revolution had taken place. "Nature" had come to connote, not divine ordinance, but human appetites, and natural rights were invoked by the individualism of the age as a reason why self-interest should be given free play. (Tawney 1960, pp.179-80)

This adoption of the Law as the fundamental source of authority in society is crucially important, since as long as a particular type and organization of work can be shown to be lawful, then that activity is for all practical purposes legitimate. The criterion of legality in other words, tends to displace all other criteria in assessing the legitimacy of a particular form of economic practice. The implications of this general 'lawful equals legitimate' framework become even more profound, when the criteria applied to the particular activities which take place within it are conducted in accordance with the principles of economic expediency described above. Once the justification of a particular form of economic practice is framed in terms of whether or not that activity fulfils these criteria, then these criteria tend to displace all other criteria for assessing whether that activity is necessary and thus justified. To a large extent, the justification of economic conduct *in terms of whether it is economically expedient*, and the attribution of legitimacy to that activity *in terms of whether it is lawful* can be seen as two of the most important characteristics of the work paradigm of modern capitalism. Weber repeatedly emphasizes this point: 'For modern rational capitalism has need, not only of the technical means of production, but of a calculable legal system and of administration in terms of formal rules' (Weber 1976, p.25); Capitalism requires a law 'which can be counted upon, like a machine; ritualistic-religious and magical considerations must be excluded' (Weber 1983, p.152). It is evident that the development of capitalism has been accompanied by an enormous expansion in those aspects of legal practice which relate specifically to the conduct of economic practice. This expansion corresponds to the increased complexity of these practices and the particular organization of work associated with them. In addition, the acceptance of limitless accumulation as the most creditable end to which productive activities are the means, has stimulated the development of a wide range of institutions which are primarily concerned with administering economic practice in accordance with the priorities of self-sufficiency, independence and individualism noted above. To this extent, notions of neighbourliness, Christian conduct and sufficiency are no longer expected nor required either to excuse wealth or to mitigate it. In their analysis of the 'financial revolution' which occurred in the UK during the late-1980s for example, Livingstone and Morison confirm that this trend has continued. They argue that 'a national reaction to the emerging world economy and the internationalization of financial markets', and attempts 'to counter the correlative demand for effective international surveillance in order to maintain investor confidence', have been followed by 'structural, jurisdictional and regulatory revision in order to constrain the primary change within acceptable parameters. Stability and certainty are thereby reinforced, without which financial markets cannot function' (Livingstone and Morison 1990, pp.47-8).

Returning then, to the question of whether conceptual or practical phenomena play a leading role in the development of work paradigms, a number of conclusions can be drawn. In the first place, the above discussion has shown that perceptions of work and the principles of justification applied to them, are intimately bound up with, and thus reflect, *practical changes in the organization of work*. The transition from feudal to early and then modern capitalism was accompanied by the emergence of a particularly coherent belief system, a defining characteristic of which was the Protestant work-ethic. Although this work-ethic contained, at least in its original religious formulation, a set of terms of reference which sought to transcend the earthly world of work with the promise of heavenly salvation, it is questionable whether this work-ethic would have been anything like as influential as it was but for the fact that it was so much in step with developments in economic practice. The power of this work-ethic did not stem from its intrinsic ethical virtues, but from the fact that a particular method of work organization had emerged to which it could be applied.

In the second place, it has been shown that once a particular organization of work has become established, the ideas and aspirations which were instrumental in its development *continue to play* a key role in maintaining the perceived justification for, and legitimacy of, that form of work. To this extent, the conceptual aspect of the work paradigm, and particularly the work-ethic it contains, may, if it has been successful in the past, help to shape future developments in the organization of work. This tends to confirm the point made in chapter four, that ideas associated with a particular organization of work may become quite deeply embedded not only within the practical organization of work itself, but also within the justificatory function of the work-ethic. The persistence of the Protestant work-ethic into the twentieth century for example, is a clear example of the potential longevity of a work-ethic. The fact that for us, this work-ethic has very little practical value in the sense that business practice in general, and the productive process in particular, have developed far beyond what was possible during the early modern period, indicates that its influence is very much confined to the realms of justification and legitimation rather than to the realms of day-to-day working. We *know about* the Protestant work-ethic, and many of us can recite some of its basic tenets of behaviour and conduct, but this does not mean that *we act* in accordance with it. A likely explanation of this longevity, relates to the point that particular recourse is made to work-ethics during periods of rapid change and transition in the labour process. On any measure the transition from modern to industrial capitalism during the nineteenth and twentieth centuries, has certainly been an era of particularly rapid transition. If the work-ethic does function as a bridge between one mode of working and another, then we should not be surprised that the Protestant work-ethic has been relied upon so persistently throughout this period. The increasingly abstract and gernalized way in which this work-ethic is articulated, is a measure of the extent to which the majority of the population may have become increasingly unwilling to accept the validity of a particular organization of work. During the late-nineteenth and early-twentieth centuries for example, the work-ethics of socialism and communism posed a considerable challenge to the competitive individualist belief system of which the Protestant work-ethic was a constituent part. These challenges were certainly fuelled by the prospect of alternative ways of working offered by technological change. The longevity of the Protestant work-ethic then, can be seen as a reflection of the increasing tempo of the 'battle of ideas' about work. Paradoxically, if these challenges had not materialised in the way that they did, then this work-ethic might have been forgotten a long time ago.

This draws attention to a third important point, that the emergence and efficacy of a particular organization of work not only depends upon the development of a perception of work which is *appropriate or sympathetic* to it, but also that this perception must be acknowledged and to some extent shared by the individuals who participate in it. It should not be assumed however, either that this mutual perception is held by *all* individuals in society, or that it derives solely from the wholehearted agreement or assimilation of the various idea-elements of which a particular concept of work is based. This brings us back to the issue of the extent to which a particular work-ethic is shared by the majority of the population. At one level, it could be argued that everyone in the early modern period embraced the Protestant work-ethic because is was the Protestant work-ethic which provided the *raison d'etre* and *modus operandi* for modern capitalism. Since we already know however, that it is highly unlikely that any belief system can claim to have such a universal hold over a particular population, the explanation for such a sense of shared recognition has to be sought elsewhere. From the analysis in this and the previous chapter, it seems most probable that apparent consensus with regard to a particular concept of work, stems from the fact that access to necessary resources *can only be obtained by participating in the organization of work as currently manifest*. It may appear that everyone believes in the Protestant work-ethic, in essence what we actually hold in common are the principles of conduct which these beliefs are used to sanction; principles which have a great deal more to do with the day-to-day business of earning a living than they do with gaining spiritual salvation.

Fourthly, this discussion has also illustrated the way in which a particular work-ethic is or is not authentic in the sense that the ideas and beliefs it puts forward do or do not accurately reflect both the expectations which people have of work, and whether in practical terms, they are conducive to the effective operation of the work paradigm as a whole. If the work-ethic fails to provide such a justification, or if this justification is made on grounds which have little or nothing to do with the practicalities of work, then it can be described as inauthentic and potentially ideological. With regard to the Protestant work-ethic, from the point of view of the entrepreneurial businessman of the early modern period, this work-ethic was authentic as it did accurately reflect the business practices of the time. From the point of view of the labouring classes more generally however, it is much more difficult to distinguish such a high degree of apparent authenticity since the benefits of early-capitalist working practice did not accrue equally to all individuals in society. As we move through the nineteenth and into the twentieth century, it can be suggested that as these inequalities not only were, but more significantly, were *seen to be* growing wider and wider, this authenticity began to weaken. Certainly by the time of the depression during the 1930s, it seems likely that any remaining authenticity had finally decayed. From this point on, a strong case can be made for arguing that the Protestant work-ethic had not only become inauthentic because of the increasing distance between the ideas and beliefs it put forward and the practical reality of automated machine manufacture, but that it had also become ideological because its remaining advocates were using it solely out of self-interest. Although it must be acknowledged that all individuals are prone to making inauthentic claims through the work-ethic, and that not all ideas about work are necessarily ideological, the Protestant work-ethic has become a particularly clear example of one that is. It is inconceivable that the disproportionately advantaged minority would have persevered so doggedly with it, if it had not been in their best interests so to do.

Finally, much of this discussion alerts us to the fact that a new or modified work-ethic only emerges when the material conditions upon which it depends have become available. Work-ethics in other words, only have tangible meaning in relation to what is practically possible. In view of the above discussion, the transition from a 'virtual' or newly emerging work-ethic into one which is effective in the concrete world of work, depends upon the willingness of the majority of the population to adopt it for practical purposes. To this extent, although 'technical' developments in the labour process determine the general direction of development of the work paradigm, the degree to which this potential can be realized, and the specific form that it takes will, *at least in part* be determined by the availability of an appropriate and popularly accepted concept of work. Whilst heeding Weber's warning against proposing an overtly 'one-sided materialist interpretation of culture and history' (Weber 1976, p.183), we can also agree with Marshall that: 'Any particular structure and pattern of economic conduct is - at least in part - a function of a number of objective circumstances and is therefore no mere application of a consistent set of principles which the capitalist brings to the transaction at the outset' (Marshall 1982, p.115).

Notes

1. See for example: George, C.H. and George, K. 1958 and Eisenstadt 1968.

2. See for example: Poggi 1983; Buss 1985; Keating 1987, and Macfarlane 1988.

3. It should also be emphasized that although Weber goes on to develop a detailed analysis of 'modern' capitalism as it developed during the eighteenth and nineteenth centuries (see Weber 1950 and 1968), the discussion in the *Protestant Ethic Thesis* relates to the potential *origins* of 'rational' as opposed to 'traditional' capitalism during the sixteenth to eighteenth centuries. To this extent, and although a number of the characteristics of capitalism distinguished by Weber inform his later work, he is not directly analysing the form and character of capitalism in his own time at the turn of the twentieth century. It is important to recognize this historical gap and not to assume that this characterization of the capitalist ideology of work is as it were, wholly contemporary.

4. This new emphasis upon individual *self-responsibility* represents a particularly significant aspect of transition as it both confirms the decay of the idea of a 'natural order' and also removes the sense of security or belonging which individuals may have felt by being part of that order. Under these new conditions, relative material disadvantage could be attributed to the failings of the individual rather than to the shortcomings of the economic and social structures. Samuel Smiles comments for example: 'It is clear that men must necessarily be the active agents of their own well-being and well-doing; and that, however much the wise and the good may owe to others, they themselves must in the very nature of things be their own best helpers' (Smiles 1958, p.57). Referring to a later period, Soper makes the point that following the Hobbesian view of man as being naturally appetitive, the variable performance of individuals in the market-place could be explained by their lack of humanity: 'Anyone then who falls short of covetousness... falls short of humanity itself' (Soper 1981, p.77).

5. For a detailed discussion of these issues see: Tawney 1960, pp.102-32.

6. Although the present aim is not to show that the economistic criteria of work discussed in chapter two above, derive directly from these principles, it will be seen that a degree of correspondence does exist between the two.

7. For Smiles, idleness is fraught with difficulties. He suggests that one of the uses of 'steady employment' is that: 'it keeps one out of mischief, for truly an idle brain is the devil's workshop, and a lazy man the devil's bolster. To be idle... is to be empty; and when the doors of the imagination are opened, temptation finds a ready access, and evil thoughts come trooping in'. (Smiles 1958, p.270).

8. In the context of the development of concepts of work, this principle is particularly important as the 'abstract' multiplication of capital comes to be seen in similar terms to the 'real' generation of productive outcomes by direct human action. The consequences of this perceptual shift within the contemporary work paradigm are discussed in the final chapter.

9. Macpherson adds: 'The possessive market society then... is a society in which men who want more may, and do, continually seek to transfer to themselves some of the power of others, in such a way as to compel everyone to compete for more power, and all this by peaceable and legal methods which do not destroy the society by open force.' (Macpherson 1962, p.59)

10. It should be noted that Weber uses the term 'rationality' in a number of different contexts and the precise meaning of the term thus alters accordingly. For a discussion of this variable usage see Andreski's introduction to Weber 1983, and Andreski 1985.

11. Weber notes for example that: 'The peculiar modern Western form of capitalism has been, at first sight, strongly influenced by the development of technical possibilities. Its rationality is to-day essentially dependent on the calculability of the most important technical factors. But this means fundamentally that it is dependent on the peculiarities of modern science, especially the natural sciences based on mathematics and exact and rational experiment.' (Weber 1976, p.24) Tawney makes a similar point: 'The exact analysis of natural conditions, the calculations of forces and strains, the reduction of the complex to the operation of simple, constant, and measurable forces, was the natural bias of an age interested primarily in mathematics and physics.' (Tawney 1960, p.249)

12. On this point Eisenstadt refers to the 'transformative capacity' of religion. He defines this as: 'The capacity of religion to legitimise, in religious or ideological terms, the development of new motivations, activities and institutions *which were not encompassed by their original impulses and views*' (Eisenstadt, 1968, p.10, emphasis added). In a similar vein, Gramsci suggests that in representing 'an historical continuity uninterrupted even by the most complicated and radical changes in political and social forms' and by 'putting themselves forward as autonomous and independent of the dominant social group', the 'traditional' intellectuals play a leading role in maintaining and embellishing the prevailing belief system. (Gramsci 1971, p.7). For a full discussion of this influence, see Ransome 1992, chapter 7.

13. Against this view, it can of course be argued that it was precisely because of this imminent jeopardy that individuals sought comfort in the expectation of spiritual salvation after death. Aside from the fact that it is very difficult to assess the extent to which this may have been so, it was certainly the case that such beliefs did not hinder the interests of the ruling classes or the Church itself.

14. For such an analysis see: Anderson 1974; Holmes 1980; Jarrett 1968, and Miller and Hatcher 1978.

15. On the development of this system of obligations and 'rights', Anderson has written: 'It was the epoch of Charlemagne himself which ushered in the critical synthesis between donations of land and bonds of service. In the course of the later 8th century, "vassalage" (personal homage) and "benefice" (grants of land) slowly fused, while in the course of the 9th century "benefice" in its turn became increasingly assimilated to "honour" (public office and jurisdiction). Grants of land by rulers thereby ceased to be gifts, to become conditional tenures, held in exchange for sworn services; and lower administrative positions tended to approximate legally to them.' (Anderson 1974, p.139)

16. Although as Weber notes, Methodism adopted important elements from the Protestant perspective, it nonetheless placed much greater emphasis on the values of pastoral care, sharing, community and education. For example in 'The Rules of the United Societies', published in 1743, John Wesley suggests that: 'All who continue in these societies should continue to evidence their desire of salvation... by doing good, by being in every kind merciful after their power; as they have opportunities, doing good of every possible sort, and as far as is possible, to all men: to their bodies, of the ability which God giveth, by giving food to the hungry, by clothing the naked, by visiting or helping them that are sick, or in prison; to their souls by instructing, reproving, or exhorting all they have any intercourse with.' (Wesley 1964. p.179) For a discussion of this influence see Thompson, E.P. 1963, chaps. 2, 3 and 11.

17. Engels paints a similar if somewhat more romanticised picture: 'Before the introduction of machinery... the workers vegetated throughout a passably comfortable existence, leading a righteous and

peaceful life in all piety and probity; and their material position was far better than that of their successors. They did not need to overwork; they did no more than they chose to do, and yet earned what they needed.' (Engels 1973, p.41)

18. Andrew Ure comments for example that: 'The factory operative, little versant in the great operations of political economy, currency, and trade, and activated too often by an invidious feeling towards the capitalist who animates his otherwise torpid talents, is easily persuaded by artful demagogues, that his sacrifice of time and skill is beyond the proportion of his recompense, or that fewer hours of industry would be an ample equivalent for his wages.' (Ure 1967, p.279) See also: Thompson, E.P. 1963, p.392, and Tawney 1960, p.270.

19. On this point Marx notes: 'For wages the lowest and the only necessary rate is that required for the subsistence of the worker during work and enough extra to support a family and prevent the race of workers from dying out. According to Smith, the normal wage is the lowest which is compatible with common humanity, i.e. with a bestial existence.' (Marx 1975, p.283; Adam Smith, *The Wealth of Nations*, vol.1, p.61)

20. This distinction is important to Weber's wider analysis as he seeks to show that from a historical perspective business enterprises may be capitalist in *form* but traditional in *spirit*: 'To be sure the capitalistic form of an enterprise and the spirit in which it is run generally stand in some sort of relationship of adequacy to each other, but not in one of necessary interdependence.' (Weber 1976, p.64)

7 The work paradigm of the late-twentieth century: changes in the practice of work

Having looked at two examples of past work paradigms, and particularly at their conceptual aspects, the task of this and the following chapter is to see how the analytical strategy developed in the first part of the book helps us understand the internal dynamics of the work paradigm of the late-twentieth century. This chapter looks at the practical aspect of this paradigm, and the following chapter at its conceptual aspect. Taking the United Kingdom as an example of an advanced economy which is currently immersed in the process of economic restructuring and transition, and following the implication developed in the proceeding chapters that changes in the conceptual aspects of work are governed, or are at least intimately connected with, changes in the way in which work is organized in practice, the object is to provide a number of clear illustrations of how the bases upon which the current concept of work has developed and matured are gradually collapsing under the weight of economic change. Whilst acknowledging that these changes may not signify a universal break with the past, in as much as established patterns of working are likely to continue to be an important feature of the future labour process, and that some aspects of our work-concept are fundamental, the thrust of the following argument is that the changes which have emerged cannot simply be regarded as temporary and gradual developments of advanced capitalistic economic practice. Rather, and given the scope of their present impact, and perhaps more importantly, of their potential future impact, these changes point quite clearly towards an irreversible transition in the organization of work.

This discussion will provide a concrete basis for the analysis in the following chapter, which critically examines the central question of whether the impact of these changes on the contemporary concept of work is sufficiently large as to suggest that a serious rupture has emerged between our conceptions of the meaning and purpose of work and the reality of work in practice. Given that these conceptions provide an important, and arguably indispensable, source of support for the perceived legitimacy of the work paradigm, evidence of such a rupture clearly has important implications for the sustainability of that paradigm.

The chapter divides into two parts. Part one briefly describes a number of key changes which have taken place in overall patterns of working in the UK during the past twenty years or so. These include changes in the distribution of employment, increases in part-time working, changes in the composition of the workforce, and increases in job insecurity and unemployment. The second part of the chapter focuses on a second, and perhaps most significant feature of recent changes, namely those associated with the emergence of the new 'technological paradigm' of 'flexibility'. The chapter concludes with a discussion of how a number of contributions to the flexibility debate highlight the importance of 'consent' as an essential element in establishing and maintaining the hegemony of a particular work paradigm. Although specific reference to a concept of work or work-ethic is largely absent from these analyses, it can be argued that people's perceptions and expectations of work have to be satisfied if the idea of consent is to have any real meaning.

Part One - Patterns of working

In historical perspective, it can be argued that the organization of work in the first industrialized societies progressed in a fairly steady way from early machine manufacture, through various higher stages of mechanization and automation, culminating in the emergence of 'mature' mass production-oriented manufacturing economies during the 1950s and 1960s. In combination with the expansion of public-sector employment in health, education and social security, a relatively settled pattern of employment had developed. Typically, work was perceived to be, and to all intents and purposes actually was, a full-time and life-long affair. Moreover, although a significant minority of women held full-time and part-time jobs, full-time life-long employment was seen to be a largely male preserve. Put crudely, for the majority of men, the expectation was that on leaving formal education at the age of sixteen, they would enter employment, probably in the locality where they had grown up, and would stay there until they retired. For the majority of women, the expectation was that they might enter employment for a period of time before entering married life. As the empirical evidence referred to in chapter three above has shown, this participation in the formal labour process was based on the premise that through employment, the individual would gain access to the resources he or she needed in order to satisfy their most pressing material and psychological needs. To the extent that patterns of employment were relatively stable, it is not unreasonable to assume that the sense of security people derived from their involvement in the mechanisms of employment also included a general understanding that this relative stability would continue more or less indefinitely. Although it is difficult to quantify in concrete empirical terms, we can infer that *the need to believe* that stability would be maintained, was in itself a key expectation of work; a need moreover, which made an essential contribution to the *perceived legitimacy* of the current organization of work.

It is now accepted that during the 1970s and throughout the 1980s, stability within the mechanisms of employment began to decay. In practical terms, the effect of this breakdown was to generate significant changes both in patterns of employment and in methods of working. Looking briefly at changes in the former during the last twenty years in the UK, three distinct developments are illustrative of the changes which have been taking place in overall patterns of working. These can be categorized in terms of changes in the distribution of employment, increases in part-time working, changes in the composition of the workforce, and increasing job insecurity and unemployment.[1]

The distribution of employment

Firstly, there has been a major decline in the proportion of the workforce employed in manufacturing industries, while the portion employed in non-manufacturing has increased significantly. In the UK for example, this amounted to a decline of nearly 3 million jobs from 8.07 million in 1971 to 5.24 million in 1989, while those in service industries rose by over 4 million from 11.6 million to 15.7 million during the same period. Expressed as a percentage of those in employment, this represented a fall in the proportion of those employed in manufacturing from 36.4 per cent to 23 per cent, and a rise in the proportion employed in services from 52.5 per cent to 69 per cent.[2] Similar changes in the aggregate distribution of employment between agriculture, industry and services have taken place in each of the larger EC countries between 1978 and 1989.[3]

Secondly, there has been a steady and accelerating increase in part-time working. Between 1981 and 1989 for example, of the overall increase of nearly 1 million jobs (from 21.8 million to 22.8 million), over 930,000 was accounted for by increases in part-time jobs compared with an increase of only 33,000 in full-time jobs.[4] During this period, the proportion of employees accounted for by men in full-time employment declined by 5 per cent (from 53.9 per cent to 48.9 per cent), while the proportion accounted for by full-time women employees increased by nearly 2 per cent (from 25.0 per cent to 26.9 per cent). The proportions accounted for by men and women working part-time have increased by 0.8 per cent and 2.3 per cent respectively. While increases in part-time working have had an impact across all industries, this has been particularly so in the service sector, where just under half of the total increase of 2.25 million jobs between 1981 and 1989 was accounted for by increases in part-time jobs. For men, full- and part-time employment in this sector increased by 403,000 and 227,00 respectively, while the number of women employed full- and part-time increased substantially by 790,000 and 800,000. The effect of these developments on the proportions of full- and part-time employment in service industries, was that while the proportion accounted for by men working full-time fell by 3.4 per cent there was a slight but steady increase of 0.8 per cent in the proportion working part-time. The proportions of women employed full- and part-time both increased by 1 per cent and 1.6 per cent respectively, representing a total gain of over 1.5 million full- and part-time jobs.[5]

Looking finally at the distribution of increases in women's employment in the service sector between 1981 and 1989, the pattern of change has followed the expansion of employment in this sector in both public and private services. Total female employment in the largest sectors of medical and health care, and education for example, increased dramatically by 33.4 per cent (an increase of over 162,000) and 28.4 per cent (an increase of over 146,000) respectively, while total employment in retail distribution, hotels and catering, business services and 'other services' increased by 17 per cent, 50 per cent, 130 per cent and 105 per cent respectively (a combined increase of 650,000 jobs). Increases in part-time employment have been even more dramatic than increases in full-time employment. In medical and health care, and retail distribution for example, part-time employment increased by 25 per cent and 19 per cent representing increases of over 112,000 and 137,000 jobs respectively.[6]

The composition of the workforce

A second important set of trends relate to changes in the composition of the workforce itself, most notably the dramatic increase in the number of women who are formerly employed in the economy. Between 1971 and 1991 for example, the total population aged between 15 and 64 for men, and between 15 and 59 for women increased by 7.9 per cent, from 33.3 million to nearly 36 million. Increases for both men and women of working age rose by almost identical amounts at 7.9 per cent and 7.85 per cent respectively.[7] Although this increase in the size of the population of 'working age' is reflected in an increase in the size of the actual workforce from 26.6 million in 1979 to 28.5 million in 1989, almost all of this rise has been accounted for by an increase of 1.8 million in the number of women who are 'economically active', compared with an increase of only 100,000 for men. These trends are also reflected in the fact that the proportion of the workforce accounted for by women has increased from 40 per cent in 1979 to 42.8 per cent in 1989.[8] Working on the basis that between 1971 and 1991 the actual workforce averaged around 76 per cent of the population of working age, and referring to population predictions up to the year 2020, we can estimate that the actual UK workforce will be around 28.9 million in 2001, 29.7 million in 2010, and 29.6 million in 2020. If the proportion of the workforce accounted for by women continues to increase at an average rate of 2.8 per cent as it did between 1979 and 1989, it can be expected that the proportion of the workforce accounted for by women will rise to 45.6 per cent by 2001, to 48.4 per cent by 2010, and to over 50 per cent by 2020. If current trends continue, it can be expected that perhaps 7 of these 15 million female employees will be working part time.[9] Population predictions also provide important information on likely changes in the composition of the workforce in terms of age. Combining data on the distribution of age groups with expected population trends into the next century, the size of the 16 to 24 age group will continue to fall until 2000 before rising again up to 2010. Over time, this trend will be reflected in a dramatic fall in the number of 25 to 39 year olds up to 2010 and of 40 to 54 year olds up to the year 2020. From around 1995 onwards, the proportion of the workforce accounted for by those aged between 55 and 64 will rise steeply by nearly 5 per cent up to 2000, over 18 per cent up to 2010, and over 10 per cent up to the year 2020. Over time therefore, the average age of the UK workforce is increasing.[10] These projections also alert us to the fact that over the next twenty years or so, the proportion of the total population who are dependent for income upon those active in the workforce, will continue to rise.

Increasing job insecurity

A third trend, relates to the persistent and rising incidence of job insecurity and unemployment. This trend is particularly important, since as noted above, a key aspect of perceptions of the legitimacy of the labour process amongst the population is based upon the expectation that relatively stable and dependable opportunities for employment are available. Although we can acknowledge that many members of the workforce have always had to contend with fluctuations in the demand for employment, and that because we are almost exclusively dependent on employment for our income, we have developed a particularly resilient capacity for believing employment prospects will improve, it can be argued that for many, this resilience is reaching breaking point as the facts of mass unemployment press ever more heavily upon us. Fluctuations in job prospects are one thing, but the prospect of indefinite unemployment is altogether more serious.

Given the overwhelmingly negative implications of rising unemployment, it is not surprising that much popular and academic debate surrounds the topic, ranging from political and ideological interpretation to arithmetic questions of how data on unemployment are gathered. Much effort has also been expended on understanding the micro- and macroeconomic causes of unemployment, much of it intended to make good some of the damage done to people's confidence about their employment prospects - 'we can understand unemployment therefore we can eliminate it'. For present purposes however, the intention is simply to illustrate that whatever interpretation one chooses to apply, and however sophisticated the level of statistical manipulation, there is no question that job insecurity and unemployment are rising, that these are now permanent rather than temporary trends which affect in real material and psychological terms an increasing majority of the UK population.

In brief then, rates of unemployment have risen substantially in the larger EC countries since 1970. Although this trend reached a peak between 1983 and 1987 before falling slightly in 1989, it is clear that unemployment rates have remained well above those of the 1970s.[11] In the UK, registered unemployment rose from 0.6 million in 1970 to over 3 million in 1985. Expressed as a percentage of the total workforce, this represents a rise from less than 3 per cent to around 12 per cent. Between

1985 and 1989 both the number and proportion of the unemployed began to decline, before rising again in 1991 to stand at over 2.2 million or 7.9 per cent.[12] By February 1993, registered unemployment had once again exceeded the 3 million mark.

Comparing the proportions of the unemployed accounted for by men and women, male unemployment has been consistently higher than female unemployment, the former rising from 1.88 per cent in 1970 to 6.02 per cent in 1991, and the latter from 0.32 per cent to 1.88 per cent over the same period. Expressed as a percentage of the total unemployed since 1979, the ratio of men to women has been around two-thirds to one-third at 70 per cent 30 per cent respectively. Reflecting the increasing economic activity of women during the 1980s, these proportions have however tended to fluctuate quite closely in response to the buoyancy or otherwise of the economy. In general terms, a pattern is emerging that during the early 1990s, female unemployment has tended to decrease more rapidly that male unemployment. This suggests that although some employers have become increasingly dependent upon the availability of women seeking full- and part-time work, these employment prospects are just as vulnerable to changes in patterns of working including decreases in demand for particular types of employee. It should not be assumed in other words, that a general trend towards part-time employment signifies reliable and stable employment prospects for people working part-time.[13]

Looking at unemployment trends in terms of age, between 1979 and 1991, the proportion of the registered unemployed under 25, fell from 33.5 per cent to 30.1 per cent, while the proportion aged 25 and over rose from 66.5 per cent to nearly 70 per cent. Amongst the under 25's, the proportion accounted for by men rose slightly from 19.3 per cent to 21.2 per cent, while that by women fell quite steeply from 14.2 per cent to just under 9 per cent. Amongst the over 25's, the proportion accounted for by men increased more rapidly than in the younger age-group from 52.3 per cent to 54.7 per cent, while the proportion accounted for by women increased from 14.2 per cent to 15.2 per cent. Since 1979 therefore, there has been an increase in the likelihood of becoming unemployed amongst the over 25's, while unemployment rates amongst the under 25's have fallen by the same amount. In addition, the likelihood of becoming unemployed has become much greater for younger males than for younger females, a trend which is also reflected in the older age group but to a slightly lesser extent. For both men and women in other words, the likelihood of becoming unemployed tends to increase with age, while younger men are more likely to become unemployed than their female contemporaries.[14]

Whilst acknowledging that levels of unemployment may be affected by increases in the number of people seeking employment rather than simply by decreases in the demand for labour, a number of features of current trends strongly suggest that increases in unemployment can only partly be accounted for by fluctuations in the supply of labour. Firstly, unemployment rates have increased more rapidly in relation both to the size of the population of working age, and to the proportion of the workforce who are economically active. Most importantly, *the largest rises* in unemployment occurred during the early to mid-1980s at a time when the size of the workforce increased *less rapidly* than it had done during the previous decade. Between 1981 and 1983 in particular, unemployment rose dramatically by two-and-a-half-times the figure in 1979 to stand at nearly 3 million, while the workforce *actually fell* by 300,000 between 1981 and 1983.[15] This strongly suggests that recent growth in the number and proportion of the workforce who are registered as unemployed cannot be accounted for in terms of cyclical demographic changes, but is a direct result of actual reductions in the demand for labour. Secondly, and confirming this relationship between economic activity and the availability of particular types of work, it has been shown that the likelihood of becoming unemployed is greater for men, and especially for older men than for women. Since a greater proportion of the workforce are concentrated in the 25-54 age group where the risk of unemployment tends to be greater, it seems likely that unemployment amongst the over 25's will continue to rise. In the context of falling employment in manufacturing industries discussed above, this suggests that men are more likely to become unemployed as a direct result of the decline in the number of jobs they have traditionally occupied. This is further confirmed by the fact that part-time employment amongst men in both the manufacturing and service sectors, has increased much less rapidly than it has for women. To the extent therefore, that a larger proportion of the workforce is accounted for by men, it is likely that rates of unemployment amongst men are likely to remain high.

Although absolute unemployment clearly has extremely negative consequences for those affected by it,[16] it is important to recognize that complete loss of employment lies an one end of a much more general phenomenon of job insecurity. Arguably, it is the emergence of this phenomenon into an almost all pervasive feature of the late modern economic period, which marks the transition after the 1970s as something more than simply another temporary 'crisis of capitalism'. Following the comments made above regarding the capacity for individuals to push thoughts of unemployment towards the backs of their minds, a number of features of current employment practice point clearly towards a virtual incorporation of job insecurity into the employment contract itself. Realistically, earlier taken-for-granted assumptions about the reliability and permanence of employment - the idea of a 'job for life' - are being displaced by terms of employment in which the individual accepts that their employment is for a fixed period of time only. This method of organizing employment relationships has developed both in terms of the sub-contracting of particular tasks to smaller specialist firms, and in terms of individual relationships between employer and employee. Where an individual is employed on a part-time, short-term or casual basis by a firm whose business depends on the needs of other businesses, (for example, a cleaning firm contracted to an office block, or a computer software supplier contracted to a manufacturing firm) it is quite evident that although that individual is formally employed, she or he is accepting a very low level of job security, compounded in many cases by the 'insecurity' the employer themselves. Under conditions where these and other forms of short-term contract-based employment relationships are coming to displace the more permanent relationships of the recent past, we can see that some degree of job insecurity is reality which affects an increasing majority of the population.

Taken together, these illustrations of developments in the redistribution of employment, of increases in part-time working, of changes in the composition of the workforce, and of increasing job insecurity and unemployment, clearly point towards a major disruption in established patterns of employment. If the typical expectation of work in the 1960s and 1970s was one of full-time life-long employment, the typical expectation in the 1990s and beyond, is likely to be one of much more temporary periods of employment, formalised around time-limited contracts, distributed amongst a range of employers.

Part Two - Technological change

A second feature of recent changes in the practice of work, and one which has certainly had an important bearing on patterns of working described in part one, is the emergence of what has be labelled a new 'technological paradigm' based on the development and application of microelectronic technologies.[17] This application has not only brought about major changes in patterns of work amongst those who are in work, it has also highlighted the plight of those who are on the fringes of employment or entirely outside it, by bringing to the fore the fundamental problem of trying to accommodate an evident reduction in the demand for formal employment (the demand of employers for employees), within a work paradigm which is based upon the expectation of life-long full-time employment. To a large extent, both the balance within established patterns of work and distribution of employment, and the balance between the availability of particular types of employment and the number of individuals seeking employment, have been profoundly altered by technologically-engendered changes in the practice of work. In some instances these imbalances have become sufficiently acute as to suggest that continued innovation and 'full' employment have become entirely incompatible.[18] In recognizing and acknowledging the accelerating impact of new technologies in working practice, contemporary analyses in labour process theory and the sociology of work more generally, have centred on the question of whether these developments signify that the economic structures of the advanced industrialized societies are passing from the phase of Fordist production based around the earlier paradigm of mechanised and semi-automated mass production, to a new, or at any rate later stage, of post-Fordism, based on the new paradigm of flexible production. Whilst considerable debate continues to revolve around the precise nature of these two stages, and of whether post-Fordism is a distinctively new phase, or simply a later modification of its Fordist forebear,[19] there is no question that these economies have entered an important period of transition, and that the momentum for change is now too firmly established to be disregarded as simply a temporary phenomenon. It will be instructive to look briefly at what the notion of 'flexibility' entails, and at some of the critiques which have been put forward which suggest that although there is evidence of change, a widespread and clearly focused transition towards 'flexibility' is more questionable.

Following Gilbert *et al.*, (1992), the flexibility debate can usefully be seen as involving three distinct but closely related strands. Firstly, and operating at a general and more overtly theoretical level, a number of authors working within what has been labelled 'the regulation school' have proposed that a transition is taking place away from the established patterns of economic organization labelled 'Fordism', toward a 'new' pattern labelled 'post-Fordism'. Secondly, Piore and Sabel (1984) have put forward the idea that at the level of the productive process itself, manufacturing industry is moving away from large-scale mass production of standardised products, towards smaller-scale production of specialized products. Thirdly, and at the level of managerial strategy, it has been argued that employers are deliberately introducing policies aimed at securing a highly skilled 'core' for performing essential tasks, while less skilled tasks are given over to a more casually employed and largely unskilled pool of 'peripheral' employees.[20] We will look at each of these strands in turn.

Fordism and post-Fordism

The regulationist perspective on the transition form Fordism towards post-Fordism (or perhaps more accurately, from Fordist to post-Fordist capitalism)[21] takes as its point of departure the fact that the capitalist mode of production has historically been able to maintain an increasing level of economic growth and relative prosperity despite the fact that it is also subject to periods of crisis. Developing the concepts of a 'regime of accumulation' and 'mode of regulation' to describe the way in which an economic system embraces not only the practicalities of the labour process, but also the economic, social and political institutions which are developed in support of it,[22] regulationists argue that the economic crises of the 1970s signified that the relatively settled methods of production and structural organization of the economy which had allowed for reliable accumulation of capital during the 1950s and 1960s, had come to an end. Since capital accumulation is the driving force of the capitalist enterprise, the avoidance of a more or less fatal decline in economic growth and prosperity, required a thoroughgoing restructuring both of the methods of production, and of the regulatory socio-political institutions and mechanisms which were conducive to these changes:

> Regulation theory characterises the postwar boom in terms of a Fordist regime of accumulation based upon techniques of mass production buttressed by a mode of regulation consisting of mass consumption and the Keynesian welfare state. The theory suggest that in recent years the process of restructuring we have been witnessing is a symptom of the "crisis of Fordism" and the emergence of post-Fordism. (Gilbert *et al.*, 1992, p.3)

Post-Fordism then, is seen as the most recent attempt by the owners of the means of production and their agents, to accommodate changes in those means, whilst at the same time manipulating the socio-political framework in such a way as to renew the process of capital accumulation. If successful, it can be expected that a new period of growth and stability will emerge. Focusing on changes in the means of production, the re-establishment of stability is tied to the transcendence of Fordism, with its reliance upon 'mass production and mass consumption and mass public provision', by post-Fordism which is characterized by:

> Homology between "flexible" production techniques, differentiated and segmented consumption patterns, a restructured welfare state and postmodernist cultural forms. The breakdown of Fordism and the emergence of post-Fordism is conceptualised primarily in terms of a search for greater levels of economic flexibility. (Gilbert *et al.*, 1992, p.3)

In political terms, and in sharp contrast to the Keynesian mode of the Fordist period, where government and state actively intervened in economic management, post-Fordist regulation is characterized by attempts by government to 'deregulate' legal and other constraints on business practices, contracts of employment and working conditions, by attempts to undermine the strength of trade unions, and arguably by increasing (or at least failing to reduce) the pool of employees who can be hired and fired at short notice (the maintenance of a reserve army) thus shifting the balance of power from employee to employer. In social and cultural terms, and again in contrast to the mass consumption and universalised domesticity of Fordism, post-Fordism is characterized by the notion of the sovereign consumer, the emergence of personalised life-styles and the withdrawal of individuals into their private worlds, what could be called the 'privatisation of personal space'.[23]

Flexible specialization

Although the regulationist approach is as much concerned with the broader historical and political dynamics of capitalist transformation and regeneration, as it is with the more immediate practicalities of the labour process, it assumes none the less, that significant changes have taken place in the practical organization of work. What after all, is post-Fordism if not a change in working practice? Given their central significance to the flexibility debate, these practicalities, many of which stem directly from innovations in microelectronic technologies, have been described in some detail. Sabel for example, describes economic transition in terms similar to those noted by the regulationists:

> Stable demand for large numbers of standard products is the cornerstone of Fordism. It makes possible long-term investment in product-specific machines.... Anything that unsettles prospects of manufacturing a certain product in a fixed way and selling it in predictably large numbers for a foreseeable price undermines the propensity to invest in the Fordist strategy.... Many signs suggest that the Fordist model of organization is being challenged by new forms of the division of labour. International competition and overlapping domestic conflicts between produces and consumers, and between workers and capitalists, are driving many large firms out of mass markets for standardised goods. To survive this challenge manufacturers have no choice but to produce more-specialised, higher-quality products. (Sabel 1984, p.194/95)

Within this analysis, the notion of 'flexible specialization' has been central. This model of economic reorganization again draws on the transition from Fordist to post-Fordist methods of production. From the 'flexible specialization' perspective, industrial development is characterized by the emergence of a number of productive techniques which in the first instance tend to co-exist within the economy. Over time however, it is argued that the craft-based techniques of the early industrial period were challenged and then overcome as automated mass production emerged during the twentieth century. During the 1970s however, a stagnation of demand for mass produced goods combined with the development and growing industrial application of highly sophisticated computer-based technologies, signified the displacement of 'rigid' automated mass production by techniques of flexible specialization. In this context, 'flexibility' refers to:

> labour market and labour process restructuring, to increased versatility in design and the greater adaptability of new technology in production. "Specialisation" relates to niche or custom marketing, the apparent end of Fordism, mass production and product standardisation. (Smith, C., 1991, p.139)

Pollert has also summarized the main characteristics of flexible specialization in terms of differences between this and the earlier paradigm of 'inflexible' mass production:

> Mass production... is based on the special-purpose machine, organised on an assembly line, operated by a semi-skilled labour force, producing standardised products for a mass market.... Flexible specialisation is a new form of skilled craft production made

easily adaptable by programmable technology to provide specialised goods which can supply an increasingly fragmented and volatile market. (Pollert (ed.), 1991, p.17)

It should be emphasized, that although the transition towards flexible specialization has been enabled by technological advance - flexibility is a key characteristic of the technology itself - the turn towards flexible specialization is also attributed to changes in the demand for goods in the market. Piore and Sabel have argued for example, that it was the saturation of mass consumer markets during the 1960s and 1970s which provided the impetus for the switch from Fordism to post-Fordism. Sabel notes for example:

> To the extent that consumers demand a particular good in order to distinguish themselves from those who do not have it, the good becomes less appealing as more of it is sold. Consumers will be increasingly willing to pay a premium for a variant of the good whose possession sets them off from the mass; and as the number of variants competing for attention and encouraging further differentiation of tastes increases, it becomes harder and harder to consolidate production of a standard product. (Sabel 1984, p.199)

Inevitably therefore, manufacturers have been obliged to respond by producing more specialized products:

> Specialised production... rests on the idea that, at the outset, customers' wants are vaguely defined and potentially diverse. The presumption is that the customer has no precise need for a particular good.... The job of the innovative firm is to find a technically and economically feasible way of satisfying this inchoate need, thus creating a new product and defining the customer's wants at the same time. (Sabel 1984, p.202)

Looking more closely at the technological dimensions of flexible specialization, three factors can be singled out. In the first place, the introduction of advanced robotics and other types of computer-controlled machinery has made it possible not only to improve the design specification and quality of products, but to produce them more quickly and more cheaply than was possible with traditional Fordist techniques:

> Instead of Fordism's specialised machinery producing standardised products, we now have flexible, all-purpose machinery producing a variety of products.... As a result, the economies of scale of mass production can now be achieved on much smaller runs, whether small

batch engineering products, or clothes, shoes, furniture and even books. (Murray 1989(b), pp.56-57)

Secondly, the assignment of routine information and data processing tasks to computer, has made it possible to displace the rigidly hierarchical and bureaucracy-bound management style of Fordism with much more responsive and fluid forms of lateral communication:

> With the revision of Taylorism, a layer of management has been stripped away. Greater control has allowed the decentralisation of work. Day-to-day autonomy has been given to work groups and plant managers. Teams linking departments horizontally have replaced the rigid verticality of Fordist bureaucracies. (Murray 1989(a), p.46)

Thirdly, in combining flexibility of production with flexibility of organization and control, flexible specialization has also brought about radical changes not only in the co-ordination of activities within an individual firm and between one firm and another, but between producer and retailer:

> Product ranges are modified more quickly, and are more internally diversified than the classic forms of production for mass consumer markets. Modern information systems allow both finer tuning of product flows and mixes in relation to changing and segmented markets, and greater producer influence over consumer demand. (Rustin 1989, p.57)

As an example of the post-Fordist approach, Murray has described the Italian clothing firm Benetton:

> Their clothes are made by 11,500 workers in northern Italy only 1,500 of whom work directly for Benetton. The rest are employed by sub-contractors in factories of 30-50 workers each. The clothes are sold through 2,000 tied retail outlets, all of them franchised. Benetton provide the designs, control material stocks, and orchestrate what is produced according to the computerised daily sales returns which flow back to their Italian headquarters from all parts of Europe. (Murray 1989(b), p.57)

Perhaps the clearest and best known application of flexible specification is found in the motor vehicles industry, where the potential benefits of this level of integration in terms of productivity, quality and product flexibility have been amply demonstrated by the Japanese system of manufacture. As Jones has pointed out, in emphasizing the standardization of components (and therefore of products) to achieve maximum throughput, the Fordist philosophy 'tended to eliminate any opportunity for responsible involvement and initiative [since] it was assumed that the worker would not report on problems, would not repair his own machines and would take no initiative for spotting and correcting faults'. As a consequence: 'Large stocks of parts had to be held between each major production operation so that parts of the system could continue to operate, while problems in other parts of the system were being diagnosed and repaired, and to insulate the system from industrial relations or other problems in the supplier firms.' (Jones 1985, p.139) Not only therefore, did the system have to take account of fluctuations in the supply of components, it also required a large number of production engineers and supervisors to oversee an army of alienated and apparently recalcitrant assembly workers, and had to spend time and resources in checking the quality of the product at the end of the production line.

In contrast, the Japanese approach sought to overcome these difficulties of supply, motivation and quality by introducing the now familiar 'just-in-time' and 'total quality control' systems. The Japanese system improved motivation by making the workforce directly responsible for their own tasks and machines. This increase in individual responsibility also solved the problem of maintaining quality, since defects could be detected and corrected actually during production rather than in retrospect. In addition, problems with fluctuations in the supply of components, and consequently with the problem of stockpiling were resolved by developing much more flexible relationships with materials and parts suppliers:

> The operations of a multi-tiered structure of component suppliers are closely integrated with the final assembler. The interdependence of each link in the supply chain, built up over many years, serves to devolve the organization of the system while at the same time mobilising all the resources of each firm to improve the total system performance. (UNIDO, *Industry and Development Global Report* 1988, p.250)

As a direct consequence of these innovations, Japanese producers have been able both to develop much greater variety within established product ranges, and to introduce entirely new models much more quickly and efficiently than their Western competitors. The UNIDO report suggests for example that the new process 'has reduced the lead time for developing a new model from 5 to 3.5 years, using about one half the number of man-hours in design and engineering. Models are replaced after only four years in Japan, as compared with every eight years elsewhere.' (UNIDO 1988, p.250)[24]

In summary, flexible specialization is seen as a response to the availability of new production methods combined with greater fluidity in likely consumer demand for non-mass produced goods. Given the apparent unsuitability of Fordist techniques for producing such a diverse range of products in limited numbers, a new technological paradigm has emerged based around the techniques of flexible specialization. There is a clear implication within this perspective, that the survival of capitalist enterprises producing consumer goods, will depend upon the extent to which they are able and willing to restructure their organization and production methods around the model of flexible specialization.

Core and periphery

The third strand of debate centres around the issue of whether employers are adopting a deliberate strategy of dividing their operations between a highly-skilled 'core' and a 'periphery' of transiently employed workers. If such a process were taking place, it would clearly have far-reaching implications for many aspects of the organization of work, not least because it could be seen as further confirmation of attempts by capital to 'divide and conquer' the workforce. It also raises complex issues over whether flexible specialization and post-Fordism will lead to a further concentration and upgrading of skills into the hands of an industrial elite, or whether the general level of skill requirements would deteriorate resulting in an increase in the proportion of unsatisfying and alienating jobs.

The core/periphery model can usefully be seen as the workforce dimension of the flexibility debate. The argument runs that if manufacturing firms adopt flexibility, this will inevitably require - and indeed cannot be achieved without - changes in the organization and activities of the workforce itself. Flexible production therefore conjures up the idea of the 'flexible firm':

> The ideal typical flexible firm is one which has attempted to secure three sorts of economic flexibility. First, numerical flexibility: the ability to change the size of the workforce quickly and easily in response to changes in demand. Second, functional flexibility: the ease with which workers can be redeployed to different tasks to meet changes in market demand, technology and company policy; and

third: financial and pay flexibility to facilitate numerical, and especially, functional flexibility. (Gilbert *et al.*, 1992, p.4)

Following Penn (1992 pp.67-8), the ideal type core/periphery model of the flexible firm developed by Atkinson and Meager (1986) takes the form of a core of functionally flexible highly- and multi-skilled workers, surrounded by two or more groups of peripheral workers. The first group is made up of semi- and unskilled workers whose numbers can be increased or decreased to give the firm numerical flexibility. The second peripheral group, is made up of various temporary, part-time, casual and un- or semi-trained workers who can also be acquired and disposed of according to fluctuations in actual and anticipated demand. Beyond these groups of employees, are various categories of workers, not directly employed by the firm, whose services can be hired if needed on a contract basis. The putative adoption of this model is seen as a response by firms and businesses to particular changes and pressures within the economy. These include a combination of generic (and inevitable) factors, such as increasing competition in the market, uncertainty about future prospects, and continuing technological advance, and particular conjunctural factors (which may or may not be permanent) including high unemployment and weak trade unions.

Gough has summarized the likely characteristics of this segmented workforce as follows:

> The core workers use advanced reprogrammable machinery and they can move between tasks. Their production is therefore flexible with respect to product change, thus enabling the short-run production of varied products at relatively low cost. They have secure employment contracts. The peripheral workforce may or may not use advanced machinery, but, at any rate, they tend to be less skilled than the core workers. Their production includes both the "remaining" production of standardised products, and the overflows of production from the core during peaks in demand. Their employment contracts are insecure. (Gough, J., 1992, pp.33-4)

In summary, the core/periphery dimension of the flexibility debate describes the employment consequences of transition towards flexible specialization in firms under conditions of post-Fordism. In its ideal type, the management of such firms would achieve numerical and functional flexibility by concentrating 'quality' employment (in terms of levels of skill, ability to move from one task to another, higher levels of pay and job security) at their core, while 'degraded' or 'down-graded' employment would be dispersed amongst a number of more heteronomous groups of workers either at the margins of the firm itself or outside the firm through contracting-out. The employment of these groups would be characterized by lower levels of skill and pay, and by high levels of job insecurity. Their value to employers rests primarily in their 'willingness' to be available and yet largely 'dispensable'.

Inconclusive evidence of flexibility?

Having outlined the three main dimensions of the flexibility debate, it will be useful to consider briefly what evidence there is that these changes are actually taking place. Taking these three dimensions in reverse order, a number of authors have suggested that it is not at all clear whether firms are actually adapting themselves to the core/periphery model of the flexible firm. Discussing the implication that management can increase flexibility by developing and controlling a core of elite workers for example, Gough has argued that the development of 'transferable' skills within the economy as a whole may make particular firms reluctant to take on the responsibility for training leading to 'underinvestment in training and under-supply of skilled labour':

> This can increase the bargaining power of skilled workers. Thus the highly socialised form of production implied by flexible integration gives workers strong potential points of resistance - in other words, inflexibility for capital. (Gough, J., 1992, p.35)

Similarly, in discussing the employment situation of research and development staff, Whittington has suggested that this group 'on the face of it a classic core group', have seen their prospects diminish rather than increase:

> Demands for different types of flexibility have not been made on discrete employment groups; rather they have been deliberately combined, so that numerical flexibility has reinforced functional flexibility. In practice, managers do not respect Atkinson's boundaries. (Whittington 1991, p.102)

Discussing the suggestion that the consolidation of a skilled core at the electronics firm Lucas would lead to a general improvement in both skills and employer/employee relations, Elger and Fairbrother are less than convinced:

> There was little evidence that the changes in work relations involved any sustained shift towards multiskilled teamworking or more harmonious relations between workers and management, but rather more of greater work pressure associated with increased responsibilities. In this respect, [these findings] also underline persistent diversity and unevenness in the patterns and processes of change. (Elger and Fairbrother 1992, p.105)

Although more decisive evidence has emerged regarding the expansion of an insecurely employed periphery (Pollert suggests for example, that: 'There is clear evidence of the growth of unemployment, and intermittent, non-permanent and vulnerable forms of work' (Pollert 1991, p.11)), numerous researchers have concluded that these forms of work are a long-standing rather than new-fangled means of organizing the labour process:

> The findings ... point to an increase in the use of insecure and indirect forms of employment. But such developments are by no means universal, being greater in some sectors than in others. The use of temporary contract, outworking and subcontractors are practices of long standing. In the majority of cases, workplaces using temporary contracts and subcontracting out service activities reported a continuation of existing practice. (Marginson 1991, p.44)

Leman has reached a similar conclusion about employment in the mail order industry:

> Temporal flexibility is on the increase in the telephone ordering departments, and is associated with an extension of peripheral, part-time female employment. There is, however, little evidence of functional flexibility or multi-skilling. There is numerical flexibility but this is not new; employment in the industry has always been cyclical....' (Leman 1992, p.132).

It seems clear then, that although changes are taking place in the organization of work, it may be somewhat premature to deduce that these constitute a decisive shift towards the model of the flexible firm. Evidence of a concentration of skills, or of a broadening of multiskilling at the core is less than decisive, while activities within the periphery may reflect longer-term trends rather than a new direction. Even at the more general level of analysis, the basic tenets of the core/periphery model may fail: the evidence Pollert suggests, implies that distinctions between such groups of workers are far from clear cut: 'Evidence on changes in the labour process lends more support to the concept of an "endangered core", and a broad dynamic of the core's expulsion from a central position, than to a picture of polarisation between a privileged elite and a periphery.' (Pollert 1991, p.12) Walsh casts doubt on the whole idea that the core is some how more important than the periphery:

> It is a naive and erroneous simplification of the flexible-firm model that only "core" workers are indispensable to the company's operations.... part-timers and casuals are central to business operations..... Part-timers' and casuals' work may be undervalued, but it is by no means peripheral to either employer or employee. (Walsh 1991, p.114)

Since the model of the core and peripherally organized flexible firm presupposes the development of techniques of flexible specification, it follows that the inconclusive (if not contradictory) evidence of the emergence of the former may cast some doubt on the transition towards the second strand of the flexibility debate, flexible specialization. Rainnie and Kraitham (1992) emphasize for example, that although the development of flexible specialization is seen as an inevitable response to the 'crisis' of mass production, this idea of managerial response assumes that management are in fact able to develop accurate strategies for the future. In reality however:

> Managerial tactics themselves (if not strategy) drawn up in one particular time frame can take an inordinate length of time to translate themselves into practical action at workplace level. By that time the external circumstances that "demanded" the shift in strategy, assumed to be timeless, can change. Thus what appears at one point to be rational can, by the time of implementation, be counterproductive. (Rainnie and Kraitham 1992, p.49)

Secondly, it has been suggested that in focusing on the technological dimensions of flexibility - on what the technology does or does not allow - exponents of flexible specialization tend to give the technology itself a determining influence over the organization of work and thus pay insufficient attention to the its human dimensions. As Smith puts it, this 'technical determinism stems from the isolation of one factor, technological state or organisational form' from the overall situation in which capitalist investment and accumulation actually takes place. Advocates of the technology-driven move towards flexible specialization compound this difficulty by tending to assume that the organization of work and labour relations will inevitably be brought into line with the technology:

> The flexible specialisation thesis is premised on technological determinism not simply because... hardware was given unusual powers to shape work organization, but rather because its promoters have invested particular combinations of labour and capital with qualities to reconcile capitalist social contradictions. They have also invested particular production or technological systems with a completeness or totality which does not mirror the ongoing production diversity within capitalism as a whole. (Smith, C. 1991, p.155)

By making such claims about a universal or paradigmatic shift from one regime of production to another, advocates of flexible specialization tend to assume: 'that it is possible to tame the market economy and that capitalist social relations are not inherently contradictory: it is possible to chose whether to continue on the old, declining path of mass production, or to reform through flexible specialisation' (Pollert 1991, pp.17-18).

Two important issues arise from this. In the first place, the model assumes that recent developments with the productive process will bring about a return to industrial harmony both between employers and employees and between one group of workers and another. It is however, extremely questionable whether capitalism ever has (or evil will) achieve such apparent harmony. It might be more realistic to accept that the inherent contradictions of capitalism will inevitably cause deep division between these groups. Recent moves towards flexibility may in fact make matters worse rather than better:

> Against the background of economic restructuring and recession, employment legislation has increased the disadvantaged and unprotected workforce, and exacerbated the already existing polarisation between the legally protected workforce and the rest.... [Employment legislation] makes sense in terms of disciplining and disempowering the workforce; it is the opposite of what one would expect if state policy aimed to reinforce the employment and organisational rights of a core workforce. (Pollert 1991, p.15)

In the second place, it was noted above that Piore and Sabel emphasized that flexible specialization developed as a response to changes in consumer demand away from mass-produced towards 'individualised' goods. As Pollert points out however, changes in consumer tastes might simply reflect changes in the types of goods which are available rather than being generated 'independently' or 'spontaneously' by consumers themselves: 'The cultivation of specific niches, whether for clothes, food or music, may become more sophisticated as competition intensifies, but this demonstrates no more than another manipulation of the mass market' (Pollert 1991, p.18).[25]

Returning to the wider dimension of the debate over Fordism and post-Fordism, it should be clear that Marxist and other propositions about the true nature and implications of moves towards flexibility find some support in the preceding arguments. Firstly, and at the level of production itself, since evidence of the emergence of flexible specialization and the flexible firm point towards bits and pieces of change rather than towards a decisive split with the past, it is realistic to see these developments in terms of a continuation of capitalism rather than a transcendence of it. Post-Fordism in other words, is the latest phase of capitalist economic organization; it is not capitalism in an entirely different form. Secondly, although liberal researchers like Sabel and others tend to represent post-Fordism in terms of the re-establishment of harmony - a revival of industrial democracy through enabling and skilful work - the present evidence points much more clearly towards a perpetuation of the contradictions of the capitalist labour process. To the extent that advocates of post-Fordism conduct their analysis at the level of 'industrial society' rather than at the level of industrial *capitalist* society, they may be guilty of putting forward an incomplete and possibly misleading picture both of the past and of the present:

> True to the nature of post-industrial theory, the radical breaks which have been constructed are based on oversimplified, reductionist straw-histories... the crude depiction of Fordist "post-war consensus" is a caricature... contrary to the image of subsequent expansion in the 1950s and 1960s being a cosy partnership of corporatist agreement, Keynesian welfare policies and rising standards of living, it was built on the exploitation of a reserve army of "flexible" labour (a parallel with today's recourse to labour market flexibility that is conveniently forgotten). (Pollert 1991, pp.22-3)

Thirdly, and looking at the political and ideological dimensions of post-Fordist capitalism, it seems clear that despite a lack of conclusive evidence of widespread change, the buzz word of flexibility provides a useful political tool with which employers and their governmental allies can herald the advent of a bright new age of innovation, progress and prosperity. By 'claiming to be a policy to the benefit both of capital and labour', this tool 'legitimises the fragmentation of labour' and 'delegitimises the progressive aspects of mass production and collective labour' (Pollert 1991, p.27).[26]

Finally, the all-encompassing image of post-Fordism in its economic and political guises has also penetrated, and in some instances coerced, the ideological and cultural spheres of society. It may well be that consumer tastes and lifestyles have changed, and that many individuals are seeking new ways of structuring and furnishing their 'private spaces'. But the underlying logic of post-Fordism remains one of producing and selling goods at a profit. The fact that methods of production and patterns of consumption have continued to develop does not in itself provide evidence of a 'new society'. If individuals feel a need to withdraw into, and seek security in a privatised and personalised world, what does this tell us about the public world from which they seek escape?

Part Three - Discussion

As the discussion part two has shown, much controversy surrounds the issue of whether the technological paradigm of flexibility is or is not being adopted as a new and universal model for the practice of work in the future. If we take a step back from these debates however, it is evident that despite their different points of departure, all parties acknowledge that a process of change is under way, and that this process is closely associated with the emergence of a new and extremely dynamic technological paradigm. Up to a point, arguments over whether or not flexibility signifies the 'final' transcendence of Fordist capitalism, whether the ideal-typical flexible firm will entirely displace previous designs, and whether the workforce will be divided between core and periphery, are all arguments about the *pace, extent and scope of change*, rather than about whether such change is actually taking place. The scale of the debate, the fact that so many writers, policy makers and practitioners are devoting so much time to these issues is in itself confirmation that the advanced industrial economies are passing from one stage to another.

It also emerges from our brief survey of the flexibility debate, that although the different *perspectives* take different points of departure, and although they develop different analyses of causality, there is a remarkably high degree concurrence in their interim conclusions as to the *key factors* involved. These relate to the two primary constituents of transition: the role of technology within the productive process, and the availability of a socio-institutional framework which supports and legitimates the accumulation of capital. Taking technology first, whether one wants to go the whole hog and argue, as do Freeman, Perez and other enthusiasts of the neo-Schumpterian approach, that the emergence of microelectronics provides in a very direct way, the primary and indispensable ingredient for a fifth Kondratiev wave of economic growth, or whether one wants to adopt a slightly more conservative view, that the present economic crisis is partly, but not exclusively determined by the new technologies, it is undeniable that the technology is available, that it will be used, and that it is not suddenly going to go away. Moreover, because the technology is inherently flexible, there are grounds for being at least as concerned with the likely trajectory of its impact on future change, as with the 'simple' question of its origins in the recent past. We are not in other words, discussing a finite development with discrete and limited application, but one with an unprecedented potential for further application.

There is also a large degree of consensus that the earlier paradigm of Fordism achieved growth and stability in the way that it did because of the parallel development of a suitable socio-institutional framework. In the UK in particular, this took the form of a Keynesian economic strategy and a proactive state bureaucracy, which brought key features of labour legislation, educational and welfare policies into line with the requirements of a mass production and mass consumption economic structure. The crisis of the 1970s was compounded by the inability of these institutions to offset the effects of falling living standards and increasing dependence on the state in the face of economic decline. Looking more closely at the idea of the socio-institutional framework, Freeman has argued that:

> The widespread generalisation of the new technological paradigms, not only in the carrier branches of the upswing but also in many other branches of the economy, is possible only after a period of change and adaption of many social institutions to the requirements of the new technology. (Freeman 1984, p.109)

During the 1950s and 1970s for example, the combination of high output and increased productivity 'depended upon the good match which then existed between the low labour cost energy-intensive technological paradigm [i.e. Fordist mass production] and the favourable institutional framework within which it was exploited [i.e. Keynesian economic policy]' (Freeman 1984, p.109). In contrast, despite continued technological innovation, the slow down in productivity and capital accumulation during the 1970s and 1980s, indicates 'some degree of "miss-match" between the new technological paradigm [i.e. flexible specialisation] and the institutional and social framework' (Freeman 1984, p.110). Following this argument, and if, as we must, we accept that technology-driven innovation will continue, a reconciliation of this miss-match will require the development of a much modified socio-institutional framework. As Freemen suggests:

> It will involve big changes in the pattern of skills of the work-force and therefore in the education and training systems; in management and labour attitudes; in the pattern of industrial relations and worker participation; in working arrangements; in the pattern of consumer demand; in the conceptual framework of economists, accountants and governments, and in social, political, and legislative priorities. (Freeman 1984, p.120)

Although as this reference illustrates, Freeman *et al.*, tend to focus on the institutional and systemic aspects of the mode of regulation, there is an important implication that this mode assumes or includes the presence of particular set of expectations of work. In a sense, the socio-institutional framework constitutes a set of mechanisms through which these expectations can be reconciled with the realities of the economic structure as manifest by the prevailing organization of the productive forces. If the mode of regulation is necessary in order to sustain capital accumulation, then it is also necessary as a means of enabling particular individuals to realise their expectations of work. This recognition of the *consensual dimension* of the mode of regulation has also been acknowledged by other participants in the flexibility debate. Some members of the regulation school for example, have referred to the necessary development of an 'hegemonic structure' which provides a linkage between the regime of accumulation and mode of regulation. Following Boyer and Mistral 1983, Esser and Hirsch explain that in their formulation:

> We use *hegemonic structure* to describe the concrete historical connection between the *mode of accumulation* and the *method of regulation*, which endows the economic form of capital reproduction (ensuring valorisation) and political-ideological (legitimation, force and consent) reproduction of the system as a whole under the domination of the ruling class(es), with relative durability. (Esser and Hirsch 1994, p.74)

Similarly, Jessop and Lipietz have added the concept of a 'mode of societalization' to the taxonomy of regulation, in order to capture the way in which the profitability of the economic system not only relies upon a sympathetic socio-institutional framework, but also upon the development of forms of socio-political interdependence and consent. In Amin's words:

> This concept refers to a series of political compromises, social alliances and hegemonic processes of domination which feed into a pattern of mass integration and social cohesion, thus serving to underwrite and stabalize a given development path. (Amin 1994, p.8)

In his analysis, Jessop defines 'mode of societalization' as the fourth referent for the terms Fordism and post-Fordism:

> A pattern of institutional integration and social cohesion which complements the dominant accumulation regime and its social mode of economic regulation and thereby secures the conditions for its dominance within the wider society. (Jessop 1994, p.252)

Although Jessop suggests that it is 'too soon' to anticipate what a post-Fordist mode of societalization would involve, he is clear that Fordist society is typically 'an urban-industrial, "middle class", wage-earning society' (Jessop 1994, p.254).[27]

Taking this analysis a stage further, Lipietz identifies the necessary development of a societal paradigm to describe 'a mode of structuration of the identities and legitimately defensible interests within the "universe of political discourses and representations"' (Lipietz 1994, p.340).[28] This field of socio-political contest forms part of the mode of regulation made up of 'the set of norms (implicit or explicit) and institutions, which continuously adjust individual anticipations and behaviours to the general logic of the regime of accumulation...:

> We might say that the mode of regulation constitutes the "scenery", the practical world, the superficial "map" by which individual agents orient themselves so that the conditions necessary for balanced economic reproduction and accumulation are met in full. (Lipietz 1994, p.339)

For Lipietz, the success and sustainability of the prevailing (work) paradigm is dependent upon the development of an hegemonic bloc which unites, in a particular socio-economic formation, the regime of accumulation and the mode of regulation. Crucially, hegemony is characterized as much in terms of political and social struggle, as it is in terms of competition between ascendant and descendent technological paradigms:

> The establishment of a mode of regulation, like its consolidation, largely depends upon the political sphere.... These struggles,

armistices and compromises are the equivalent in the political domain of competition, labour conflict and the regime of accumulation in the economic sphere. Defined by their daily conditions of existence, and in particular by their place in economic relations, social groups do not engage in a struggle without end. *Social bloc* is the term to delineate a stable system of relations of domination, alliances and concessions between different social groups (dominant and subordinate). A social bloc is *hegemonic* when its interests correspond with those of a whole nation. In any hegemonic bloc the proportion of the nation whose interests are discounted has to be very small. (Lipietz 1994, pp.339-40)[29]

Applying this scheme to recent developments in capitalist society, Lipietz describes in familiar terms, how the Fordist or 'progressivist paradigm':

> Offered a conception of progress which itself rested upon three pillars: technical progress (conceived as technological progress unconditionally driven by "intellectual workers"); social progress (conceived as progress in purchasing power while respecting the constraint of full employment); and state progress (the state conceived as guarantor of the general interest against "encroachments" of individual interests). And this triple progress was supposed to weld society together, by advancing goals worthy of collective pursuit. (Lipietz 1994, p.342)

He goes on to suggest that the collapse of this paradigm during the 1970s - its loss of hegemonic solidarity - ushered in a new phase of 'economic liberalism' or 'liberal-productivism' founded upon 'the cult of the enterprise':

> The clarion call of the Western intelligentsia the first half of the 1980s was: we must be competitive! And to that end the initiative of entrepreneurs must be freed. And if the social consequences are unfavourable? Too bad. We must be competitive! To what end? Because free enterprise dictates that we be competitive. And so the story unfolded. (Lipietz 1994, p.343/4)

From this perspective then, the transition from Fordist to post-Fordist capitalism, corresponds to a breakdown in one form of socio-economic hegemony or social bloc, and attempts by the owners and controllers of the means of production to re-establish their hegemonic domination on a new footing. Whilst accepting that this crisis of hegemony originates in, or at the very least, becomes a real possibility because of, practical developments in techniques of production and the organization of work, it also comes about as a result of a breakdown in the perceived legitimacy of the paradigm. What unites these two factors, is that all those involved are seeking to protect their *economic interests*:

> The fit between "hegemonic bloc", "regime of accumulation" and "mode of regulation" becomes visible *as long as the interests constituting the consensus on which the hegemonic bloc is built and reproduced are economic interests*. (Lipietz 1994, p.340, emphasis added)

Arguably, unless people feel, or come to feel more intensely, that their economic interest are under threat, then loss of hegemony and paradigmatic crisis are unlikely to occur. Neither a revolution in the means of production - in this instance the emergence of microelectronic technology, nor a change in the political philosophy of the dominant group, *which had no detrimental effect* on standards of living, or on the prospect that these standards would gradually improve, would necessarily represent a significant challenge to societal hegemony. If either of these factors *did have* such an effect, then it is very likely that a significant challenge would emerge. If *both* the regime of accumulation *and* the mode of regulation suffer a loss of hegemonic legitimacy at the same time, there is a real possibility that the entire socio-economic edifice could collapse.

We are now in a position to return to the question which guided the discussion in this chapter, namely whether recent changes in the practice of work justify the claim that the bases upon which the current concept of work is based have begun to collapse. In the first place, and following the contours of the flexibility debate discussed in part two, we are certainly justified in concluding that technologically induced changes in the means of production have had a profound effect on the practice of work. Whilst conceding that the results of this impact on particular firms and industries have to be regarded as somewhat provisional, there is no question that a new technological paradigm has emerged, and that this paradigm has the potential to further accelerate changes in the pattern and organization of work. As people's daily working life - and indeed non-work life - becomes more and more acutely affected by the experience of working with the new technologies, it is likely that perceptions of what work will be like in the future will also be affected.

In the second place, changes in patterns of work described in part one, demonstrate that many established characteristics of the distribution and availability of employment are in transition. If we accept that earlier perceptions of the nature of work developed against this background - that they largely corresponded with the patterns of work which prevailed at the time - then it is not unreasonable to conclude that if these patterns change, then perceptions of work will also change. In concrete form, we can suggest that the transfer of employment away from manufacturing industries and occupations to services, has dispelled the idea, always in part a myth, that 'proper' work involved 'real men' in the production of materials and manufactured commodities through muscular effort, 'blood, sweat and tears'. To this we can add the fact that the passing of many large-scale primary industries such as coal mining and steel manufacture, has resulted in a severe decline in the idea of an occupational community. Together with the generally much more geographically fragmented and fluid nature of employment opportunity, this has undermined the expectation of living and working in one locality more or less for life. Similarly, work is no longer seen as a largely male preserve, and as a full-time and life-long activity, but as an activity which involves at least as many women as it does men, and that various forms and combinations of temporary, contract-based and part-time employment have superseded the idea of a 'job for life'. In at least these four key respects, the stereotype of the industrial worker has certainly collapsed.

Following the logic of the Gramscian perspective discussed above, we can suggest that, although technical change in work-tasks and the redistribution of employment directly affected the working lives of many people, these were, at least up to a point, accommodated within the prevailing progressivist paradigm and did not challenge the basis of it; it was not a major threat to progressivist hegemony. Somewhat more serious however, has been the collapse of the idea of *secure* employment. Whereas changes in the distribution of employment could have been accepted as variations and modifications to the general norm of secure employment - jobs lost in one area would be compensated for by increased employment elsewhere - both the threat and the reality of unemployment have been much more difficult to reconcile with earlier assumptions about secure employment. It is not just that the nature of work has changed, but whether or not it will be available at all *in whatever form*. Undoubtedly, this development has lowered the general threshold of resilience to the perceived threat of unemployment, as a growing majority of the population have had to reorient themselves away from the assumption of job security towards job insecurity. Whilst this change has had a profound impact upon the practical aspect of work, its effect has been greatly multiplied because of the way it has been combined with, and up to a point has actually caused, a general breakdown in a number of beliefs and expectations which were central to the mode or regulation. As we have seen, the inability of the Keynesian and more recently of the liberal-economist state to preserve and protect people's standard of living, and to act as guarantor of employment opportunity in the face of economic decline, has largely failed to meet the expectations which people had of it. Since we know that the hegemonic bloc of progressivist capitalism is based upon the realization of economic interests, and that the economic interests of the majority are simply that they should have access to means for satisfying their real material needs, it is difficult to reach any other conclusion than that a loss of actual employment opportunity, together with a loss of material support to mitigate its effects, will have a profoundly negative effect on people's sense of trust and belief in the continuing utility of the work paradigm.

In the third place, and following on from this, there is strong support for the suggestion that a fully hegemonic work paradigm crucially depends on a high degree of consent amongst the population. When a number of theorists speak of the 'adaption of many social institutions', of the need for a 'favourable institutional framework', of 'big changes in the conceptual framework', of 'a pattern of mass integration and social cohesion' of 'institutional integration and social cohesion', of 'the set of norms which continuously adjust individual anticipations and behaviours to the general logic of the regime of accumulation', they are alerting us to the fact that participation in the mechanisms of employment is not simply 'automatic' or 'mechanical' but also depends upon the expression of belief and expectation. Within this realm of ideational understanding, resides a set of ideas and beliefs about work, upon which the perceived legitimacy of the work paradigm largely depends. If crucial aspects of these beliefs and expectations come under threat, and accepting that people cannot simply dispense with the needs which give rise to them - we cannot choose to do without material resources - resent changes in the practice of work point quite directly to an impending crisis in the conceptual aspects of the contemporary work paradigm.

Notes

1. The analysis presented in the first part of this chapter draws on material previously published in Ransome 1995.

2. See *Social Trends* no.21 (HMSO) 1991, table 4.11.

3. See: *Eurostat Annual Review 1976-1985* (EEC Brussels 1986), tables 3.4.13-18; Eurostat: *Basic Statistics of the Community* (EEC Brussels 1988, 1989 and 1991), tables 3.17 and 3.18.

4. Based upon *Census of Employment* 1981, 1984, 1987, 1989. Final results published in *Employment Gazette*: December 1983; September 1987; October 1989, and April 1991, table 1.

5. Based upon *Census of Employment* 1981, 1984, 1987, 1989. Final results published in *Employment Gazette*: December 1983; September 1987; October 1989, and April 1991, tables 1 & 5.

6. See: *Census of Employment* 1981, 1984, 1987, 1989. Final results published in *Employment Gazette*: December 1983; September 1987; October 1989, and April 1991, table 5.

7. See: *Annual Abstract of Statistics* no.127 (HMSO) 1991, table 2.5.

8. See: *Annual Abstract of Statistics* no.127 (HMSO) 1991, table 6.1.

9. See: *Eurostat Demographic Statistics* (EEC Luxembourg 1990), pp.220-225 and Ransome 1995, table 3.16.

10. See: *Eurostat Demographic Statistics* (EEC Luxembourg 1990), pp.220-225 and Ransome 1995, table 3.12.

11. See: *Social Trends* no.18 (HMSO) 1988, table 4.21; no.21 (HMSO) 1991, table 4.25.

12. See: *Annual Abstract of Statistics* no.117 (HMSO) 1981; no.127 (HMSO) 1991, table 6.1.

13. See: *Annual Abstract of Statistics* no.117 (HMSO) 1981; no.127 (HMSO) 1991, table 6.1.

14. See: *Employment Gazette*, (HMSO) Oct 1980; Feb 1984; Oct 1987; May 1990, Jan 1992 table 2.5.

15. See Ransome 1995, ch5.

16. See Ransome 1995, ch 6.

17. The term 'technological paradigm' has been developed by Freeman and Perez, to describe how long-waves of capitalist development are driven by a process of invention, investment and innovation in new technologies. Following Freeman, the primary elements of the most recent paradigm - the fifth wave - are: '(i) The shift towards information-intensive rather than energy and materials-intensive products and processes... (ii) the change from relatively inflexible dedicated mass production systems, towards much more flexible systems, capable of manufacturing a diverse range of output as efficiently as a single homogeneous product... (iii) new patterns of business organization implying "systemation rather than automation".' (Freeman C. 1985, p.x.; Perez 1985) See also: Perez 1983 and Dosi *et al.*, 1988. An historical account tracing the four waves is given by Mager (1987). He dates these as follows: 1787-1843 (peaking in 1814); 1843-1896 (peaking in 1864); 1896-1949 (peaking in 1920), and 1949-2003 (peaking in 1973).

18. For a discussion see Ransome 1995 chs. 4&5. Case-study evidence in presented in: Kendall *et al.*, 1980; Francis, A. 1986; Bosworth 1983; Marstrand 1984; Gill 1985; Burke and Rumberger (eds.), 1987; Northcott and Walling 1988, and Knights and Willmott (eds.), 1988.

19. Jessop writes for example: 'A minimum condition for referring to post-Fordism is to establish the nature of the continuity in discontinuity which justifies the claim that it is not just a variant form of Fordism but does actually succeed Fordism. Without significant discontinuity, it would not be *post*-Fordism; without significant continuity, it would not be post-*Fordism*.' (Jessop 1994, p.257)

20. It should be noted that although I am following Gilbert *et al's* analysis here, other authors have attached slightly different labels to the perspectives which have contributed to the Fordism/post-Fordism debate. In his introduction to these debates for example, Amin (1994), divides his analysis between the regulationists, the neo-Schumpterians, and the flexible specialization approach. Mark Elam

(1994) prefers the labels neo-Marxist (referring to the regulationists), neo-Schumpterian, and neo-Smithian (referring to Piore and Sabel's work on the emergence of flexible specialization). In the conclusion to this chapter, it will be argued that although each approach differs in its emphasis and in its analysis of causality, there is a high degree of correspondence between these perspectives regarding the *key factors* involved. The alternative points of departure in other words, tend to lead towards very parallel conclusions.

21. See: Aglietta 1979; Lipietz 1985 and 1987; Jessop 1992(a), 1992(b).

22. Esser and Hirsch for example, define these terms as follows: 'Each capitalist development of society is characterized by a specific *mode of accumulation* (accumulation regime) and a *method of regulation* associated with it. By "mode of accumulation", we mean a form of surplus value production and realization, supported by particular types of production and management technology.... This includes investment and capital devaluation strategies, branch structure (in particular the ratio between the producer goods sector and consumer goods sector), wage condition, consumer models and class structures, the relations between the capitalist and non-capitalist sectors of work in society and the mode of integration into the international market. [Mode of] regulation describes the way in which the elements of this complex relationship between production and reproduction are related to each other socially, i.e. based on the behaviour of the social participants.... It includes a multifaceted configuration of economic and sociopolitical institutions and norms, which gives a certain equilibrium and stability to the reproduction of the system as a whole....' (Esser and Hirsch 1994, pp.73-4)

23. In his analysis of the political consequences 'privatism and autonomy', Lodziak draws attention to the double-sided nature of this phenomenon: 'It is clear that the experienced lack of autonomy steers people towards the private sphere, and can result in apolitical self-absorption. But there is also a sense in which privatism can be seen to reflect an attempt to exercise autonomy. We can take heart from this because it means that our capacity for autonomy is still alive. But more than this, opportunities are opening up for the development of this capacity in the private sphere. If this opportunity is seized future generations will be better able to avoid self-absorption, and

will be less satisfied than the present ones with restricting their exercise of autonomy to the private sphere.' (Lodziak 1995, p.91)

24. For an illustrative example of the adoption of the just-in-time system in the UK, see Turnbull 1988. For a discussion of the impact of these developments on working relationships, see Hyman and Streek 1988.

25. Whilst acknowledging the logic of Pollert's comment on this point, it is worth noting that as standards of living improve, individual consumers are likely to have an increasing surplus income which can be disposed of in purchasing 'non-necessary' goods. Under these conditions, it would not be surprising if their wants for more diverse types of goods would also increase. Increased demand for product diversity is an effect of increasing affluence as much as it is an effect of 'manipulation'. Discussing the impact of flexible specialization in retailing, Murray has noted a shift from 'manufacturer's economies of scale' to 'retailer's economies of scope': 'The economies come from offering an integrated range from which customers choose their own basket of products. There is also an economy of innovation, for the modern retail systems allow new product ideas to be tested in practice, through shop sales, and the successful ones then to be ordered for wider distribution. Innovation has become a leading edge of the new competition. Product life has become shorter for fashion goods and consumer durables.' (Murray 1989(a), pp.43-4). Under these circumstances, the technology creates a kind of feedback loop between consumer and producer, which some might argue, is to the benefit of the consumer.

26. The 'ideological' uses of the concept of flexibility are discussed in the following chapter.

27. For a more detailed explanation see Jessop 1992(a) and 1992(b).

28. Lipietz is drawing on Jenson 1989 for part of his analysis.

29. This analysis draws heavily on concepts developed by Antonio Gramsci. For a full account of these see Ransome 1992.

8 A critique of the current concept of work

The previous chapter has provided an overview of a number of important changes which have taken place in the practical organization of work during the last twenty years or so. Taking the UK as an example of an advanced economy which is currently passing through a period of economic transition, it has been shown that changes in traditional patterns of working, together with the introduction of a new technological paradigm signify that a number of the bases upon which the contemporary concept of work were bases have begun to collapse. It has also emerged, that there is considerable agreement that the conceptual aspect of work is heavily implicated in the sustainability or otherwise, of the overall hegemony of this work paradigm. In particular, a number of theorists have pointed to the *consensual* dimensions of the work paradigm, and to the fact that continued participation in the mechanisms of employment in part depends on whether people believe that this participation will provide them with an opportunity to peruse their economic interests. For the majority, these interests can be understood in terms simply of the need to provide themselves and their dependants with the necessities of life. Using a number of the principles developed in earlier chapters, the object of this chapter, is to develop a closer understanding of why the contemporary concept of work has been largely unable to accommodate changes in the practice of work. Whilst acknowledging the immediate potency of these practical changes, it will be argued that the present crisis in the concept of work is closely associated with fundamental deficiencies *within the concept of work itself*. The inability of the contemporary concept of work to respond adequately to changes in the practice of work has highlighted these deficiencies, thus exposing it to a level of scrutiny which its advocates had previously been able to avoid. It can further be suggested, that these inadequacies have not only instigated a crisis in the *present* concept of work, but are seriously inhibiting the emergence of a *reformulated* perspective on work; a perspective which could respond more fully to evident and widespread changes in the practice of work.

The critique of the contemporary concept of work put forward in this chapter is organized around two central themes. In part one, we will look again at the question of the criteria which are currently applied to working activities. Of particular importance, will be the question of whether these criteria can continue to allow individuals to exercise the fundamental principles of action/work, and the key expectations of work outlined in chapters two and three. Part two develops a critical scrutiny of the contemporary work-ethic. If, as was argued in chapter four, a work-ethic functions to provide an intellectual/moral justification for a particular organization of work - a justification which plays a leading role in preserving the overall hegemony of the work paradigm - we have to ask whether the contemporary work-ethic has outlived its usefulness in this respect. The overall aim will be expose the arbitrariness of the current concept of work, the falsity of the terms of reference upon which it is based, and the inherent, and increasingly ideological nature of the work-ethic which it sustains. Finally, in part three, a number of suggestions will be put as to how a new concept of work might emerge and what its key characteristics might be.

Part One - The arbitrariness of the contemporary criteria of work

It was argued, in chapter two, that the definition of work derives from a number of basic criteria. These define work as predominantly public mental and or physical activities, which are seen to be economically expedient, carried out in return for monetary payment. Within capitalism, the criterion of financial payment has become the most often used means of distinguishing between work and non-work activities; for all practical purposes in contemporary capitalist society, *work is paid work*. It was also argued, that although the criteria of the economistic definition of work have become dominant, this dominance may not necessarily imply that the criteria upon which it is based are inherently more appropriate or expedient than other criteria. Rather, this dominance relates to the *prevailing use* of a particular set of terms of reference which *give priority* to particular criteria. In broad terms, we can distinguish between terms of reference which give priority to systemic requirements - that is, to sustaining a particular historical manifestation of the means of production, and what can be labelled humanist terms of reference which focus on the satisfaction of individual human needs. Within a particular historical conjuncture, it is possible for both these sets of terms of reference, and therefore for both sets of criteria, to co-exist. Indeed, some criteria are present across a number of different terms of reference. In practical terms, we operate with a mixture of criteria drawn from a range of terms of reference, although in the present context, economistic criteria tend to prevail. It was further suggested, that the practical application or operationalization of criteria of work depends upon the active and shared consent of the population. For a particular criterion to be effective, people have to be willing to abide by it and to live with its consequences. This consent is expressed both in practical terms - it governs our day-to-day working activity, and in conceptual terms in as much as we assume that other people are acting in a similar way for similar reasons. Criteria of work then, are social phenomena which derive their usefulness through practical application in a shared social context.

Looking at the nature of the criteria themselves, it was suggested in chapter three, that distinctions can be made between arbitrary (temporary) criteria, and absolute (permanent) criteria, on the basis of whether or not the criteria accurately reflect the basic principles which underlie the human predisposition to act. Derived from the humanist terms of reference, these principles are that work is a manifestation of the basic human need for expression through action, that it is an expression of human creativity, that it is a profoundly social activity, and that it is deliberately undertaken in pursuance of the satisfaction of needs. If a particular criterion accurately recognizes and reflects one or more of these principles, then, according to these terms of reference, it can be regarded an absolute rather than arbitrary criterion. To the extent that they do reflect the basic principles of action, absolute criteria are permanent criteria which will be sustained even during periods of rapid change in either the practical organization of work (regime of accumulation) and/or in the terms of reference which are being applied (mode of regulation). Arbitrary criteria are much more vulnerable to such changes. Taking this as our point of departure, it can be argued that the criteria which are currently used to distinguish working activities from non-working activities have become increasingly arbitrary, precisely because they fail to acknowledge, and indeed in some cases, actually contradict, these basic principles of action. In part as a consequence of changes in the practice of work described in the previous chapter, and in part because of the fundamental weakness of the economistic terms of reference themselves, the extent of this arbitrariness has become increasingly transparent resulting in an actual and perceived crisis in the continued usefulness of these criteria.

Firstly then, and beginning with the (universal) principle that work is simply a manifestation of the basic human need for expression through action, it can be argued that key aspects of the contemporary criteria of work are arbitrary, because they impose an artificial distinction between one type of activity and another. According to economistic terms of reference, activities which are described as work tend to be seen a *distinct and separate from*, general human activity. This approach fragments and separates one category of activity from another, purely on the basis of whether or not these activities are public, expedient and financially rewarded. Adopting the humanist terms of reference however, we know that 'work' actually denotes a wide range of activities, not all of which fulfil the economistic criteria given above. Work-as-paid-work is therefore *an aspect* of work in the economic sense, and 'work' as a whole is *an aspect* of activity in general. This fragmentation has at least two important consequences for people's experience of work. In the first place, the *intrinsic aspects* of activity tend to be subjugated by the *extrinsic* resulting in a profound devaluation of the notion of human agency itself. Gorz argues for example, that because the intrinsic qualities of work are devalued, individuals are coerced by a complex mechanism of 'incentive regulators' (understood in terms of 'money, security, prestige and/or power attached to the various functions'), and 'prescriptive regulators' (which 'force individuals, on pain of certain penalties to adopt functional forms of conduct' (Gorz 1989, p.35), which only offer 'compensations *outside work* for the constraints, frustrations and suffering inherent in functional labour itself' (Gorz 1989, pp.43-4). This transcendence of the worker/producer by the worker/consumer lies at the heart of the consumer-ethic of post-Fordism, wherein individuals seek a 'private' realm of individuality and difference:

> It constitutes an incentive to withdraw into the private sphere and give priority to the pursuit of "personal" advantages, and thus contributes to the disintegration of networks of solidarity and mutual assistance, social and family cohesion and our sense of belonging. (Gorz 1989, p.47)[1]

In the second place, and because of the priority given to extrinsic utility and the payment criterion, *all activities* tend to be evaluated in terms of the criterion of extrinsic evaluation. The perceived value and worth of economic expediency becomes the dominant means of assessing the worth and value of all activities *irrespective of whether those activities are categorized as work in other respects, or indeed of whether they are categorized as work at all.* If we are prepared to adopt the economistic terms of reference, and to accept that intrinsic satisfactions are only of secondary importance, the more or less universal application of the expediency criteria would not be unduly problematic. Unfortunately from this point of view however, it is clear that individuals do attach great significance to the intrinsic aspects of their working activities, and experience a profound sense of resentment if these are not acknowledged and rewarded.

Secondly, and taking the principle that work is deliberately undertaken in pursuance of the satisfaction of needs - a satisfaction which is the prerequisite for all other activity - we need to consider again whether the economistic terms of reference make sufficient allowance for this. In pre-capitalist economic systems the productivity of an activity and indeed the point of engaging in that activity, could be assessed straightforwardly in terms of whether or not it resulted in the satisfaction of a need:

> There is no point in working more than is required to satisfy one's *felt needs*. Nor is there any point in seeking maximum productivity, in counting one's time, in rationalizing work when one can meet one's needs by working according to one's natural rhythm. Counting and calculating itself is useless from this perspective. *The limited nature of needs constitutes an obstacle to economic rationality.* (Gorz 1989, p.111, original emphasis)

Within capitalism however, the principal criterion and underlying motive of the economistic definition of work is the accumulation of surplus value. Since profit has no 'determinate goal' other than its own perpetuation, advocates of this conception of work must continuously seek to ensure that consumption progressively outpaces the satisfaction of felt needs:

> *Consumption would have to be in the service of production.* Production would no longer have the function of satisfying existing needs in the most efficient way possible; on the contrary, it was needs, which would increasingly have the function of enabling production to keep growing.... *It is to the extent that consumption frees itself from felt needs and exceeds them that it can serve production, that is, serve the 'needs' of capital.* (Gorz 1989, pp.114/119, original emphasis)

In his analysis of industrial society at the turn of the twentieth century, Tawney places particular emphasis upon the acceptance of the principle of limitless accumulation. This principle and the purposelessness which it sustains, characterizes modern capitalist society as an 'acquisitive society':

> Such societies may be called Acquisitive societies, because their whole tendency and interest and preoccupation is to promote the acquisition of wealth.... It is an invitation to men to use the powers with which they have been endowed by nature or society, by skill or energy or relentless egoism or mere good fortune, *without enquiring whether there is any principle by which their exercise should be limited....* (Tawney 1982, p.32, emphasis added)

Whereas in pre-capitalist society, the instruments of production and therefore the right of access to their products, were seen in concrete terms as providing for immediate necessity and some security for the future, within capitalism, perceptions of access to the instruments of production and the perception of the worth and value of their products, have been replaced by a much more abstract and purposeless perception of work for its own sake:

> The enjoyment of property and the direction of industry are considered, in short, *to require no social justification*, because they are regarded as rights which stand by their own virtue, *not functions to be judged by the success with which they contribute to a social purpose*. (Tawney 1982, p.28, emphasis added)

This general confusion of ends with means is symptomatic of the economistic terms of reference. The purposes and outcomes of work and the meaning attributed to them, are not, as noted above, evaluated in terms of particular and concrete ends, but in terms of the desirability of economic activity *per se*:

> In fact the *summum bonum* [the greatest good] of this ethic, the earning more and more money... is thought of so purely as an end in itself, that from the point of view of the happiness of, or utility to, the single individual, it appears entirely transcendental and absolutely irrational. Man is dominated by the making of money, by acquisition as the ultimate purpose of his life. Economic acquisition is no longer subordinated to man as the means for the satisfaction of his material needs. This reversal of what we should call the natural relationship... is evidently as definitely a leading principle of capitalism as it is

foreign to all peoples not under capitalistic influence. (Weber 1976, p.53)

The justification that all acquisitive activity is valid, irrespective of its actual usefulness, and that all activity can be evaluated in terms of the criterion of economistic pragmatism, inevitably reinforces the perceived legitimacy, indeed virtue, of limitlessness: '[Men] are never satisfied, nor can they be satisfied. For as long as they make [the principle of wealth] the guide of their individual lives and of their social order, nothing short of infinity could bring them satisfaction' (Tawney 1982, p.42).

From the humanist point of view, any economic system adopting a concept of work which effectively denies that needs can be satisfied, must necessarily become arbitrary since it abolishes any notion of satisfaction or sufficiency. Work therefore becomes a process directed towards its own perpetuation rather than towards any discernible finite goals. As such 'it cannot, by its very nature, define the limits of its own applicability' (Gorz 1989, p.127). The displacement within capitalism of use-values by exchange-values has therefore resulted in a situation where the satisfaction of needs has become an almost incidental aspect of work.

Up to a point, we should accept that the Fordist regime of accumulation did not seek to deny that work was a means of needs satisfaction. In effect, it maintained a more or less satisfactory balance between terms of reference which supported the requirements of the economic system for accumulation, and terms of reference applicable to the satisfaction of individual needs. We could go so far as to say that its success was in fact dependent upon the maintenance of this balance. However, the subsequent crisis of accumulation, together with declining standards of living (or at least with a considerable slow-down in the rate at which they had been improving) has brought the conflict between these two priorities out into the open. In light of structural constraints upon employment opportunities discussed in the previous chapter, it is difficult to reach any other conclusion than that assumptions about the perpetuation of work for its own sake - meaning in effect, working in response to systemic requirements rather than to individual needs - has become both practically and conceptually inappropriate. One effect of this exposure however, has been to reinstate the general understanding that work itself is a means to an end rather than an end in itself, an understanding which may have become partially obscured under conditions of relative prosperity. Not only does the very real threat of loss of income through job insecurity focuses the mind on this basic fact, it also raises the question of whether the current mechanisms of income distribution are *the only means* through which these fundamental aims can be achieved. It reminds us that the mechanisms through which we gain income are *less important* than the gaining of that income.

Thirdly, and turning to the principle that work is a profoundly social activity directed at achieving common goals, it can be argued that the economistic criteria of work tend to be arbitrary in as much as they give priority to individual rather than to communal interests, and tend to fragment the social aspects of work. This is an extremely complex issue, since from an economistic point of view, it could be argued that in their working lives, most people are willing to tolerate a wide range of levels of social contact at work, and in any case the majority do work as part of a wider social group. For many however, the experience of working within the capitalist division of labour does infringe upon the human predisposition towards the social dimensions of working, with the result that the contemporary organization of work is a fragmenting rather than a unifying experience. In more broadly conceptual terms, this process of fragmentation may also obscure the notion of common interests. Tawney notes for example, that the perceived legitimacy of unlimited accumulation is mutually reinforced and driven by the limitlessness of self-interest:

> By fixing men's minds, not upon the discharge of social obligations, which restricts their energy, because it defines the goal to which it should be directed, but upon the exercise of the right to pursue their own self-interest, it offers unlimited scope for the acquisition of riches, and therefore gives free play to one of the most powerful of human instincts. (Tawney 1982, p.32)

Individual agency is not directed towards the common good, but is carried out purely on the basis of individual self-interest. Under these circumstances, even if common goals are achieved as an effect of the exercise of self-interest, the prioritizing of the latter over the former makes it much more difficult not only to specify what these common goals are, but also to judge when they have been satisfied.

In his critical analysis of the Marxist expectation that the division of labour will provide a basis for social integration and consent, Gorz has argued that 'functional integration' and the 'functional sub-division of tasks',[2] will not result in social integration and greater co-operation, but points towards fragmentation and disharmony. Although Gorz's comments are primarily directed against the Marxian presumption that developments in productive technique contain the seeds of a profound 'liberation of work', they are equally valid against liberal-bourgeois arguments which suggest that the emergence of increasing flexibility will increase industrial harmony. He argues that this optimism is based upon a confusion between liberation *in* work and liberation *from* work:

> Liberation *within* work, is for Marx and Marxists, particularly those in workers' organizations, the necessary prerequisite for liberation *from* work; for it is through liberation *within* work that the subject capable of desiring liberation *from* work and of giving it a meaning will be born.... If this is the case, if liberation *within* work (which is always partial and relative) is at stake in the workers' struggle, this means *the development of the forces of production does not of itself bring about either this liberation or its historical and social subject.* (Gorz 1989, p.95, original emphasis)

For Gorz therefore, the liberation from work is to be found *outside* rather than *within* the realm of formal paid employment. Because capitalist economic practice is based upon a detailed division of tasks, the continued existence of this arrangement of the productive forces is necessarily dependent upon, and therefore creates a demand for, 'a functional specialization of tasks in all areas' (Gorz 1990, p.40), a tendency which as we saw in the previous chapter, is likely to become more and more evident. Unfortunately however, these specialisms do not as it might sometimes appear, provide individuals with greater opportunities for autonomy and control over their own work and its products, but actually increase their powerlessness:

> Specialization always stands in contradiction to the free all-round unfolding of individual capacities, even if it demands initiative, responsibility and personal commitment to the job. A computer specialist, a maintenance worker, a chemicals worker or postman cannot experience and develop themselves in their work as creative human beings.... In the course of their work the operatives can hardly influence at all the decisions which relate to the character, determination, use-values and social utility of the end products. (Gorz 1990, p.40)

In contemporary society therefore, the increasing specialization of tasks within the organization of work, may not in fact be a particularly liberating experience leading to greater harmony and commonality.

In summary, it can be argued that although the criteria of work derived from the economistic terms of reference have become deeply embedded in the contemporary concept of work, and have achieved a considerable degree of success in sustaining the perceived legitimacy of that concept, a general decline in the availability of formal paid employment has exposed them to close scrutiny. Whilst it has already been noted in chapters two and three, that a degree of ambiguity accompanies the application of these criteria as a means of distinguishing work from non-work (in particular the distinction between public and private, and between official and unofficial activities), closer analysis shows that many of these criteria are also quite arbitrary. Under conditions of high job security and low unemployment, this arbitrariness did not significantly undermine the practical validity of these criteria, as the details of what counted as work were less important than the fact that those who wanted employment could find it. Now that these conditions have been reversed, the issue of how we categorize a particular activity as work proper has become much more pressing. At one level, the economistic terms of reference still hold good as long as we are willing to accept that systemic requirements are given priority over individual needs, and that the key criterion of work is that it is simply an activity for which one gets paid more or less irrespective of other considerations such as quality of creative experience or expression of common purpose. Arguably, we actually have little choice but to accept these conditions, since, at present, participation in the mechanisms of formal employment is the only means through which we can gain access to the resources we need in order to survive. At another level however, it is becoming increasingly apparent that the prevailing criteria of work will have to be reassessed in order to accommodate, in practical terms, a decline in the availability of secure employment. The humanist criteria of work, and the principles of action from which they derive, indicate some of the bases upon which such a reassessment could be made.

Part Two - The contemporary work-ethic: the ideology of economic rationality

The discussion in part one raises the issue of what impact the decaying usefulness of the economistic criteria of work might have upon the consensual dimension of work. Whilst people will continue to participate in the mechanisms of employment, and thus express an at least minimal level of pragmatic 'consent', it is much more questionable whether such consent will be maintained at the more general level of ideational understanding. In the same way that the criteria of work are being exposed to close scrutiny, so too is the work-ethic of which they are a constituent part. Recalling the discussion in chapters five and six, a work-ethic reflects the more general ideas about the nature of society and of the role of the individual within it, and may therefore play a significant role in maintaining an intellectual/moral justification for a particular organization of the productive forces. It was also pointed out, that a distinction can be made between idea-elements in the work-ethic which simply represent an ideational reflection of the practical experience of working, and those which are ideological. Ideological idea-elements can be identified by considering whether or not they accurately reflect both the expectations which people have of work, and are fully in tune with, and make a significant contribution to, the practical organization of work. Whilst we can accept that many ideas about work are in some sense 'ideological', an overtly ideological work-ethic is one which attempts to justify the maintenance of a particular organization of work, even if such an organization *is no longer a practical possibility*.

With regard to the contemporary work-ethic, there are grounds for suspecting that recent changes in the practice of work have highlighted the fact that many of the claims it makes are becoming increasingly untenable. Beginning with the content of the contemporary work-ethic, a number of its key idea-elements can be identified. Firstly, and at the level of broad ideas about the meaning and purpose of work, it includes a combination of bourgeois economic rationality characterized by the perceived legitimacy of limitless accumulation, the absorption of a utilitarian philosophy of economic expediency backed up by the practices of the law, and an increasingly abstract perception of work and its purposes and products. In terms of more immediate ideas and beliefs, if we expect work to provide opportunities for income, security, creativity, and social contact, the work-ethic encompasses the idea that these expectations can be met. Relative prosperity during the 1960s, resulted in a consolidation of this idea giving rise to the further expectation that secure employment would be available more or less indefinitely. This belief was reinforced by the knowledge that a temporary relapse of this situation would be underwritten by income benefits from the state. Economic prosperity also gave rise to two further work-related ethics, namely a consumer-ethic and a leisure-ethic. In both cases, these sets of ideas were premised on the assumption that the ideational and ideological claims of the work-ethic were valid: the promise that the capitalist labour process could literally 'deliver the goods' had been kept.

As shown in the previous chapter, recent changes in the practice of work together with a loss of economic stability and certainty, have considerably undermined a number of these ideas. Beginning with bourgeois economic rationality itself, a key feature of this system was the claim that economic prosperity and individual prosperity would progress more or less hand in hand. In this sense 'progress' was driven as much by individual initiative as it was by technological and other developments in the organization of work. Following the crises of the 1970s however, it has become increasingly evident that individual efforts are in fact extremely vulnerable to systemic crises in the economic structure. The claim that nation states and corporations, let alone particular individuals can maintain control over prosperity has become less and less convincing. In the ideational sphere, this rupture in a basic tenet of the work-ethic stimulated a more or less frantic attempt by a number of governments - notably the Thatcher administration in the UK and the Reagan administration in the USA - to restore the validity of the work-ethic by reviving the ideas of economic liberalism and entrepreneurialism. It was not that the 'prosperity contract' between individual effort and economic structure had failed, but that individuals were simply not trying hard enough. Moreover, individuals who failed to achieve prosperity, only had themselves to blame and had in effect forfeit the right to expect the state to help them.

Whilst this shift in the attribution of responsibility away from the economic system towards individuals, could be accepted as legitimate by those sectors of the population who felt that their economic position and prosperity were more or less secure - principally the urban-industrial middles classes of Jessop's analysis - it is questionable whether this process of legitimation extended to those who were more fully exposed to job insecurity and unemployment. For these individuals, the expediency or otherwise of the productive system had to be assessed more immediately in terms basic material survival. Living at the sharp end of industrial restructuring, changes in patterns of employment, and the imposition of short-term employment contracts, opportunities for creativity an social contact had to be subjugated to the need for income alone. Whilst the idea of financial security may have remained attractive, the reality was one in which such security was becoming more and more elusive.

Throughout the late-1980s, it can be argued that a revival of the liberal-entrepreneurial work-ethic was sufficient to form a bridge between the assumptions of the past and the new reality. The modified work-ethic served to obscure in people's minds, the true extent of the crisis in the regime of accumulation. This borrowing of faith would eventually be repaid with a return to prosperity in the not too distant future. The fact that the balance between material coercion and ideational consent had been shifted towards the former, acted as a guarantee that people would continue to participate in the (albeit modified) mechanisms of employment because they actually had no choice but to do so.

During the 1990s however, it has become increasing clear that a return to economic security cannot be achieved simply by working harder and by being prepared to adapt to increasing flexibility in the practice of work. As argued in the previous chapter, key changes in patterns of working, the distribution of employment and most particularly, in the availability of full-time life-long secure employment, have rendered any expectation of simply returning to a full employment economy of the kind which existed in an earlier period, practically absurd. Claims that the service sector would increase employment by colonizing a realm of previously un-paid work within the 'private' household - the idea that 'these tasks should occupy the greatest number of people and absorb as much working time as possible, but in the form, in this instance, of commercial services' (Gorz 1989, p.155) - can be seen as a last ditch attempt to sustain the myth of full employment.

Within the ideational sphere of the work-ethic, the temporary legitimacy which was sustained by appealing to the (self)interests of the industrial-urban middle classes has become progressively weakened by this confrontation between the idea of full employment and the reality of job insecurity. A key factor here, has been the fact that the bases of their own prosperity are also being eroded by changes in the organization of work. Where once they may have felt that their own employment prospects would be largely unaffected, this is no longer the case. In simple terms, the central idea of employment has shifted from an assumption of secure employment (1960s), to the expectation of secure employment (1970s), to the hope of secure employment (1980s). For those living in the 1990s, the ideology of secure employment has been replaced by the idea of employment as a largely insecure, short-term affair. For many, the idea of prosperity is no longer something which can be taken for granted, but has become instead an idea about degrees of insecurity, of short-term protection rather than enduring surety. In analytical terms, it is not unreasonable to conclude that many of the economistic ideas about work which have persisted until the recent past have progressed from marginal authenticity, and marginal ideologicality, through increasing inauthenticity and increasing ideologicality, to patent inauthenticity and absolute ideologicality.

Where then, does this leave the idea of an hegemonic work paradigm, based on the presumption of intellectual/moral consent? At its most basic, we can say that the perceived legitimacy of the contemporary work paradigm has always been more apparent than real. 'Consent' is not so much a product of intellectual/moral belief, as it is of having to accept the need to participate in the mechanisms of employment because there is no real alternative. We can identify three important sources of this pragmatic 'consent'. In the first place, people develop an understanding of the meaning and purpose of work on the basis of a fairly uncomplicated realization of their material and psychological needs. As long as the economic structure continues to provide them with adequate means of satisfying these needs, as long that is, that it allows them to fulfil their expectations for income, security, creativity and social contact, then arguably, there is no real need to develop a more abstract concept of work. In the second place, and within the productive process itself, an element of agreement or 'consent' is necessary in order that the practicalities of work can be organized in a reasonably orderly way. Since it is extremely doubtful whether the capitalist division of labour and organization of work have ever been seen as fully legitimate by those who are obliged to participate in it, we can understand the minimal degree of commitment to it in terms of practical necessity. Consensual participation in the labour process does not so much signify a wholehearted belief that this is the only and best way of realizing economic interests, as that these are the ones which are currently available. It also signifies a recognition that a systematic and regulated organization of employment and income distribution are necessary in order to provide all individuals with access to the means of survival. Thirdly, and at a slightly more abstract level, there is an important sense in which a growing majority of the population have a vested interest in the current form of the organization of work - an interest which has a strongly future orientation - which makes them reluctant to consider what the alternatives may be. For many, the experience of relative affluence signifies that they believe, and actually do have, a lot more to loose than their chains. Although this reluctance could with some justification be interpreted as a demonstration of popular 'consent' for the continuation of the present system of employment and income distribution, it could equally be interpreted as much more defensive form of 'consent' by default. In the UK for example, the collapse of the private housing market during the 1990s has left so many households with such a high level of debt to mortgage lenders, that they would find it extremely difficult, if not completely impossible, to countenance any further reorganization of work because of the threat of complete economic disaster.[4] Overall then, we can suggest that the perceived legitimacy of the current work paradigm has very little to do with agreement about elusive and ill-defined intellectual and moral considerations beyond the fact that these relate specifically to the realization of economic interest through the fulfilment of basic needs. Somewhat paradoxically, attempts by the ideologues of Fordist and post-Fordist capitalism to appeal ever more vigorously to the 'higher' moral and intellectual meanings and purposes of work, have in reality been met by an increasingly explicit restatement of the fact that work is simply a means to an end. If that end cannot be achieved by current means, then new means will have to be developed. Put bluntly, if secure employment is no longer the common experience, can it any longer provide a basis for common understanding and consent?

To summarize the discussion in this chapter so far, it has been argued that by attempting to replace the relationship between activity and the satisfaction of determinate needs by an assumption of the 'need' for production more or less for its own sake, by tending to subordinate the perceived worth and value of all activities to the criterion of economic expediency, and by subordinating the needs of individuals to the requirements of the economic system, the current concept of work operates with a number of criteria of work which are inherently arbitrary. In the same way that this arbitrariness is demonstrated by an inability to acknowledge the fundamental principles and motives which underlie human productive activity, the contemporary work-ethic can be shown to be ideological because it no longer reflects an accurate understanding of changes in the practice of work. In the context of a reducing requirement for labour, it would seem that trying to maintain a belief in, let alone trying to provide opportunities for, full-time and life-long employment has become an increasingly unrealistic endeavour. On this understanding, and on the basis of available evidence, the contemporary concept of work can be described as ideological in that it offers expectations which cannot be fulfilled. The validity and legitimacy of the contemporary concept of work in other words, has been seriously reduced as it lags behind, and fails to accommodate itself, to evident changes in contemporary working practice.

Part Three - Towards a new concept of work

Although this critical analysis has painted a somewhat gloomy picture of the current state of the work paradigm, the discussion has also highlighted the potential for a practical solution to these difficulties. Beginning with its theoretical premises, we have established that the relationship between the practice of work and the concept of work is dynamic and flexible, that it is reciprocal, and that it is not only bound to change over time, but actually has a propensity for change. In the present conjuncture, the inherent flexibility of new ways of working strongly suggests that the process of developing and introducing a new work paradigm can take advantage of, rather than simply be a victim of, changes in technique and work organization. Moreover, because the redesign of work in practice can more or less easily accommodate new ideas about work, these ideas could have a guiding influence - we can give priority to the ideational aspects of work in the confident expectation that practical solutions to their implementation can be found. With regard to the arbitrariness of the current criteria of work, it can be suggested that arbitrariness does not in itself inhibit the emergence of an new work paradigm, as long as we are clear what its underlying terms of reference are. There is no substantive reason why the categorization of some activities as work and others not can continue to be made on grounds which have little to do with the nature of the activity itself. The crucial point is to acknowledge at the outset, that people need opportunities for income, security, creativity and social contact, and that they cannot do without these opportunities. The precise form which is given to 'work', is less important than are the quality of its content and its ability to provide people with a secure income.

Moving on to the more immediate practicalities of the present situation, there is overwhelming evidence that the present crisis in the work paradigm largely stems from the increasing irrationality of attempting to reconcile the assumption that productive activity can only be understood and 'measured' in terms of formal full-time and life-long paid employment, with the reality of a consistently falling demand for activities which can be categorized in this way. The 'problem' in other words, stems from the fact that contemporary capitalist society operates with a simplistic and inadequate perception of what should constitute 'work'. To this extent, and assuming that recent technological innovation is unlikely to be reversed, finding a realistic and lasting solution to the problem of unemployment *is at least as much to do with changing the definition and concept of work as it is to do with changing the way that work is organized in practice*. Since the development of the work paradigm is organic and dynamic, it is reasonable to expect that this dynamism will be reflected in the conceptual aspect of the paradigm. Although these changes have been slow to emerge, it is possible to predict, on the basis of observable changes currently under way, a number of ways in which the current work paradigm may develop in the medium term.

In the first place, it is likely that since high levels of output can be achieved within the context of an already reduced *and reducing* need for labour, the trend away from full-time employment will result in a more fluid perception of how much time we actually need to spend 'at work' as currently defined. In turn, this may lead not only to a new perception of the balance between work and non-work time, but also of the arrangement of activities within work itself. It is going to be the case for example, that an increasing number of people will be able to fulfil their working obligations within a time framework which is appropriate to their *own needs* as well as to the 'needs' of industry. Although it is acknowledged that the nature of the activity will dictate the extent to which these new structures of time may or may not be possible, it is nonetheless the case that particularly within information-intensive occupations, the potential for part-time working, job sharing and working from home is increasing.[3]

In the second place, and in recognition of the fact that the number of activities which currently fall into the category of work is decreasing, it is crucial that the criteria by which activities are judged to be necessary, useful, and expedient, must become more flexible. The rigid association between individual expediency and simplistic extrinsic instrumentality will become, and will be seen to be, increasingly inappropriate. As part of this process, a greater appreciation could emerge of the importance and necessity of a wide range of activities which currently fall outside 'work'. These might include activities which have earlier been described as 'concrete' and 'autonomous' many of which take place within the private sphere but which are nonetheless profoundly necessary and productive in both material and psychological terms.

A greater recognition of the 'productivity' of autonomous activities could lead to important changes in the perception and conduct of work itself. If the definition of work derives from a number of discernible criteria, it follows that a change in these criteria would result in a new definition of work. On the assumption that the perceived worth and value of apparently non-work autonomous activities derives from the fact that they relate to, and provide an opportunity for, the expression of the basic predisposition to be productively active, (if they did not then it is unlikely that anyone would engage in them) it can be argued that these concrete and non-arbitrary criteria could provide a new basis not only for distinguishing between which activities are and which are not necessary, but also of the most expedient means of carrying them out. Developing and applying a new and non-arbitrary definition of work in other words, would stimulate a fresh appraisal of the ends to which 'work' is the means, and of the worth and value of these ends themselves. At the same time, it would go some way towards restoring the separation which is currently perceived to exist between the realms of work and non-work; the criteria of work-as-productive activity would displace the criteria of work-as-paid-work. These changes would certainly constitute the development of a much more flexible, and in the circumstances, much more expedient conception of what constitutes 'work'.

In the third place, and once the principle had been established that the purposes of 'work' are relatively finite, a wider and much more positive understanding could develop of the evident and potentially very positive advantages of technologically engendered changes in patterns of work. This would not only include an acceptance of the reducing need for full-time and life-long employment itself, but of the possibility that at least some types of work could be organized in quite different ways. Any suggestion that a reduction in the need for one particular category of activity, namely 'work', will result in a plunge towards mass inactivity and anomie is quite absurd. The point is, that within the confines of the present concept of work, this particular realm of activity is simply not as large as it used to be:

> Work and the work-based society are not in crisis because there is not enough *to do*, but because *work in a very precise sense* [i.e. work-for-a-wage] has become scarce, and the work that is to be done now falls less and less into that particular category. (Gorz 1989, p.153, original emphasis)

The adoption of flexible manufacturing systems, the displacement of large-scale manufacturing plants by small-scale sub-contractors, the reorientation of organizations around an information intensive core, and the development of new networks of communication, can all be taken as clear examples of the forms that such developments might take. It should however be emphasized that many spheres of productive activity may still have to be organized in much the same way as they are at present. The provision of basic utilities, the transportation systems, the maintenance of large plants in the processes industries such as steel and other basic manufacturing materials, chemicals, fuels and food-stuffs, and some labour-intensive services such as health care and education, are at least in some respects, relatively inaccessible to further technological change. It is nonetheless the case, that although *the form* of these organizations may remain unchanged, *the content* of the activities which take place within them can and in some cases already has, been altered significantly.

Finally, a key feature of this process of conceptual change will be the exercise of far greater choice over how necessary commodities and services are produced. A more flexible concept of work could play a leading role not only in how current technologies are implemented, but in how they might continue to develop. Again these changes would not only affect the practice of work itself, but also the balance between one realm of productive activity and another. If for example, the possibility of further reductions in 'the need to work' were not only acknowledged and accepted, *but became a guiding aim of the work paradigm* (in place that is, of the present 'aim' that 'production' as such is necessarily 'a good thing'), and if other non-work but nonetheless 'productive' activities acquired greater 'public' validity and thus personal and social 'worth', then innovations which further reduce the need for particular types of activity could be implemented much more smoothly and rapidly. Although there is some justification in the view that factors other than technological innovation, such as demographic change and a contraction of consumer demand, have contributed to the decline in employment, it must be acknowledged that if policies *deliberately aimed at further reductions in employment* were introduced, then technological innovation would not be a hindrance, but would play a central role in achieving this aim.

Despite the fact that the potential for such changes already exists, and for many has already become a practical reality, it is undoubtedly the case that the emergence of a new concept of work and the transition towards a new work paradigm is likely to be extremely problematic. Following the principal contention of this book that the full benefits of technological innovation not only point towards, but will increasingly come to depend upon, the development of a new concept of work, questions arise as to whether such a concept can develop and be introduced in practice sufficiently quickly. Although some features of the new concept of work have already started to emerge 'automatically' in response to the immediate demands of the new technological paradigm of flexibility, it is likely that some form of regulatory intervention will be required if the conceptual aspect of the work paradigm is to catch up with, and play a leading role in, further practical developments. Although space precludes a detailed analysis of the precise form of this intervention, it is possible to outline briefly the kind of framework within which it might take place.

Following Marx's observation that: 'mankind always sets itself only such tasks as it can solve; since, looking at the matter more closely, it will always be found that the task itself arises only when the material conditions for its solution already exist or are at least in the process of formation' (Marx 1977, p.390), the first priority should be to establish an independent national agency to look firstly at the task, and to develop policies aimed at its solution. Since, as Gramsci argues, 'the ensemble of the material forces... can be ascertained and measured with mathematical exactitude and can therefore give rise to observations and criteria of an experimental character' (Gramsci 1971, p.466), the first aim should be to develop a detailed analysis of the amount of labour which is actually required to maintain productive output at present levels. Having ascertained these maximum labour requirements, and by comparing them with data on the size of the workforce, it would then be possible to calculate the number of hours that each individual would have to contribute to the pool of *necessary labour*. Although it would subsequently be necessary to subdivide these tasks so as to ensure that particular skill requirements could be met, this could be achieved within the general framework of a limited and finite requirement for such activities. Given the degree of sophistication in gathering information which is already exercised by the administrative agencies of the state, establishing a register of skills and a 'time-account' to record how much necessary labour each individual had contributed or 'owed', would be relatively straightforward. In developing what he calls 'a new politics of time', Gorz suggests for example, that:

> As average working time falls to 30, 25 and 20 hours a week, it will become necessary to introduce even more flexible arrangements: for example, 'retirement advances' available at any age in return for an equivalent postponement of final retirement... or "time saving-accounts", allowing people who have worked more in previous years to stop or reduce work for a year without loss of earnings. (Gorz 1982, p.142)[5]

It can further be argued that increasing specialization and thus standardization of tasks will lead to an increase in demand for interchangeable and flexible skills and a decrease in rigid and task-specific skills. In the context of greater interchangeability, a larger number of people would, at least in some instances, be able to work in a greater variety of occupations.

Having determined these limits, policies would have to be developed aimed at making the transition, in the first instance, from work-as-formal-paid-employment, to work-as-necessary-labour. Two aspects of this transition would require particular attention. Firstly, solutions would have to be found to the problem of reducing the number of 'surplus' hours currently devoted to formal paid employment. Although the present mechanism of income distribution acts directly against this possibility, since income largely depends upon the number of hours worked, it is nonetheless the case that under different circumstances, and with the legislative backing of the state, employers' and employees' organizations could introduce programmes for reducing and redistributing this surplus.

The second and most problematic aspect of transition, centres around the problem of *income*. If access to necessary resources is almost exclusively achieved through the medium of monetary income, and if this income can only be gained by participating in the mechanisms of formal employment, then the introduction of a new relationship between work and non-work time *necessarily requires the development of a new mechanism for income distribution*. Although the above discussion has indicated some of the principles upon which such a new mechanism might be based, including for example, the fact that many working activities are now less concerned with the direct transformation of materials into products, than with supervising the production process itself, that the working activities of a growing number of individuals in service occupations, cannot be measured in terms of 'product' and 'output' because of the nature of the work they do, and that most individuals now receive a proportion of their income in the form of holiday pay, maternity leave and pensions, when they are not 'at work' at all, *it is of paramount and urgent importance to develop a new mechanism for income distribution.* To the extent that this mechanism is presently manifest through the institutions of formal paid employment, and to the extent that these institutions have entered a period of profound change, it is not unreasonable to suggest that the continued legitimacy of the capitalist mode of production depends upon finding a solution to this problem.

Having indicated some of the immediate and practical difficulties which an accelerated introduction of the new work paradigm would require, and having suggested that solutions to them will have to be developed and introduced through the regulatory institutions of the state, it must be acknowledged that in the longer term, a successful transformation of the work paradigm will require concentrated effort within the political and ideational spheres. In Gramsci's terminology, it will be necessary to transcend particular 'economic-corporate' interests, and move towards the development of a new 'intellectual and moral unity':

> An appropriate political initiative is always necessary to liberate the economic thrust from the dead weight of traditional policies - i.e. to change the political direction of certain forces which have to be absorbed if a new, homogeneous politico-economic historical bloc, without internal contradictions, is to be successfully formed. (Gramsci 1971, p.168)

It remains to be seen whether a new concept of work of the kind discussed here will provide the basis of the new intellectual/moral social order. It seems certain however, that the legitimacy of such an order will depend upon the expediency of the work paradigm upon which it is based, and that this expediency will in turn depend upon the extent to which it acknowledges the basic expectations which individuals seek to fulfil through 'work'.

A century on from the publication *The Division of Labour*, Durkheim's closing comments seem particularly appropriate:

> What we must do to relieve this anomy is to discover the means for making the organs which are still wasting themselves in discordant movements harmoniously concur by introducing into their relations more justice by more and more extenuating the external inequalities which are the source of evil.... Because certain of our duties are no longer founded in the reality of things, a breakdown has resulted which will be repaired only in so far as a new discipline is established and consolidated. In short, our first duty is to make a moral code for ourselves. Such a work cannot be improvised in the silence of the study; it can arise only through itself, little by little, under the pressure of internal causes which make it necessary. But the service that thought can and must render is in fixing the goal that we must attain. That is what we have tried to do. (Durkheim 1933, p.409)

Notes

1. For an analysis of 'privatism' see Lodziak 1986 and Ransome 1987. For a discussion of the 'consumer society' see, Macfarlane, A. 1987.

2. Gorz defines this functionality as: 'Any conduct which is rationally programmed to attain results beyond the agents' comprehension, irrespective of their intentions.' He contrasts this form of 'hetero-determined collaboration', with the relationships produced by autonomous or 'self-regulated integration' based on 'the ability of individuals to self-organize by coordinating their conduct with a view to obtaining a result by their collective action.' (Gorz 1989, pp.32-3).

3. Walton reports for example, that: 'It is estimated that 250 US companies have some form of work at home programme, with roughly 10,000 telecommuting employees, and that an equal number of people work independently out of electronic cottages.... If, as forecast, 80 per cent of business people end up with personal computers on their desks, more and more of these desks will be outside the traditional business office'. (Walton, P. 1985) For further discussion of these trends see Dey, I. 1989.

4. Quoting a recent report by Shelter, the UK charity for the homeless, the *Times* reported that: 'More than 130,000 mortgage borrowers significantly risk losing their homes in the near future.... The study found that 250,000 owner-occupiers - one in twenty - owe more than six months' repayments. Only a quarter of these are reducing their arrears and the remaining 188,000 face an increasing risk of losing their homes, including 130,000 in significant difficulty. Although the number in long-term debt fell by 65,620 last year [1994], that was largely because 49,210 properties were repossessed.' (The *Times*, 1 June 1995, quoting from *Which Way Out*, London: Shelter)

5. For more details of Gorz's views on this topic see Gorz 1985, pp.101-10, and Gorz 1989, pp.191-215.

Bibliography

Abercrombie N. and Turner, B.S. (1982), 'The Dominant Ideology Thesis', in Giddens, A. and Held, D., (eds.), (1982), pp.396-414. Originally published 1978 in *British Journal of Sociology*, 29(2), pp.149-70.

Aglietta, M. (1979), *A Theory of Capitalist Regulation*, London: New Left Books.

Amin, A., (ed.), (1994), *Post-Fordism: A Reader*, Oxford: Blackwell.

Anderson, P. (1974), *Passages from Antiquity to Feudalism*, London: New Left Books.

Andreski, S. (1985), *Max Weber's Insights and Errors* (International Library of Sociology), London: Routledge, Chapman and Hall.

Annual Abstract of Statistics, Central Statistical Office: no.108 (1972); no.112 (1976); no 117 (1981); no.118 (1982); no.119 (1983); no.21 (1985); no.127 (1991), London: HMSO.

Anthony, P.D. (1977), *The Ideology of Work*, London: Tavistock.

Aquinas Selected Political Writings, (1970). Edited and introduced by A.P.D. D'Entreves, translated by J.G.Dawson, Oxford: Basil Blackwell.

Aquinas, T. *Summa Theologiae*. Translated by the Fathers of the English Dominican Province, London: R. and T. Washbourne (1918).

Arber, S and Gilbert, N. (1992), *Women and Working Lives*, London: Macmillan.

Aristotle, (1950), *Politics*. Translated by H.Rackman. London: Heinemann; Cambridge, Mass.: Harvard University Press.

Atkinson, J. and Meager, N. (1986), *Changing Working Patterns: How companies achieve flexibility to meet new needs*, London:National Economic Development Office (NEDO).

Baechler, J., Hall, J.A. and Mann, M., (eds.), (1988), *Europe and the Rise of Capitlaism*, Oxford: Basil Blackwell.

Beechy, V. and Perkins, T. (1987), *A Matter of Hours: Women, Part-time Work and the Labour Market*, Cambridge: Polity Press.

Beynon, H. and Blackburn R.M. (1972), *Perceptions of Work: Variations Within a Factory*, London: Cambridge University Press.

Blackburn, R.M. and Mann, M. (1979), *The Working Class in the Labour Market*, London: Macmillan.

Blauner, R. (1964), *Alienation and Freedom: The Factory Worker and his Industry*. Chicago: University of Chicage Press.

Blum, F. (1953), *Towards a Democratic Work Process*, New York: Harper and Bros.

Bosanquet, N. (1983), *After the New Right*, London: Heinemann.

Bosworth, D.L., (ed.), (1983), *The Employment Consequences of technological Change*, London: Macmillan.

Boyer, R. and Mistral, J. (1983), *Accumulation, Inflation, Crises*, Paris: PUF

Braham, P., Rhodes, E. and Pearn, M. (1981), *Discrimination and Disadvantage in Employmnet: The Experience of Black Workers*, London: Harper and Row.

Brown, J.A.C. (1954), *The Social Psychology of Industry: Human Relations in the Factory*. Penguin.

Brown, R.K., Curran, M. and Cousins, J. (1983), *Changing Attitudes to Employment?*, (research paper no.40), Department of Employment: HMSO.

Bulmer, M., (ed.), (1975), *Working-Class Images of Society*, London: Routledge and Kegan Paul.

Burke, G. and Rumberger, R.W., (eds.), (1987), *The Future Impact of technology on Work and Education*, London: Falmer Press.

Burns, T., (ed.), (1969), *Industrial Man: Selected Readings*, Harmondsworth: Penguin.

Buss, A.E. (1985), *Max Weber and Asia: Contributions to the Sociology of Development*, London: Weltforum Verlag.

Callinicos, A. (1985), *Marxism and Philosophy*, Oxford: Oxford University Press.

Calvert, P. (1982), *The Concept of Class: An Historical Introduction*, London: Hutchinson.

Calvin, Thomas. *Institutes of the Christian Religion*. Trans. J.Allen, 1838, vol. ii.

Census of Employment, 1981, 1984, 1987 and 1989, final results published in *Employment Gazette* December 1983, September 1987, October 1989 and April 1991.

Centre for Contemporary Cultural Studies, (1978), *On Ideology*, London: Hutchinson.

Clark, S. (1992), 'What the F---'s Name is Fordism', in Gilbert *et al.*, (1992), pp.13-30.

Clutterbuck, D., (ed.), (1985), *New Patterns of Work*, Aldershot: Gower.

Cockburn, C. (1985), *Machinery of Dominance: Women, Men and Technical Know-How*, London: Pluto Press.

Coombs, R.W. 'Long-Term Trends in Automation', in Marstrand, P., (ed.), (1984), pp.146-62.

Cullen, I., Hammond, S. and Haimes, E. (1980), *Employment and Mobility in Inner Urban Areas*, Principal Report to the SSRC of Project HR 5884, London: Bartlett School of Architecture and Planning.

Dallago, B. (1990), *The Irregular Economy: The 'Underground' Economy and the 'Black' Labour Market*, (SPRU) Aldershot: Gower.

Davis, L.E. and Werling, R. (1960), 'Job design factors', *Occupational Psychology*, vol. XXXIV, no.2, pp.109-32.

Day, R.B. (1976), 'The Theory of the Long Clcle: Kondratiev, Trotsky, Mandel', *New Left Review*, no.99 (Sep-Oct 1976), pp.67-82.

Dex, S. (1985), *The Sexual Division of Labour: Conceptual Revolutions in the Social Sciences*, Brighton: Harvester Press.

Dey, I. (1990), 'Flexible "Parts" and Rigid "fulls": The limited revolution in work-time patterns', *Work, Employment and Society*, vol.3 no.4, pp.465-90.

Dosi, G., Freeman, C., Neson, R., Silverberg, G. and Soete, L., (eds.), (1988), *Technical Change and Economic Theory*, London:Frances Pinter

Durkheim, E. (1933), *The Division of Labor in Society*. Translated by G. Simpson, London: Glencoe Free Press. Originally published in 1893.

Durkheim, E. (1952), *Suicide: A study in Sociology*. Translated by J.A. Spaulding and G. Simpson, edited and introduced by G. Simpson, London: Routedge and Kegan Paul. (Second edition). Originally published 1897.

Eagleton, T. (1991), *Ideology: An Introduction*, London: Verso.

Edwards, R. (1979), *Contested Terrain: The Transformation of the Workplace in the Twentieth Century*, London: Heinemann.

Eisenstadt, S.N. (ed) (1968), *The Protestant Ethic and Modernisation: a Comparative Perspective*, New York.

Elam, M. (1994), 'Puzzling out the Post-Fordist Debate: technology, markets and institutions', in Amin, A. (ed.), (1994), pp.43-70. Originally published in *Economic and Industrial Democracy*, (1990), vol.11 no.1, pp.9-37.

Elger, T. and Fairbrother, P. (1992), 'Inflexible flexibility: A case study of modularisation', in Gilbert *et al.*, (1992), pp.89-106.

Elkan, W. (1979), 'Views from three other Disciplines: Economics', in Wallman, S., (ed.), (1979), pp.25-30.

Employment Gazette, Department of Employment, Oct 1980,Feb 1984, Oct 1987, April 1989, May 1990 and Jan 1992, London:HMSO

Engels, F. (1934), *Ludwig Feuerbach and the Outcome of Classical German Philosophy*, London: Martin Lawrence.

Engels, F. (1973), *The Condition of the Working Class in England: From Personal Observation and Authentic Sources*, London: Lawrence and Wishart. First English edition published in 1892.

Ernste, H. and Meyer, V., (eds.), (1992), *Flexible Specialization and the New Regionalism*, London: Pinter.

Esser, J. and Hirsch, J. (1994), 'Post-Fordist regional and urban structure', in Amin, A. (ed.), (1994), pp.71-97. Originally published in *International Journal of Urban and Regional Research*, 1989, vol.13, no.3, pp.417-36.

Eurostat, *Annual Review 1976-1985*, (EC Brussels: 1986).

Eurostat, *Basic Statistics of the Community*, (EC Brussels: 1988; 1989; 1991).

Eurostat *Demographic Statistics*, (EEC Luxembourg 1990).

Fagin, L. (1979), 'Views from three other Disciplines: Psychiatry', in Wallman, S., (ed.), (1979), pp.31-6.

Feuerbach, L (1957), *The Essence of Christianity*. Translated from the second German edition by M.Evans (George Elliot), London: Chapman's Quarterly Series, vol.6, 1854. Reprinted 1957, London: Kegan Paul; New York: Harper and Row.

Firth, R. (1979), 'Work and Value: Reflections on Ideas of Karl Marx', in Wallman, S., (ed.), (1979), pp.178-79.

Fox, A. (1980), 'The meaning of work', in Salaman and Esland., (eds.), (1980), pp.139-191.

Francis, A. (1986), *New Technology at Work,* Oxford: Clarendon Press.

Franklin, B. (1874), *The Life of Benjamin Franklin, Written by Himself.* Edited by J. Bigelow, Philadelphia: J.B. Lippincott & Co.

Fraser, R. (ed.), (1968), *Work: Twenty Personal Accounts*, Harmondsworth: Penguin Books. (First Published in *New Left Review*, 1965, 1966, 1967).

Freeman C. 'Keynes or Kondratiev ?', in: Marstrand P., (ed.), (1984), pp.103-23.

Freeman, C. (ed.) (1985), *Technological Trends in Employment: vol.4 Engineering and Vehicles*. (SPRU) Aldershot: Gower.

Freeman, C., Clark, J.A. and Soete, L. (1982), *Unemployment and Technical Innovation: A Study of Long Waves and Economic Development*, London: Frances Pinter.

Friedman M. (1962), *Capitalism and Freedom*, Chicago: Chicago University Press.

Friedman M. and Schwartz A.J. (1963), *A Monetary History of the United States*, Princeton: Princeton University Press.

Fromm, E. (1942), *The Fear of Freedom*, London: Routledge and Kegan Paul.

Fromm, E. (1955), 'The Human Implications of Instinctivistic Radicalism', *Dissent* vol.2, no.4, pp.342-49.

Fromm, E. (1956a), 'A Counter Rebuttal', *Dissent* vol.3, no.1, pp.81-3.

Fromm, E. (1956b), *The Sane Society*, London: Routledge and Kegan Paul.

Gamble, A. (1988), *The Free Economy and the Strong State: The Politics of Thatcherism*, London: Macmillan.

George, C.H. and George, K. (1958), 'Protestantism and Capitalism in pre-Revolutionary England', *Church History*, vol.27, pp.351-71.

Giddens, A. (1980), *The Class Structure of the Advanced Societies*, London: Hutchinson.

Giddens, A. and Held, D., (eds.), (1982), *Classes, Power, and Conflict: Classical and Contemporary Debates,* London: Macmillan.

Gilbert, N., Burrows, R. and Pollert, A., (eds.), (1992*), Fordism and Flexibility: Divisions and change*, Basingstoke: Macmillan

Gill, C. (1985), *Work, Unemployment and the New Technology*, Cambridge: Polity Press.

Godelier, M. (1977), *Perspectives in Marxist Anthropology*, Cambridge: Cambridge University Press.

Godelier, M. (1980), 'Language and History; Work and its Representations: A Research Proposal', *History Workshop Journal*, issue 10 (Autumn 1980), pp.164-74.

Goldthorpe, J.H., Lockwood, D., Bechhofer, E. and Platt, J. (1968), *The Affluent Worker: Industrial Attitudes and Behaviour*, Cambridge: Cambridge University Press.

Gorz, A., (ed.), (1976), *The Division of Labour: The Labour Process and Class-structure in Modern Capitlaism*, Brighton: Harvester Press.

Gorz, A. (1982), *Farewell To The Working Class: An Essay on Post-Industrial Socialism*. Translated by M. Sonenscher, London: Pluto Press. Originally Published 1980, as *Adieux au Proletariat*. Paris, Editions Galilee.

Gorz, A. (1985), *Paths to Paradise: On the Liberation from Work*. Translated by M.Imre, London: Pluto Press.

Gorz, A. (1989), *Critique of Economic Reason*. Translated by G. Handyside and C. Turner, London: Verso. Originally published as: *Metamorphoses du Travail*: Quete du sens, Galilee, 1988.

Gorz, A. (1990), 'The New Agenda', *New Left Review*, no.184, (Nov-Dec 1990), pp.37-46.

Gough, I. (1972), 'Marx's Theory of Productive and Unproductive Labour', *New Left Review*, no.76, (Nov-Dec 1972), pp.47-72.

Gough, J. (1992), 'Where's the value in "post-Fordism" ?', in Gilbert *et al.,* (1992), pp.31-45.

Gramsci, A. (1977), *Selections from the Prison Notebooks*. Edited and Translated by Q. Hoare and G. Nowell Smith, London: Lawrence and Wishart.

Hall, S. and Jacques, M., (eds.), (1983), *The Politics of Thatcherism*, London: Lawrence and Wishart.

Hall, S. and Jacques, M., (eds.), (1989), *New Times: The Changing Face of Politics in the 1990's*, London: Lawrence and Wishart.

Hamilton R. and Barrett M., (eds.), (1987), *The Politics of Diversity: Feminism, Marxism and Nationalism*, London: Verso.

Hammond, N.G.L. (1959), *A History of Greece to 322 BC*, Oxford: Clarendon Press.

Harding, P. and Jenkins, R. (1989), *The Myth of the Hidden Economy*, Milton Keynes: Open University Press.

Hayek F A. (1980), *Unemployment and the Unions*, London: Institute of Economic Affairs.

Herzberg, F (1968), *Work and the Nature of Man*, New York: Staples Press.

Hirst, P. (1989) 'After Henry', in Hall, S. and Jacques, M. (eds.), (1989), pp.321-29. Originally published in *New Statesman and Society*, (21 July 1989).

Holmes, U.T. Jr. (1980). *Medieval Man; His Understanding of Himself, His Society and the World, Illustrated from his own Literature*. Studies in the Romance Languages and Literatures No.212, Chapel Hill: University of North Carolina.

Huizinga, G. (1970), *Maslow's Need Hierarchy in the Work Situation*, Groningen: Wolters-Noordhoff Publishing.

Hyman, R. and Streeck, W., (eds.), (1988), *New Technology and Industrial Relations*, Oxford: Basil Blackwell.

Jahoda, M. (1979), 'The Impact of Unemployment in the 1930's and the 1970's', *Bulletin of the British Psychological Society*, vol.32.

Jahoda, M. Lazarsfeld, P.H. and Zeisel, H. (1971), *Marienthal: The Sociography of an Unemployed Community*, Chicago: Aldine Atherton Inc. Originally published 1933.

Jarrett, B. (1968), *Social Theories of the Middle Ages, 1200-1500*, London: Frank Cass and Co Ltd. Originally published 1926.

Jenson, J., (1989), 'Paradigms and political discourse: protective legislation in the USA and France before 1914', *Canadian Journal of Political Science*, 22, 235-58.

Jessop, B. (1992a), 'Post-Fordism and Flexible Specialization: incommensurable, contradictory, complementary, or just plain different perspectives?', in Ernste and Meyer (eds.), (1992), pp.25-44.

Jessop, B. (1992b), 'Fordism and post-Fordism: critique and reformulation', in Scott and Storper (eds.), (1992), pp.43-65.

Jessop, B. (1994), 'Post-Fordism and the State', in Amin, A. (ed.), (1994), pp.251-279.

Jessop, B., Bonnett, K., Bromley, S. and Ling, T. (1988), *Thatcherism: A Tale of Two Nations*, Cambridge: Polity Press.

Jones, D. 'Vehicles', in Freeman (ed.), (1985), pp.128-87.

Kamenka, E. (1970), *The Philosophy of Ludwig Feuerbach*, London: Routledge and Kegan Paul.

Keating, M.C.P. (1987), *Clerics and Capitalists: A Critique of Weber's Protestant Ethic Thesis*, (Salford Papers in Sociology and Anthropology No.2), University of Salford.

Kendall, P.M.H., Crayston, J., Malecki, A.M.J., Wallace, A.S. and Wheatley, T.F. (1980), *The Impact of Chip Technology on Employment and the Labour Market*, London: Metra Consulting Group.

King, D. S. (1987), *The New Right: Politics, Markets and Citizenship*, London: Macmillan.

Knights, D and Willmott, H., (eds.), *New Technology and the Labour Process*, Basingstoke: Macmillan.

Kondratiev, N. (1935), 'The Long Waves in Economic Life', *Review of Economic Statistics*, 17, pp.105-15.

Lane, C. (1988), 'Industrial change in Europe: The Pursuit of Flexible Specialisation in Britain and West Germany', *Work, Employment and Society*, vol.2 no.2, pp.141-68.

Larrain J. (1979), *The Concept of Ideology*, London: Hutchinson.

Larrain, J. (1983), *Marxism and Ideology*, London: Macmillan.

Lawrence, P. (1964), *An analysis of time Allocation and Labour Supply in the rural village sector of Melanesia*, London: Brunel University. Multigraph.

Leman, S. (1992), 'Gender, technology and flexibility in the UK mail order industry', in Gilbert *et al.*, (1992), pp.118-133.

Lipietz, A. (1985), *The Enchanted World: Inflation credit and the world crisis*, London: Verso.

Lipietz, A. (1987), *Mirages and Miracles: the crisis of global Fordism*, London: Verso.

Lipietz, A. (1994), 'Post-Fordism and Democracy', in Amin, A. (ed.), (1994), pp.338-357.

Livingstone, S. and Morison, J., (ed.), (1990), *Law, Society and Change*, Aldershot: Gower.

Lockwood, D. (1975), 'Sources of variation in working-class images of society', in Bulmer, M. (1975), pp.16-31. Originally published 1966, *Sociological Review*, vol.14, no.3, pp.249-267.

Lodziak, C. (1986), *The Power of Television a Critical Appraisal*, London: Frances Pinter.

Lodziak, C. (1995), *Manipulating Needs, Capitalism and Culture*, London: Pluto Press.

Logan, J. (June 1985), *Reflections Series*, no.54. Nottingham Trent University.

Lukács, G. (1968), *History and Class Consciousness: Studies in Marxist Dialectics*. Translated by R. Livingstone, London: Merlin Press.

Luther, Martin, *Ermahnung zum Frieden auf die zwolf Artikel der Bauerschaft in Schwaben* (1525), in *Werke*, vol.xviii, p.327.

Macfarlane, A. (1987), *The Culture of Capitalism*, Oxford: Basil Blackwell.

Macfarlane, A. (1988), 'The Cradle of Capitalism: The Case of England', in Baechler, J., *et al.*, (1988), pp.185-203.

Mackenzie, G. (1973), *The Aristicracy of Labour: The position of skilled craftsmen in the American class structure*, Cambridge: Cambridge University Press.

Macpherson, C.B. (1962), *The Political Theory of Possessive Individualism*, Oxford: Clarendon Press.

Mager, N.N. (1987), *The Kondratieff Waves*, New York: Praeger.

Mann, M. (1982), 'The Social Cohesion of Liberal Democracy', in Giddens, A. and Held, D. (eds.), (1982), pp.373-95. Originally published in *American Sociological Review*, vol.35, no.3, pp.423-39.

Marcuse, H. (1956), 'A reply to Eric Fromm', *Dissent* vol.3, no.1, pp.79-81.

Marcuse, H. (1964), *One Dimensional Man*, London: Abacus.

Marginson, P. (1991), 'Change and continuity in the employment structure of large companies', in Pollert (ed.), (1991), pp.32-45.

Marglin, S.A. (1976), 'What do Bosses Do ?: The Origins and Functions of Hierarchy in Capitalist Production', in Gorz, A. (ed.), (1976), pp.13-54.

Marshall, G. (1982), *In Search of the Spirit of Capitalism: An Essay on Max Weber's Protestant Ethic Thesis*, London: Hutchinson.

Marstrand P. (ed.), (1984), *New Technology and the Future of Work and Skills*. Proceedings of a Symposium organised by Section X at the Annual Meeting of the British Association for the Advancement of Science, August 1983, London: Frances Pinter.

Marx, K. (1954), *Capital I*, London: Lawrence and Wishart.

Marx, K. (1959) *Capital III*, London: Lawrence and Wishart.

Marx, K. (1963), *Early Writings*. Translated by T.B. Bottomore, London: C.A. Watts and Co.

Marx, K. (1975), *Early Writings*. Introduction by L.Colletti, translated by R.Livingstone and G.Benton, Harmondsworth: Penguin.

Marx, K. (1977), 'Grundrisse', in *Selected Writings*, edited by D. McLellan (1977), pp. 345-387.

Marx, K. (1977), 'The Early Writings', in *Selected Writings*, edited by D. McLellan (1977), pp. 3-127.

Marx, K. (1977), 'The Poverty of Philosophy', in *Selected Writings*, edited by D. McLellan (1977), pp. 195-215.

Marx, K. and Engels, F. (1970), *The German Ideology, Part One* (with selections from Parts Two and Three, together with Marx's 'Introduction to a Critique of Political Economy'). Edited by C.J. Arthur, London: Lawrence and Wishart.

Maslow, A.H. (1970), 'A Theory of Human Motivation', in Vroom, V.H. and Deci, E.L., (eds.), (1970). Originally published 1943, in *Psychological Review*, vol.50, pp.370-96.

Mayo, E. (1933), *The Human Problems of an Industrial Civilisation*, New York: Macmillan.

McLellan, D., (ed.), (1977), *Karl Marx Selected Writings*, Oxford: Oxford University Press.

Miller, E. and Hatcher, J. (1978), *Medieval England: Rural Society and Economic Change 1086-1348*, London: Longman.

Mills, C. Wright. (1953), *White Collar: The American Middle Classes*, New York: Oxford University Press.

Molyneux, M. (1979), 'Beyond the Domestic Labour Debate', *New Left Review*, no. 116, (July-August 1979), pp.3-27.

Murray, R. (1989a), 'Fordism and Post-Fordism' in Hall, S. and Jacques, M., (eds.), (1989), pp.38-53. Originally published in *Marxism Today*, (October 1988).

Murray, R. (1989b), 'Benetton Britain: The New Economic Order, in Hall, S. and Jacques, M., (eds.), (1989), pp.54-64. Originally published in *Marxism Today*, (November 1985).

Neale, R.S. (1983), *History and Class: Essential Readings in Theory and Interpretation*, Oxford: Basil Blackwell.

Newby, H. (1979), *The Deferential Worker: A Study of farm Workers in East Anglia,* Harmondsworth: Penguin.

Northcott, J and Walling, A. (1988), *The Impact of Microelectronics*, London: PSI.

Pahl, R.E., (ed.), (1988), *On Work: Historical, Comparative and Theoretical Perspectives*, Oxford: Basil Blackwell.

Palmerston (1850), Don Pacifico Debate, House of Commons. Quoted in: Briggs, A and Saville, J., (eds), (1967), pp.154-77.

Parker, S. (1972), *The Future of Work and Leisure*, London: Paladin.

Parkin, F. (1979), *Marxism and Class Theory: A Bourgeois Critique*, London: Tavistock.

Penn, R. (1992), 'Flexibility in Britain during the 1980s: Recent empirical evidence', in Gilbert *et al.*, (1992), pp.66-80.

Perez, C. (1983), 'Structural Changes and the Assimilation of New Technologies in the Economic and Social Systems: A Contribution to the Current Debate on Kondratiev Cycles', *Futures*, October 1983. (See also *Futures*, vol.13, no.4 (August 1981) Special Issue.

Perez, C. (1985), 'Micro-electronics, long-waves and world structural change', *World Development*, vol.13, no.3.

Phillips, A. and Taylor, B. (1986), 'Sex and Skill: Notes Towards a Feminist Economics', in Hamilton, R. and Barrett, M. (eds.), (1986), pp.232-51.

Piore, M.J. and Sabel, C.F. (1984), *The Second Industrial Divide*: Possibilities for Prosperity, New York: Basic Books.

Plant, L. Lesser, M. and Taylor-Gooby, P. (1980), *Political Philosophy and Social Welfare: Essays on the Normative Basis of Welfare Provision*, London: Routledge and Kegan Paul.

Pogi, G. (1983), *Calvinism and the Capitalist Spirit: Max Weber's 'Protestant Ethic'*, London: Macmillan.

Pollert, A. (1988), 'The "Flexible Firm": Fixation or Fact ?', *Work, Employment and Society*, vol2, no.3, pp.281-316.

Pollert A., (ed.), (1991), *Farewell to Flexibility ?,* Oxford: Blackwell.

Poulantzas, N. (1975), *Classes in Contemporary Capitalism.* Translated by D.Fernbach, London: New Left Books.

Rainnie, A. and Kraitham, D. (1992), 'Labour market change and the organisation of work', in Gilbert *et al.*, (1992), pp.49-65)

Ransome, P. (1987), 'Productive Activity: a Marxist concept of need and an examination of privatism in contemporary capitalist society', *Reflections Series* no.57. Nottingham Trent University.

Ransome, P. (1988), 'To what extent can Recent Literature on the 'Boundary Problem' be viewed as Productive Labour ?'. Unpublished Working Paper, (Cambridge).

Ransome, P. (1991), 'Andre Gorz *Critique of Economic Reason*', book review, *Theory and Society*, vol.20, pp.560-65.

Ransome, P. (1992), *Antonio Gramsci: A New Introduction*, Hemel Hempstead: Harvester Whearsheaf.

Ransome, P. (1995), *Job Security and Social Stability: the impact of mass unemployment on expectations of work*, Aldershot: Avebury.

Rohrer, R.H. and Sherif, M. (1951), *Social Psychology at the Crossroads*, New York: Harper and Row.

Rose, M. (1975), *Industrial Behaviour: Theoretical development since Taylor*, London: Allen Lane.

Rose, M. (1985), *Re-Working the Work-ethic: Economic Values and Socio-Cultural Politics*, London: Batsford Academic and Educational.

Rustin, M. (1989), 'The politics of Post-Fordism: Or, the trouble with 'New Times', *New Left Review* no.175, (May/June 1989), pp.54-77. A shortened version was subsequently published as 'The trouble with 'New Times' in Hall and Jacques (eds.), 1989, pp.303-20.

Sabel, C.F. (1984), *Work and Politics: The division of labour in industry*, Cambridge: Cambridge University Press. (First published 1982).

Sabine, G.H. (1951), *A History of Political Theory*, London: Harrap.

Salisbury, R. (1962), *From Stone to Steel*, Melbourne: Melbourne University Press.

Sayers, S. (1987), 'The Need to Work', *Radical Philosophy*, no.46. (Summer 1987), pp.17-26. Reprinted in Pahl, R.E., (ed.), (1988), pp.722-41.

Schein, E.H. (ed.), (1987), *The Art of Managing Human Resources*, Oxford: Oxford University Press.

Schumpeter, J.A. (1989), *Essays on Entrepreneurs, Innovations, Business Cycles, and the Evolution of Capitalism*. Edited by R.V. Clemence, Oxford: Transaction Publishers.

Schwimmer, E. (1979), 'The Self and the Product: Concepts of Work in Comparative Perspective', in Wallman, S., (ed.), (1979), pp. 287-315.

Sève, L. (1978), *Man in Marxist Theory and the Psychology of Personality*. Translated by J.McGreal, Hassocks: Harvester Press. Originally published 1974.

Smiles, S. (1958), *Self-Help; With Illustrations of Conduct and Perseverence*, London: John Murray. Originally published 1859.

Smith, Adam, *The Wealth of Nations*, 2 vols., Everyman Edition.

Smith, C. (1989), 'Flexible Specialisation, Automation and Mass Production', *Work, Employment and Society*, vol.3 no.2, pp.203-20.

Smith, C. (1991), 'From 1960s automation to flexible specialisation: a *deja vu* of technological panaceas', in Pollert, A., (ed.), (1991), pp. 138-157.

Social Trends, Central Statistical Office: No.14 (1984); No.18 (1988); No.19 (1989); No.21 (1991). London: HMSO.

Soper, K. (1981), *On Human Needs: Open and Closed Debates in a Marxist Perspective*, Brighton:Harvester Press.

Tawney, R.H. (1960), *Religion and the Rise of Capitalism: An Historical Study*, (Holland Memorial Lectures, 1922). London: John Murray. Originally published 1926.

Tawney R.H. (1982), *The Acquisitive Society,* Brighton: Wheatsheaf. Originally published 1921 by G.Bell and Sons.

Taylor, F.W. (1911), *Principles of Scientific Management*, New York.

Thompson, E.P. (1963), *The Making of the English Working Class*, London: Voctor Gollancz.

Thompson, E.P. (1967), 'Time, Work-Discipline, and Industrial Capitalism', *Past and Present* no.38, pp.56-97.

Thompson, J.B. (1984), *Studies in the Theory of Ideology*, Cambridge: Polity Press.

Thompson, J.B. (1990), *Ideology and Modern Culture*, Cambridge: Polity Press.

Tilgher, A. (1930), *Homo Faber: Work Through the Ages*. Introduction by R. Gross and D. Canfield Fisher Translated by D. Canfield Fisher, (1958 edition).

Troeltsch, E. (1912), *Die Soziallehren der Christlichen Kirchen and Gruppen*, Tubingen. English Trans. by O.Wyon (1931), *The Social Teaching of the Christian Churches*, 2 vols. London.

Turnbull, P.J. (1988), 'The Limits to "Japanisation" - Just-in-Time, Labour relations and the UK Automobile Industry', *New Technology, Work and Employment*, vol3. no.1, pp.7-20.

United Nations Industrial Development Organisation (UNIDO), *Industry and Development Global Report*: 1988/1989 (Vienna 1988

Ure, A. (1967), *The Philosophy of Manufactures. Or an exposition of the Scientific, Moral and Commercial Economy of the Factory System of Great Britain*, London: Frank Cass. Originally published 1835.

Vernant, J-P. (1965), *Mythe et pense chez les Grecs*, Paris: Maspero.

Vroom, V.H. and Deci, E.L., (eds.), (1970), *Management and Motivation*, Harmondsworth: Penguin Books.

Wadel, C. (1979), 'The Hidden Work of Everyday life', in Wallman, S., (ed.), (1979), pp.365-84.

Walker R. and Guest R. (1952), *Man On the Assembly line*, Cambridge, Mass.: Harvard University Press.

Wallman, S., (ed.), (1979), *The Social Anthropology of Work*. Association of Social Anthropologists of the Commonwealth (ASA), Monograph No. 19, London: Academic Press.

Walsh, T. (1991), '"Flexible" employment in the retail and hotel trades', in Pollert (ed.), 1991, pp.104-115.

Walton, P. (1985), 'Job Sharing', in Clutterbuck, D., (ed.), (1985), pp.127-36.

Walton, P. and Gamble, A. (1972), *From Alienation to Surplus Value*, London: Sheed and Ward.

Warr, P. and Wall, T. (1975), *Work and Well-Being*, Harmondsworth: Penguin.

Weber, M. (1950), *General Economic History*. Edited by F.Knight, Glencoe Illinois: Free Press.

Weber, M. (1968), *Economy and Society*. Edited by G.Roth and C.Wittich, Totowa N.J.: Bedminster.

Weber, M. (1976), *The Protestant Ethic and the Spirit of Capitalism*, Translated by T.Parsons, London: Allen and Unwin. This translation originally published in 1930.

Weber, M. (1983): *Max Weber on Capitalism, Bureaucracy and Religion: A Selection of Texts.* Edited and in part newly translated by S. Andreski, London: Allen and Unwin.

Wesley, J. (1964), *John Wesley*, edited by A.C. Outler, New York: Oxford University Press.

Whittington, R. (1991), 'The fragmentation of industrial R & D', in Pollert (ed.), (1991), pp.84-103.

Williams, G. (1960), 'The Concept of Egemonia in the Thought of Antonio Gramsci', *Journal of the History of Ideas*, vol.21, pp.586-99.

Williams, R. (1976), *Keywords: A Vocabulary of Culture and Society*, London: Croom Helm.

Wood, S. (1988), 'Between Fordism and Flexibility ? The US Car Industry', in Hyman, R and Streek, W (eds.), (1985), pp.101-127.

Wright, E.O. (1978), *Class, Crisis, and the State*, London: New Left Books.